The Transformation of the World Economy

Robert Solomon

Second Edition

palgrave

Published in Great Britain by
MACMILLAN PRESS LTD
Houndmills, Basingstoke, Hampshire RG21 6XS and London
Companies and representatives throughout the world

A catalogue record for this book is available from the British Library.

ISBN 0–333–73481–5 hardcover
ISBN 0–333–73482–3 paperback

Published in the United States of America by
ST. MARTIN'S PRESS, INC.,
Scholarly and Reference Division,
175 Fifth Avenue, New York, N.Y. 10010

ISBN 0–312–22111–8 clothbound
ISBN 0–312–22112–6 paperback

Library of Congress Cataloging-in-Publication Data
Solomon, Robert.
The transformation of the world economy / Robert Solomon. — 2nd
ed.
p. cm.
Includes bibliographical references and index.
ISBN 0–312–22111–8 (cloth). — ISBN 0–312–22112–6 (pbk.)
1. Economic history—1970–1990. 2. Economic history—1990–
I. Title.
HC59.S564 1999
330.9'048—dc21

98–53537
CIP

First edition (*The Transformation of the World Economy, 1980–93*) 1994
Reprinted 1996
Second edition 1999

This book is printed on paper suitable for recycling and made from fully managed and
sustained forest sources.

Transferred to digital printing 2001

Printed and bound by Antony Rowe Ltd, Eastbourne

THE TRANSFORMATION OF THE WORLD ECONOMY

This book is due for return on or before the last date shown below.

Contents

List of Tables and Figures

Tables

Figures

Preface

This book – a revised and updated edition of *The Transformation of the World Economy, 1980–93* – deals with the remarkable changes that have occurred in and between the various regions and countries of the world economy in the past two decades.

An explanation is in order regarding the amount of attention, and therefore the number of pages, devoted to different countries. They may be roughly in proportion to the countries' size in the world economy, as measured by their gross domestic product (GDP). If so, that was not done deliberately. The reader will find more detail about developments and about the process of policymaking in the larger industrial countries than in most developing countries and countries in transition from centrally-planned economies. The reason for that is the greater availability of information (or accessibility to me) about the policymaking process in the industrial countries. For example, I had the good fortune to stumble upon Favier and Martin-Roland's *La Décennie Mitterrand*, which provides an amazing amount of detail concerning the policymaking process in France, including the discussions around the table in the Elysée between the President of the Republic and cabinet ministers. This is not a case of Say's Law – supply creates its own demand – in which I used material because of its availability. Rather, I found, and I hope the reader will agree, that the material was revealing in helping one understand the transformations that occurred in France under Mitterrand.

Among countries other than those in the industrial world – a term, incidentally, that is going out of fashion and, in the case of the International Monetary Fund, is being replaced by 'advanced countries' and includes four Asian nations plus Israel – the amount of space is roughly in line with the degree of transformation that has occurred since 1980. Clearly much more has happened in China than in Korea, in India than in Egypt, in Mexico than in Colombia.

It was obviously impossible to cover every country. Thus I chose not to include Canada, largely because it underwent much less of a change than other nations. The same is true for Italy, the Scandinavian countries, Pakistan, the Philippines, Australia and New Zealand. I have also omitted a detailed account of Spain, even though it

xi

changed greatly, simply because of the need to maintain balance in the treatment of different parts of the world.

The data used in this work come mostly from a limited and well-known number of publications: IMF, *International Financial Statistics* and *World Economic Outlook*; World Bank, *World Development Report*; and OECD, *Economic Outlook*. Where a source is not given for data, it is in one of these publications.

I am grateful to the following friends and colleagues for constructive help on various chapters of the first edition of the book: Joseph Berliner, Susan Collins, Anne Cugliani, Harry Harding, Martin Kohn, Joseph Minarik, Fred Pryor, Alexis Rieffel, and John Van Oudenaren.

I have not burdened them or any of my Brookings colleagues with drafts of the revised edition, except for my dear, diligent in-house editor, Fern Solomon. I thank her as well as Mr T. M. Farmiloe and Ms Karen Brazier at Macmillan.

ROBERT SOLOMON

1 Introduction

The world has undergone dramatic changes since the end of the 1970s. This book uses a broad brush to trace the economic transformation, in its political context, that has occurred in the three areas into which the globe is often divided for economic purposes: industrial countries, former centrally-planned economies now in transition, and developing countries. Actually, one of the significant changes has been a blurring of those very distinctions.

The transformation has several aspects. The principal one was a shift toward greater reliance on market forces in all three areas as governments became less involved in economic processes: markets were deregulated, import barriers were lowered, income taxes were reduced, state-owned enterprises were privatised and central planning, where it existed, gave way to direction by the price system. Another change was that 'globalisation' in both industry and finance was intensified. World trade continued to grow faster than world output. And there now exist 'world products': for example, a computer or an automobile may now be assembled from parts made in a number of countries. The international mobility of capital increased greatly, binding national financial markets closer together. The 1990s witnessed an enormous rise in the flow of capital to 'emerging markets' which brought benefits as well as problems – even crises. A consequence of these developments was a heightening of the interdependence among nations and of the perception of that interdependence. That heightened perception shows up in intensification of regional trading and financial arrangements – as in the European Union (formerly the European Community), the North American Free Trade Agreement (NAFTA), and the Asia Pacific Economic Cooperation (APEC) forum. It is also evident in the completion of the negotiations in December 1993 on the GATT (General Agreement on Tariffs and Trade), the most comprehensive worldwide trade liberalisation in history and its replacement by the World Trade Organisation (WTO) in January 1995.

The results of these transformations are not all favourable, but they will have lasting influence.

What initiated the changes? Partly the answer is a dissatisfaction with what had come earlier. The 1970s was a decade of discontent.

1

Stagflation – an unhappy combination of too much inflation and rather stagnant economies – prevailed in industrial countries. Centrally-planned economies were less and less able to provide their citizens with rising standards of living; there is compelling evidence that the larger the share of state-owned enterprises in an economy, the lower tends to be its rate of growth.[1] Many developing countries had become more industrialised, often with the help of loans from banks abroad. But they were burdened with debts and often hobbled by the heavy hand of governmental controls.

In looking for an explanation for these transformations, one has to recognise the influence of the revolution in telecommunications and computer technology. Television encouraged rising expectations, both economic and political, as people saw 'how the other half lives'. A striking instance was the series of revolutions in Eastern Europe in 1989, in which television played a significant role. In the Soviet Union, the process of economic reform 'was launched by a revolution in consumer desires and the idealization of Western consumption patterns'.[2] In China, in the throes of rapid economic reform,

> the constant refrain among urban Chinese is that they can no longer keep up with the quickened pace of life. They are confused by shifting values and outlooks on such fundamentals as careers, as traditional beliefs clash with more modern – often Western – ideas picked up from radios and satellite dishes all over China.[3]

It is reported that hundreds of thousands of satellite dishes 'are sprouting, as the Chinese say, like bamboo shoots after a spring rain'. The result is that the Communist Party's monopoly on news is crumbling.[4]

The increase in migration from poorer to richer countries, not only from developing nations to industrialised ones but within Europe, also owes something to the existence of television. In the early 1990s it could be said that 'a spectre is haunting Europe' – namely the possibility of mass emigration from Russia and the other republics of the former Soviet Union if political and economic instability should worsen there. That danger subsided later in the decade but may have intensified again in 1998.

The computer has also bound the world closer together. It flashes new information around the planet instantaneously. Among other effects, it made possible the use of new financial instruments – derivatives – that facilitate larger and faster flows of funds from country to country in response to profit opportunities, differences in interest rates or expected changes in exchange rates.

History is also affected by the chance emergence of new political leaders at times when they can have an impact. In our period economic transformation was shaped by Margaret Thatcher, Ronald Reagan, François Mitterrand, Felipe Gonzalez, Mikhail Gorbachev, Boris Yeltsin, Lech Walesa, Václav Klaus, Deng Xiaoping, Zhu Rongji, Carlos Salinas de Gortari, Fernando Henrique Cardoso, and Carlos Menem, among others. In the same period the Ayatollah Khomenei, Saddam Hussein and Mobutu Sese Seko also influenced world events but did not play a significant role in the economic transformations we are concerned with.

We owe to the late Isaiah Berlin the distinction between hedgehogs and foxes among statesmen (and, it must be added, stateswomen): 'The fox knows many things, but the hedgehog knows one big thing', wrote the Greek lyric poet Archilochus of the 7th century BC. Berlin first applied this analogy to 'writers and thinkers' in an essay on Tolstoy.[5] In his later essay on Franklin Roosevelt, Berlin, without mentioning hedgehogs and foxes, observed that there are

> two contrasting types of statesmen, in each of which occasionally men of compelling stature appear. The first kind of statesman is essentially a man of single principle and fanatical vision. Possessed by his own bright, coherent dream, he usually understands neither people nor events. He has no doubts or hesitations and by concentration of will power, directness and strength he is able to ignore a great deal of what goes on outside him. This very blindness and stubborn self-absorption occasionally, in certain situations, enable him to bend events and men to his own fixed pattern...
>
> The second type of politician possesses antennae of the greatest possible delicacy, which convey to him, in ways difficult or impossible to analyse, the perpetually changing contours of events and feelings and human activities round them – they are gifted with a peculiar, political sense fed on a capacity to take in minute impressions, to integrate a vast multitude of small evanescent unseizable detail, such as artists possess in relation to their material. Statesmen of this type know what to do and when to do it, if they are to achieve their ends, which themselves are usually not born within some private world of inner thought, or introverted feeling, but are the crystallisation, the raising to great intensity and clarity, of what a

large number of their fellow citizens are thinking and feeling in some dim, inarticulate, but nevertheless persistent fashion.[6]

Among the first type of statesman I would include Thatcher and Reagan, while Mitterrand, Gorbachev and Yeltsin are (or were) more like the fox who knows many things. Václav Klaus appeared to be a hedgehog in his determination to transform the Czech Republic into a democratic free-market economy. Mao Zedong was very much a hedgehog while Deng Xiaoping was a fox, as is his successor Jiang Zemin. Salinas and Menem appear to be fox-like, but they single-mindedly pursued economic reform. Blair and Clinton, and probably Lionel Jospin, appear very similar to Berlin's characterisation of the fox.

The aim of this book is to bring out the transformations of the world's economies that have occurred since 1980 while these and other governmental leaders were in office. An effort is made to describe the essential changes that occurred and the interactions among nations as those changes worked themselves out. The book does not purport to be a comprehensive history. Rather its ambition is to highlight as far as can now be judged those events and developments that have had or will have a lasting impact in transforming the world economy.

It is obvious that this is an unfinished story. The world will continue to evolve.

2 The Way it Was in 1980

History is a continuum, but it contains nodal points – periods of outstanding and lasting significance. The years 1979–81 brought political changes that were to have substantial impacts on economic policies and developments in many countries and would begin to transform the world economy. This narrative therefore starts with the opening of a new decade – the 1980s – one that was to contrast starkly with the 1970s. In this chapter a wide-angled snapshot view is presented of how the three segments of the world economy looked in 1980.

Many still speak or write of 'third world countries', by which is meant the developing countries of Latin America, Africa, the Middle East and Asia. They are also often referred to as less-developed countries – LDCs. The identity of the 'first' and 'second' worlds is less well known. The first world consists of the industrial nations of North America and Western Europe plus Japan, Australia, and New Zealand. The second world countries were those with centrally-planned economies: the Soviet Union, China, and Eastern Europe, along with North Korea, and Cuba.

One of the many changes during the 1980s was the blurring of this way of categorising countries. A number of LDCs were industrialising rapidly and were becoming less and less distinguishable from those usually classified as industrial. In fact, as noted in the Preface, the International Monetary Fund has dropped the term 'industrial countries', replacing it with 'advanced countries' which include the 23 former industrial countries plus Hong Kong, Israel, Korea, Singapore, and Taiwan. It need hardly be mentioned that striking, historic reforms began in Eastern Europe, the former Soviet Union and China. Centrally-planned economies are becoming market economies, though the transition is difficult and one for which there is no precedent. Just as Karl Marx did not spell out how a capitalist economy was to be transformed into a socialist one, writers in the tradition of Adam Smith have not given us a blueprint for changing a command economy, in which most industry is in the hands of the government and economic decision-making is centralised, into a market economy where, broadly speaking, the 'the invisible hand' does the regulating and most means of production are owned privately. Nevertheless, the transition has proceeded and many of the so-called

5

second world nations are beginning to resemble those in the first world. An instance of that was the reaction of the Russian stock market to the Asian crisis in 1997–8, along with markets in the advanced countries.

Among the advanced countries too there were significant modifications in economic policy, structure and performance in the 1980s, beginning with Margaret Thatcher's programme in the United Kingdom but also including the United States, France, Germany, Japan and others.

The decade began in the midst of the second oil shock to the world economy. The fall of the Shah of Iran in 1979 led to a cessation of Iran's oil exports. The price of oil rose steeply – from about $13 per barrel in 1978 to $32 per barrel in mid-1980. As had become evident in 1974–5, when the oil price quadrupled, an increase in the price of oil has an economic effect on oil-importing countries similar to the imposition of a substantial sales tax. The price of the product goes up and consumers have less income available to spend on other goods and services. The result is a bout of inflation, at least temporarily, and sluggish economic expansion if not recession.

Thus, 1980 was not a good year for the world's economies. In the industrial countries, output, measured by gross domestic product (GDP), increased only 1.5 per cent, compared with an average of 3.9 per cent in the four previous years. Inflation averaged 12.4 per cent. The 'misery index' – the rate of unemployment plus the rate of inflation – was at a high level. In the developing countries, surprisingly, output continued to expand vigorously; the real GDP of the so-called non-oil developing countries rose 6.0 per cent in 1980, slightly above the average for 1970–9. But this was not to last. In Eastern Europe economic growth almost came to a halt in 1979–81.

Important political changes marked the opening of the era of the 1980s. In the United States, it was the last year of the less-than-successful Carter presidency. The country was struggling with inflation, declining output, and an acute shortage of gasoline. Carter's difficulties were to be magnified by the seizure of American hostages in Teheran.

In November 1980, Ronald Reagan won the presidential election on a platform that promised to reduce the role of the Federal government (partly by shifting functions back to the states), to cut non-defence spending and tax rates, to balance the budget, to overcome inflation, to accelerate deregulation, and through these supply-side measures to renew economic growth.

In the United Kingdom, the political turnover came in May 1979 with a Conservative electoral victory and Mrs Thatcher's accession to 10 Downing Street as the first woman prime minister in Britain's history. She quickly set to work in an effort to cure the economy of some chronic ills: high inflation and low productivity growth. This was to be accomplished by firm monetary and fiscal policies, a smaller role for government, reduced power of trade unions, deregulation, and denationalisation.

In France, François Mitterrand, after two earlier unsuccessful attempts, won the presidential election in May–June 1981, replacing Valéry Giscard d'Estaing. And the 'union of the left' – the Socialist and Communist Parties – achieved a majority in the National Assembly. Mitterrand's campaign was based largely on a promise to reduce unemployment, which was about $7\frac{1}{2}$ per cent in 1981, compared with less than 3 per cent in the early 1970s. Mitterrand intended to speed up the growth of the economy and shorten the working week. He was also committed to nationalising some banks and additional industries.

The political shift in Germany came in 1982, when the coalition between the Free Democrats and Helmut Schmidt's Social Democrats was dissolved and Helmut Kohl, head of the more conservative Christian Democrats, took over as Chancellor of the new coalition. Schmidt had been a towering figure on the international scene in the 1970s. He and Giscard – both former finance ministers – were largely responsible for the establishment in 1979 of the European Monetary System (EMS) with its Exchange Rate Mechanism (ERM). This in turn created the momentum toward economic and monetary union that became evident in the later 1980s. But Schmidt faced serious domestic economic problems in 1980–2: growing unemployment, a large budget deficit and high inflation by German standards. That is what led to the dissatisfaction of the Free Democrats and the end of their coalition with the Social Democrats.

Japan, which is completely dependent on imports for its oil supply, was hard-hit by the first oil shock but was less affected in 1979–81. In 1980 Japan's balance of payments showed a current-account deficit of almost $11 billion. It was not evident as the decade opened that Japan would in a few years develop a massive surplus on current account and that its business and financial institutions would become major investors in the United States and elsewhere. In economic policy a move toward deregulation began, starting with the abolition of exchange controls in 1980. Japan's political landscape continued to be dominated throughout the 1980s by the Liberal Democratic Party (LDP) – a party that was divided into fiercely competitive factions and was said to be neither liberal nor democratic nor a party. This gave rise to a number of political corruption scandals over the years. Oddly enough, the factional differences did not involve policy issues. They arose from the fact that political constituencies elected more than one representative to the Diet.

Italy continued to experience frequent changes of government but economic policy did not change radically.

In Spain, an attempted military coup in February 1981 was thwarted with the help of King Juan Carlos. In December 1982 Felipe Gonzalez, a Socialist, became prime minister and presided over an economic renaissance as Spain undertook structural reforms and pursued policies that led to a high growth rate and attracted large amounts of capital from abroad, especially from its partners in the European Community, which Spain joined in 1986.

In Eastern Europe and the Soviet Union, too, change was in the air. In Poland, the Gdansk shipyard workers held a strike in 1980 and secured the legal right for workers to form independent unions and to strike – unprecedented in the Soviet bloc. The reforms brought a massing of Soviet troops on the common border and the threat of invasion. Lech Walesa emerged as a charismatic leader. In Hungary economic reform had been proceeding for some time. I heard János Kádár, in a private meeting with the Group of Thirty in Budapest in 1982, say that although he had been a Communist all his life, he had come to the conclusion that central planning did not work in a modern economy. In the Soviet Union, Leonid Brezhnev was obviously failing and would die in November 1982, to be succeeded by Yuri Andropov, who started the process of political and economic transformation.

Mao Zedong, China's paramount leader, died in 1976. At the end of 1978 Deng Xiaoping initiated a series of economic reforms in the agricultural sector and in foreign trade. In the mid-1980s the economic reform process – moving toward a market economy – was to be applied in the industrial sector and the Chinese economy was to achieve remarkably rapid growth rates.

In the third world, the oil-exporting countries, especially those in the Middle East, were once again piling up foreign exchange earnings. The current-account surplus of the OPEC nations, which had reached $68 billion in 1974, had virtually disappeared by 1978, mainly as the result of massive imports. As the oil price shot up again in 1979–80, the OPEC current-account surplus reappeared and was to reach $108 billion in 1980. Investment, both governmental and private, increased after the first oil shock and again after the second. The heightened economic activity brought with it a need for additional labour, which was satisfied by immigration. OPEC's large current-account surplus of 1979–80, like the one in 1974–5, was equal to about 1.3 per cent of the GNP of the rest of the world. The mirror image of this surplus was the combined current-account deficit of industrial and oil-importing developing countries.

The non-oil developing countries, whose terms of trade worsened in both oil shocks, consisted of at least three groups. In one group were about a dozen or so middle-income nations – mainly in Latin America. They had been borrowing from commercial banks in the industrial countries throughout most of the 1970s, invested heavily and grew fairly rapidly. This process was regarded as a 'recycling' of the OPEC surpluses. As the oil exporters acquired foreign exchange arising from their current-account surpluses, they placed the funds in bank deposits or short-term securities in the industrial countries. This enabled the banks to increase their lending especially to developing countries. The latter were then in a position to incur and finance enlarged current-account deficits. Thus, the OPEC surplus provided the means for its own financing. What else could the OPEC countries with large current-account surpluses do with their accruing foreign exchange reserves but use them abroad to make direct investments, buy securities, acquire bank deposits, or give grants to other countries? The smoothness of this recycling process in 1974–8 refuted some of the apocalyptic predictions made after the first oil shock.

Whether recycling would proceed so smoothly after the second oil shock was not clear. The way it worked, most of the lending and investing by the OPEC nations was in the financial centres of Europe, North America, and Asia. The funds then had to be redistributed to countries in deficit. While some of the redistribution took the form of foreign aid grants by industrial-country governments to low-income LDCs and funds were available for loans by official multilateral institutions, a principal mode of recycling was extension of credit by commercial banks in the industrial countries to middle-income developing countries.

A major question in 1980 concerned the sustainability of such lending by commercial banks. If it did not continue, the recycling channels would become clogged and the implications for both the LDCs that were heavy borrowers and the rest of the world would be less than favourable. The LDCs would not only have to reduce their imports, which would have a depressive effect in the industrial countries, but might also find it difficult to continue servicing their debts.

Among a number of the Latin American LDCs, military governments existed in 1980. In fact Argentina, Chile, Guatemala, Paraguay and Uruguay were condemned for human rights violations by the Council on Hemisphere Affairs. The continent was to undergo a tidal movement toward more democratic regimes in subsequent years.

Another, smaller, group of non-oil LDCs consisted of the so-called 'newly industrialised countries' (NICs) of Asia: Hong Kong, South Korea, Singapore, and Taiwan. They had been growing rapidly for some time, based on high rates of investment and strong export expansion. But they had a combined current-account deficit of $9 billion in 1980. Most other countries in the region – except Indonesia, an oil exporter – also had current-account deficits. In Korea the successful economic performance occurred under the presidency of General Park Chung Hee, who took power in a military coup in 1961. He was assassinated in October 1979, just when the second oil shock was depressing the economy and labour unrest was being expressed in demonstrations and strikes. Park was succeeded by another general, Chun Doo Hwan, and Korea remained under a military government, against which tens of thousands of students protested in 1980, followed by the imposition of martial law.

Singapore, a city state smaller than New York City, developed rapidly in the 1960s and 1970s under Prime Minister Lee Kuan Yew. Among other policies, he encouraged incoming direct investment with the result that much of Singapore's output comes from foreign-owned firms. In 1980 Singapore was in the early stages of its 'second industrial revolution' aimed at the development of high technology industries.

The third, and numerically greater, group of oil-importing developing countries – those with relatively low incomes – had to rely on official assistance from governments and multilateral institutions to help finance their enlarged deficits. These countries are in south Asia and Africa. There is a great diversity, both political and economic, among them.

In India, Indira Gandhi became prime minister for the second time in January 1980. The economy was one of the most highly regulated outside the Communist bloc, and its growth rate in the years 1965–80 was relatively low as compared with other developing countries.

Another political change early in the decade was in Egypt, where the slain Anwar Sadat was succeeded as president by Hosni Mubarak. His country was the beneficiary of heavy financial assistance from the United States, owing to Sadat's participation in the Camp David peace accord with Israel in 1979.

With the major exceptions of Gabon and Nigeria, most southern African countries were adversely affected by the rise in oil prices in 1979–80. The years ahead would not be kind to their populaces.

Our narrative begins in an atmosphere of uncertainty, political and economic, as the three areas of the world economy were being affected for a second time by a dramatic rise in the price of oil. In the OPEC countries, particularly those in the Middle East, there was a sense of economic power as the wealth came pouring in, but perhaps also an inquietude as events in Iran unfolded and its war with Iraq broke out in September 1980.

3 Changing Philosophies of Economic Policy

The 1980s began with an external shock to most economies as the world price of oil rose by about 150 per cent. The years around 1980 also witnessed numerous changes in political leadership, as was noted in the previous chapter. Many, though not all, of the political shifts brought fundamental policy modifications. In some cases – Thatcher and Reagan especially – the new leaders were hedgehogs rather than foxes and acted to impose a new ideology that was closer to orthodoxy than what it replaced. In other cases the alteration in policies – also toward greater orthodoxy – came about through the force of circumstances and under the leadership of foxes like Mitterrand in France and Gonzalez in Spain. These are four selected examples from among the industrial countries. As our story unfolds we shall encounter other instances of striking shifts away from interventionist policies based on changes in economic philosophy – sometimes carried out by ideological hedgehogs and sometimes by pragmatic foxes.

3.1 THATCHER AND REAGAN

Margaret Thatcher and Ronald Reagan, who have been called 'soul mates', were strong believers in free markets. They each initiated a series of policies that were designed to free up their economies and thereby improve economic performance by reducing the role of government. However one judges their success, there is little doubt that they had a major impact on their own countries and on the policies of many other countries.

Even casual observation reveals a number of striking similarities between 'Thatcherism' and 'Reaganomics'. Both Thatcher and Reagan asserted primacy over the power of trade unions, Reagan by breaking the air controllers' strike early in his administration and Thatcher by putting down a miners' strike in 1985. Union membership fell in both countries during their terms of office. Both emphasised supply-side policies, especially reductions in income taxes, but the favourable effects on economic growth promised by these policies are difficult to detect. Both pursued deregulation, with mixed results. Both left their successors with recessions to contend with and both were critical – Thatcher openly and Reagan by inference – of their successors. And, incidentally, both survived assassination attempts: Reagan was wounded by gunshot in 1981 and Thatcher escaped a bombing that killed five others in 1984.

In office, Thatcher and Reagan differed in many ways. She was not only a hard worker but often took on tasks that might well have been left to her ministers or staff. Reagan was above all that. He was amiable but unfocused except for a few strongly-held beliefs. She was analytical; he operated by instinct. He loved to use jokes and anecdotes; she was rather humourless. He had a soft heart; she could be hard as nails. She was a natural orator. Reagan's style, as Nigel Lawson put it,

> was that of the actor he once was. He knew his lines perfectly, and had rehearsed and polished them endlessly, with the result that everything, from the generalizations to the anecdotes, came across with impressive fluency, obvious sincerity, and complete command. But take him off the ground covered by his script, and he often had difficulty in grasping the point.[1]

What Thatcher and Reagan shared as government leaders was a simple tenet: get the government off the backs of the people and let 'the magic of the market place' prevail.

3.2 THATCHER'S BRITAIN

The tone and substance of what was to happen in economic policy formation in many countries were foreshadowed beginning in May 1979 when Margaret Thatcher became prime minister. The daughter of the owner of two grocery stores who was also a local politician in Grantham, the town of her birth, Margaret Thatcher was educated at Oxford, reading chemistry and later becoming a tax attorney. She was intelligent, hard working and tough. The sobriquet 'iron lady', coined in the Soviet Union in 1976, came into wide use. But the lady is also very feminine. François Mitterrand is said to have described her as having 'the eyes of Caligula and the lips of Marilyn Monroe'.[2] Her personal qualities helped her to dominate the British government for twelve years. She was also lucky in that not long after she took office Britain became a net exporter of oil from the North Sea fields.

It is said of some people that they may be wrong but are never in doubt. Margaret Thatcher is probably in that genre. I met her a year and a half before she became prime minister, when she visited the Brookings Institution. I was struck by her strong-mindedness, her keen intelligence, her knowledge of economics and her ability to make her presence felt and to take charge of a meeting.

What she took charge of on entering Number 10 was an economy that had been in trouble through a good part of the 1960s and 1970s. Plagued by inflation that was aggravated by persistent upward trade-union pressure on wages and by slow productivity growth – attributable in part to 'overmanning' – Britain had been forced to devalue sterling in 1967, to leave the EC exchange-rate snake in 1972, to borrow from the IMF in 1976–7 and to put up with widespread strikes in 1979.

At the time of the election in May 1979, the economy had been expanding at a good clip but inflation was in double digits, partly driven by wages rising by more than 15 per cent per year for most of the decade. Unemployment, though well above the levels of the first half of the 1970s, was somewhat lower than in 1976–8.

The broad economic aims of the Thatcher government are set forth in Chapter 2. In the words of Sir Alan Walters, economic adviser to Mrs Thatcher, 'The objective was to get a market economy functioning efficiently without suffocating government intervention.'[3]

The instruments for achieving the objectives were a strict monetarist policy like that espoused by Milton Friedman (he was, in fact, one of her advisers), a medium-term financial strategy to lower the budget deficit, restraint on wages, legislation to alter the way trade unions operated and a pound sterling that was appreciating under the influence of high interest rates and strong export earnings from oil.

One of the basic differences in economic philosophy between Thatcher and Reagan was that she held strongly to the need to balance the budget whereas Reagan merely paid lip-service to that principle. Ironically, Thatcher's Britain demonstrated in the later 1980s that a country can develop a large current-account deficit even when its budget is in surplus.

Both Thatcher and Reagan were succeeded by members of their own party who shared their values but were less colourful and less single-minded.

John Major, whom Thatcher characterised in her memoirs as 'modest', 'untested', and inclined 'to accept the conventional wisdom', had to endure a recession in 1991–2 and a sterling crisis in 1992 that forced Britain to take its currency out of the ERM.

The dissatisfaction that developed paved the way for Tony Blair and 'New Labour' to win a large majority in the election of May 1997. Thatcher's impact was certainly evident in the transformation of the Labour Party that Blair and his colleagues had brought about. It was symbolic of the new philosophy that one of the first actions of the Blair government was to make the Bank of England independent.

3.3   REAGAN'S AMERICA

Born to a poor family in midwest America, Reagan was a mediocre student at Eureka College but a good athlete. He became a sports announcer on radio and then moved on to Hollywood. Membership in, and presidency of, the Screen Actors Guild developed his negotiating skills and stimulated his interest in politics. That interest was strengthened when he became host of General Electric Theatre and a lecturer for the company. Originally a New Deal Democrat, he gradually moved to the right and in 1964 made a nationally-televised speech in Barry Goldwater's campaign for the presidency. In 1966 he was elected governor of California and that eventually brought him into national politics.[4]

Ronald Reagan took up residence in the White House about a year and a half after Margaret Thatcher came to power. While she moved into Downing Street with a coherent notion of what she wanted to accomplish as regards economic policy and how to go about it, Ronald Reagan's views were less distinct.

Part of Reagan's appeal, not only to members of his own party but also to those who had usually voted for the other party ('Reagan Democrats'), was his ability to characterise America in glowing terms, to help his countrymen 'to stand tall'. One of his favourite ways of doing this was to describe his country as 'a city upon a hill', which comes from the Gospel According to St Matthew and was used in a sermon preached in 1630 by John Winthrop, a governor of Massachusetts Bay Colony.

Reagan's basic aims, like Thatcher's, were to lower inflation and to speed up economic growth. These were to be accomplished by reducing government spending while strengthening national defence, cutting taxes, lightening the 'burden' of Federal regulation, and encouraging 'a monetary policy on the part of the independent Federal Reserve System which is consistent with these policies'.

President Reagan's appointments to high office in his first administration reflected his lack of single-mindedness. His Treasury Secretary, Donald Regan, had been head of Merrill Lynch and was not a man with a strong ideological bent. He never received a single word of policy guidance from the President, nor had a one-on-one meeting with him as Treasury Secretary. It was taken for granted by the President that his Secretary of the Treasury had absorbed his campaign pledges.[5] Reagan's Chairman of the Council of Economic Advisers, Murray Wiedenbaum, was – and is – a well-known economist who is certainly not an ideologue. David Stockman, Director of the Office of Management and Budget, appeared to be idiosyncratic in both his behaviour and his policy views. He too has reported that Reagan 'gave no orders, no commands; asked for no information; expressed no urgency'.[6] But three Treasury appointees were men with burning convictions. The Under Secretary for Monetary Affairs, Beryl Sprinkel, was known as a single-minded monetarist, a faithful disciple of Milton Friedman. The Under Secretary for Tax Policy, Norman Ture, and the Assistant Secretary for Economic Policy, Paul Craig Roberts, were both orthodox supply siders.

Although this diffusion existed in the early days of the Reagan tenure, the supply-side philosophy had a powerful influence on the President, on his team, and on a number of members of Congress – most notably Representative Jack Kemp of upstate New York. Outside the administration, Arthur Laffer and Jude Wanniski used their well-honed talents for publicity to popularise the supply-side view, as did George Gilder in his book *Wealth and Poverty*.[7]

What is the supply-side view all about? Its main thesis is that what drives economies are incentives to engage in economic activity – incentives felt by workers, by savers, and by investors. The way to strengthen these incentives is to reduce marginal tax rates.

No economist will disagree with the proposition that incentives are important. What distinguished the small but vociferous band of supply siders in and around the first Reagan Administration was their rejection of the main-stream belief held by both Keynesians and monetarists that aggregate demand is a major – if not the major – determinant of output, income, employment, and prices. This rejection was spelled out in a confused way in a book by the *Wall Street Journal* editorial page editor, Robert Bartley.[8]

The supply siders claimed that cutting marginal tax rates would lead to large increases in employment, in saving, and in investment while also reducing the rate of inflation. All that seemed to matter was tax rates. Even the budget deficit could be ignored, either because of a Laffer curve effect – the view propounded by economist Arthur Laffer that tax cuts would induce such a large increase in incomes that growth of tax revenues would rise despite the lower tax rates – or the Paul Craig Roberts argument that issuing bonds is equivalent to taxing the public as a way of financing the budget deficit.[9] The latter argument, it may be noted, must have been reconsidered; it does not appear in a book that Roberts published after he left office.[10]

While supply siders tended to ignore the budget deficit, they were not alone. Other conservative thinkers were also tolerant, if not welcoming, of the budgetary imbalance on the grounds that deficits create persistent political pressure to reduce government spending. Olivier Blanchard, of the Massachusetts Institute of Technology, identifies this as the 'centerpiece' of the Reagan conservative strategy, distinguishing it 'from its European counterparts and their strategy of fiscal austerity'.[11]

One of the many oddities in the case put forward by the supply siders was a surprising neglect of the role of corporations in capital formation. Reductions in marginal tax rates were supposed to lead to greater investment. The bulk of investment in the United States, and other industrial countries, is carried out by corporate business. But the supply siders were concerned almost entirely with cutting the taxes paid by individuals.

It is difficult to determine how seriously this group of ideologues was taken at higher levels of the administration. There was a good deal of in-fighting among the White House, the Office of Management and Budget, and the Treasury, as is described in detail in Craig Roberts' book. And the supply siders were not fully united; Roberts rejected Laffer's curve and regarded Wanniski as a bull in a china shop. What is clear is that the supply siders helped to engineer the massive tax cut enacted in 1981 – the so-called Kemp–Roth legislation. That the ideology had influence at a high level is illustrated by a hyperbolic statement in a speech by Treasury Secretary Regan in early 1981 to the effect that supply-side economics is a new economic paradigm comparable to Sir Isaac Newton's approach to physics, which 'changed mankind's understanding of the universe'.[12]

The failure of the Reagan tax cuts to produce the results promised by the supply siders induced two types of rationalisation. One was to blame the Federal Reserve's restrictive monetary policy – especially Chairman Paul Volcker, who became Paul Craig Roberts's favourite whipping boy – for repressing the economy. This argument was, of course, inconsistent with the supply-side view that aggregate demand is unimportant. The other response was to claim that the promised results were realised. For example, Jude Wanniski wrote in 1991 that the Reagan tax cuts were responsible for making the US economy one-third bigger than a decade earlier.[13] What he failed to point out is that the economy grew even faster in the two previous decades. Robert Bartley went even further in exaggeration; he measured economic expansion from the bottom of the 1981–2 recession to the peak in 1990 and compared that with the growth rate from the peak year 1973 to the recession year 1982, thereby claiming to demonstrate the beneficial effects of supply-side policies.[14]

In general, the promised effects on investment and saving are impossible to discern in the available statistics. Some increase in labour supply occurred but much of it was due to factors other than tax reform.[15]

While Ronald Reagan was anxious to lighten the tax burden on the American public, he was also eager to strengthen the country's defences against what he was later to call 'the evil empire'. The result was that Federal defence expenditures rose from 23.2 per cent to 26.5 per cent of total budget outlays in the eight Reagan years.

The growing budget deficits that resulted from the combination of tax cuts and rising military outlays were to have major effects on the US economy, on the dollar's exchange rates, on the balance of payments and on America's trade partners in both the industrial and developing worlds. From 1980 to early 1985, the average value of the dollar in terms of the currencies of other industrial countries rose by 80 per cent. Can one imagine any other country putting up with that? Such a large currency appreciation would probably have toppled a government more sensitive to the foreign trade position and less addicted to the belief that markets are always right. That view was to change in 1985 when James Baker became Secretary of the Treasury.

Deregulation was another significant plank in the Reagan platform, though it started under President Carter in the oil and airline industries. The deregulation of saving and loan associations – widening their scope to invest well beyond their traditional field of residential housing – has been assigned some of the blame for the crisis that afflicted those institutions in the latter part of the 1980s. But other aspects of deregulation have been widely applauded – for example, liberalisation in telecommunications and natural gas.

In line with reducing the role of government in the economy, Treasury Under Secretary Sprinkel made it known in May 1981 that the United States would henceforth intervene in foreign exchange markets 'only when necessary to counter conditions of disorder in the market'. This decision was based on the view that

> markets have become more efficient in evaluating and adjusting to new information. Significant and frequent intervention by governments assumes that a relatively few officials know better where exchange rates should (or shouldn't) be than a large number of decision makers in the market, and that public funds should be put at risk on the basis of that assumption.[16]

In general, then, although both Thatcher and Reagan succeeded in moving their economies toward greater market-orientation, their macroeconomic policies left something to be desired, as we shall see in the next chapter.

It is difficult to discern an economic philosophy during the four years of the presidency of George Bush, aside from his campaign pledge, 'Read my lips: no new taxes'. In a four-part survey of economic policymaking in the Bush years, published just before the election of 1992, the *Washington Post* reported that

> President Bush's top economic advisers have worked for nearly four years without agreeing on an overall philosophy or plan and have been divided by personal animosity and turf fights that are fierce even by Washington standards, according to more than two dozen sources inside and outside the administration.

The same report tells us that Treasury Secretary Nicholas Brady was 'muddled', Office of Management and Budget Director Richard Darman was brilliant, had an 'acid tongue' and was in conflict with other members of the administration; and Council of Economic Advisers Chairman Michael Boskin was often left out of the policy-making circuit. The President is said to have complained that 'it is hard at times to sort out or make sense of the advice he receives from his economic team'.[17]

The election of William J. Clinton in 1992 ushered in a very different approach to government. Clinton ran for office on a programme calling for 'change' and he lost no time, after assuming office, in proposing a reduction in the budget deficit and starting an unsuccessful effort to reform the health care system of the United States. In economic policy, his first year featured passage by Congress of his proposal to reduce the budget deficit modestly – from 4 per cent to 3 per cent of GDP over a five-year period and passage of the North America Free Trade Agreement (NAFTA). He had the good fortune to preside over a remarkably prosperous economy, which, among its other effects, helped to produce a much faster decline in the budget deficit and a surplus in 1998 and subsequent years. The Congressional elections of 1994 resulted in a Republican majority that carried on many of the Reagan beliefs. In that atmosphere, Clinton declared at one point that 'the era of big government is over'.

3.4   MITTERRAND'S FRANCE

François Mitterrand, who had unsuccessfully run for the Presidency of the Republic against de Gaulle in 1965 and Giscard in 1974, finally came to power in the elections of May–June 1981, along with a Socialist majority in the National Assembly. The first Mitterrand government, under Prime Minister Pierre Mauroy, included four Communist ministers. This political upheaval, while it may have shocked some of the chanceries of the world, oddly enough was greeted by Washington and Moscow in almost identical language. The official statements from Reagan's White House and Brezhnev's Kremlin both dwelt on the traditional ties between their countries and France and expressed assurance of continued good relations. 'Brezhnev could have signed Reagan's message and vice versa.'[18]

In contrast to the consistency over time of Thatcher and Reagan, Mitterrand came into office with one economic philosophy but within a year was forced to switch to another. He and his government had to move toward the right, adopting a policy of *rigueur*. By the late 1980s French economic policy was not very different from that in Great Britain and the United States.

But at the outset the Mitterrand Government moved in the opposite direction from Thatcher and Reagan. In fact, Thatcher began a programme of privatisation while the French National Assembly was debating the Mitterrand nationalisation proposals. President Mitterrand presented several justifications for the nationalisations. In a press conference in September 1981, he declared that nationalised industries play a pilot role in industrial policy, noting that since 1976 public investments had increased more than 50 per cent compared with only 1 per cent in the private sector. Also, nationalised industries are an arm of defence of French production comparable with de

Gaulle's nuclear strategy: a French *force de frappe*. In a more nationalistic mode, Mitterrand said that nationalisation would keep French companies from coming under 'international control'. He went on to state: 'I am opposed to an international division of labour and production, a division decided not from our shores and obeying interests that are not our own.' Thus, 'for us nationalisation is a weapon to protect France's production apparatus'.

This statement was reminiscent of French policy in the 1960s when Charles de Gaulle, as President of the Republic, opposed foreign direct investment in France. He had to abandon that policy as new foreign plants were established in neighbouring countries from which they could ship their products to France under the rules of the Common Market.

While the nationalisations were being debated in the Parliament, the French franc was devalued in the EMS (4 October 1981) by 3 per cent. This was a warning shot across the bows of the Mitterrand Socialist armada, whether or not it was realised at the time.

Other policy changes introduced by the new government were an increase in the minimum wage and higher family and housing allowances, a one-year 10 per cent surtax on high incomes (affecting about 2 million out of 15 million taxpayers), and a bitterly-resented tax on wealth over 3 million francs (affecting about 200 000 taxpayers).

While the economic philosophies of the Reagan and Mitterrand governments could not have been more different, they both adopted measures that increased the budget deficit substantially.

Another action of the Mitterrand government was to try to reduce unemployment by cutting the work week, lowering the age of retirement to 60 years, providing a fifth week of paid vacations, among other measures that Prime Minister Mauroy characterised as 'social advances'. The work week was initially cut to 39 hours but the aim, which was not pursued, was to go all the way to 35 hours by 1985. Despite these measures, the unemployment rate rose from 7.4 per cent in 1981 to 12.4 per cent in 1997.

This combination of policies was hardly designed to strengthen the foreign exchange value of the franc. France already had a current-account deficit in 1980, which increased in 1981–2, reaching $12 billion. The franc suffered periodic bouts of weakness, which caused concern to Minister of Finance Jacques Delors. The weak franc and the balance-of-payments deficit were to be the Achilles' heel of Mitterrand's initial policies and were to lead to a complete turnaround.

Mitterrand was succeeded in May 1995 by Jacques Chirac. The rise in unemployment was a major reason for dissatisfaction and Chirac invoked legislative elections in 1997 in which, as he hardly intended, the leftist parties won a majority and Lionel Jospin became prime minister.

3.5 JAPAN

Policies changed in Japan in the course of the 1980s but less dramatically than in Britain, the United States, and France. And alterations in the basic philosophy of policy were slight. Still Japan moved toward a less-regulated and less export-orientated economy. Exchange controls were removed in 1980. Partly under pressure from the United States, Japan liberalised its financial markets and institutions. A number of administrative reforms lightened the heavy hand of government on the economy. And some privatisation, including the giant Nippon Telephone and Telegraph Company (NTT), took place. Prime Minister Nakasone (1982–7) is said to have been influenced by Margaret Thatcher.

In the 1970s, Japan had the highest growth rate among the major industrial countries. The economy slowed along with others in the early 1980s. Yet, Japan's fiscal policy moved toward restraint at that time in a reaction against large budget deficits.

Japan had a temporary current-account deficit as the decade began, under the impact of the steep rise in the price of oil. A current-account surplus reappeared as early as 1981 and grew to large proportions as the decade wore on. As a result, Japanese financial institutions and other investors became major capital exporters, especially to the United States. These investments included some conspicuous acquisitions – notably the Rockefeller Center in New York – that aroused some resentment among Americans, most of whom had forgotten that their fellow-countrymen had done something quite similar in Europe in the 1950s and 1960s.

By 1987 Japan's current-account surplus had become embarrassingly large. That was one reason for a shift in focus to the domestic economy. The Mayekawa report, published in 1986, recommended that Japan give priority to encouraging domestic demand and solving some of its problems at home. A substantial programme of domestic spending was inaugurated in 1987. Together with a stimulative monetary policy, it set off the boom – the bubble economy – that Japan experienced in the next few years. That gave way in the 1990s to a falling stock market, a drop in property values, and the most severe recession in Japan's post-war history.

Over the years, Japanese policymakers have been torn between pressure to deal with short-term cyclical problems and their concern about the long-term problems associated with the 'greying of Japan' – that is, the low birth rate and the prospect that 'of the major industrial countries, Japan will experience the most rapid increase in the share of the elderly in the total population in the coming decades.' The old-age dependency ratio is projected to rise from 12.1 per cent in 1990 to at least 25.5 per cent in 2020.[19]

3.6 GERMANY

Germany at the beginning of the new decade found itself with a stagnant economy, too much inflation, higher unemployment and a larger budget deficit than it was accustomed to. The Kohl government, when it took over in October 1982, was determined to improve this situation. Emphasis was placed on reducing the budget deficit ('consolidating' was the popular word for this) by holding down expenditures, on reforming the tax system so as to encourage private investment and on stimulating housing construction.

Yet as two German scholars wrote:

in contrast to both the UK and US experience, the change in government in 1982 did not represent a complete break with the past. The Schmidt government had already been pledged to a policy of fiscal consolidation, which was then more forcefully pursued by its successor. The main difference was that the Kohl government was less hamstrung by internal divisions, and from the very beginning its fiscal policies appeared to be more decisive than those that the Schmidt government pursued in 1982.[20]

It is fair to say, therefore, that the switch from Schmidt to Kohl did not have anything like the earth-shaking effects on economic policies that occurred in Britain, the United States, and France. The big change in the West German economy came only with unification with what was East Germany.

3.7   COUNTRIES IN TRANSITION

It goes without saying that the philosophy of economic policy has changed radically in the former Soviet Union, Eastern Europe and China. Mikhail Gorbachev started the process with *glasnost* and *perestroika,* but his heart was not in thoroughgoing economic reform. Boris Yeltsin struggled to bring it about but it is a painful process. The countries of Eastern Europe have made considerable progress but differ in the extent to which they have succeeded in reforming their economies. China has undergone tremendous economic changes since 1978 without explicitly abandoning communism. In one way or another these countries are abandoning central planning and shifting towards market-based systems.

3.8   DEVELOPING COUNTRIES

In 1980 the many third world countries were in different stages of development, ranging from the high income Asian 'tigers' (Korea, Hong Kong, Taiwan and Singapore) to some very poor countries in Africa. In the early decades after the Second World War, many developing countries, reacting to colonialism and anxious for economic progress, adopted socialist philosophies, established state-owned enterprises, discouraged direct investment from abroad and pursued import substitution behind high tariff walls and quantitative import controls.

The period since 1980 brought a basic change in orientation towards free-market economies in east Asia, India and much of Latin America. The policy of import substitution gave way to more open trade. Beyond that, numerous developing countries launched themselves on a process of more basic reform involving less state intervention in their economies and more effective policies in what came to be called 'the Washington consensus'.[21] This may help to account for the fact that in the recession of the early 1990s the industrial countries were given a boost in demand as developing countries maintained rapid growth rates and rapid import expansion. But the economic and financial crisis that overcame the east Asian countries in 1997 reversed that process.

4 America and Britain

This chapter and the following one trace developments – both macro-economic and structural – in a number of major industrial countries from 1980 on. Chapter 6 will be devoted to the interactions among these economies. The purpose is not to review history comprehensively but to bring out major changes and to take note of the more lasting impacts – the legacies – of Margaret Thatcher, Ronald Reagan, François Mitterrand, and other national leaders. The initial focus is on the United States since it is the largest economy with the greatest impact on other countries.

4.1   UNITED STATES

Developments in the United States since 1980 were strongly affected by fiscal policy that produced a large and persistent budget deficit.

Macroeconomic Evolution

The combination of the tax reductions enacted in 1981 and the build-up of defence outlays produced a budget deficit that increased from $74 billion in fiscal year 1980, the last year of the Carter presidency, to $185 billion in 1984, when recovery from the recession of 1981–2 was well under way, and $221 billion in 1986. The structural, or cyclically-adjusted, budget deficit – which abstracts from the effects of recession – increased from 1.8 per cent of potential GDP in 1981 to a peak of 4.8 per cent in 1985.

Meanwhile the Federal Reserve System, under the chairmanship of Paul Volcker, had begun in 1979 to combat inflation with a highly restrictive monetary policy. Inflation in the United States had crept up in the late 1970s, partly under the influence of substantial wage increases in the automobile and steel industries. But inflation accelerated with the advent of the second oil shock. Consumer price advances exceeded 11 per cent in 1979 and 13 per cent in 1980, the highest rate of inflation since 1947, with the single exception of the year 1974, when the previous oil shock had its effect.

Paul Volcker, who was hardly a monetarist, was shrewd enough to persuade his policymaking colleagues at the Federal Reserve to adopt a quantitative approach to the implementation of monetary policy, based on target growth rates for the monetary aggregates. While interest rates soared – the Treasury bill rate was above 15 per cent and the prime rate on bank loans reached 20.5 per cent in the summer of 1981 – the Federal Reserve was able to minimise the political heat by sticking to its announced money supply targets.[1]

The oil-price increase and tight money created, or at least contributed to, the recession in which real GDP fell by more than 2 per cent and unemployment reached 9.7 per cent in 1982. That recession carried the US economy to its lowest point in post-war history in terms of idle labour and unused industrial capacity.

It is also noteworthy that a significant fraction of the fall-off of GDP was accounted for by the reduction of exports of goods and services. While Americans had ample reasons to become aware of international interdependence after the two oil shocks, this experience added another dimension. The decline of US exports was the result not of arbitrary action by OPEC but of three other factors: appreciation of the dollar by some 36 per cent from 1980 to late 1982, the slashing of imports by Latin American countries owing to the debt crisis which erupted in the summer of 1982, and the slowdown in economic activity and therefore in imports in other industrial countries. The trough of the recession came in the third quarter of 1982.

The Reagan tax reductions – embodied in the Economic Recovery and Tax Act of 1981 (ERTA) – provided for cuts in marginal tax rates of individuals and families by 5 per cent in 1981, 10 per cent in 1982, and another 10 per cent in 1983, cumulating to 23 per cent. The maximum marginal rate was reduced from 70 to 50 per cent. For corporations, depreciation allowances were liberalised (this was partly reversed in 1982) and the investment tax credit was extended to cover additional types of equipment.

The Federal Reserve began to ease monetary policy around the middle of 1982 and interest rates came down sharply from their record high levels as the growth rate of the money supply doubled. The prime rate on bank loans fell from 16.5 per cent at midyear to 11.5 per cent in December and the yield on long-term Treasury bonds declined from 13 to 10 per cent, bringing with it a drop in mortgage interest rates.

With both fiscal and monetary policy shifting toward stimulus, consumers and businesses stepped up their spending. Housing starts rose and automobile sales increased sharply in the latter part of 1982.

The recovery was also aided by a significant reduction in the rate of inflation. Consumer prices, which had risen in double digits in 1980 and 1981, advanced only 1.2 per cent in the second half of 1982 (Figure 4.1). To some extent, the price rise was bound to taper off. What the United States and other oil-importing countries were experiencing was a jump in the price of oil, not a continuing advance. As long as wages did not respond fully to the sharp upswing in consumer prices – and they did not – there was no reason for prices to continue to climb rapidly. In addition, the appreciation of the dollar (lowering the cost of imports) and the recession itself helped to bring about the deceleration of inflation.

The economy recovered vigorously in 1983–4 and maintained a satisfactory rate of growth during the next five years, when GDP increased on average by 3.4 per cent per year. The rate of inflation averaged 3.6 per cent annually in the years 1985–9, with an upward trend during the period.

The economic expansion that began in 1982 brought with it some financial and economic excesses. That was the 'go, go' era of speculative construction of office buildings based on readily supplied credit, of mergers and acquisitions, of leveraged buyouts and hostile takeovers of corporations, of 'junk bonds', of computerised trading in stocks, of illegal stock market transactions that sent several notorious operators to gaol and of a rapid run-up in stock prices. From 1982 to mid-1987, stock prices tripled as measured by the Dow Jones industrial average. In the first eight months of 1987, they rose 40 per cent. The ratio of prices to earnings, which had been about 17 in the 1960s and 11 in the 1970s, increased sharply in the 1980s to a peak above 23 in August 1987. Part of the explanation lay in the issuance of large amounts of debt – especially bonds – by corporations, some of the proceeds of which were used to buy up outstanding shares of their common stock – to the extent of about $100 billion per year in 1984–9.

It is clear that what was going on in the stock market was a speculative bubble: a market in which each investor knew that the inflated price of stocks was unsustainable but hoped to be able to sell before the predictable downturn. This phenomenon is also known as 'the greater fool theory'. The day of reckoning came on 19 October 1987 – Black Monday – when stock prices fell 23 per cent in a near panic.

What brought on the sharp drop? The main explanation is that the market rose too steeply and a reversal was inevitable. But other forces were also at work. Interest rates in the United States had risen sharply in 1987; the yield on 10-year US Government bonds went up from

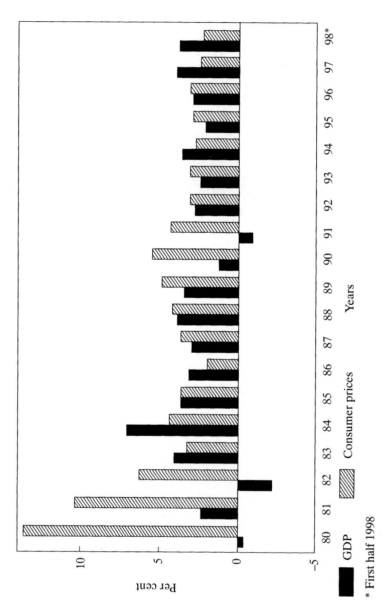

Figure 4.1 Growth and inflation, 1980–98

$7\frac{1}{4}$ per cent in March to over 10 per cent in mid-October. A rise in interest rates tends to depress stock prices for two reasons: corporate earnings are adversely affected and investors are attracted away from stocks to bonds.

The advance in interest rates in turn can be attributed to expectations of a further depreciation of the dollar. As is discussed in Chapter 6, the Group of Seven finance ministers and central bank governors agreed in early 1987 – at a meeting at the Louvre – to stabilise exchange rates; in particular, to reverse the policy initiated at their meeting at the Plaza Hotel in New York in 1985 and put a stop to the decline of the dollar. As events unfolded in 1987, this new policy became less and less credible. To sustain it, central banks had to intervene heavily in foreign exchange markets buying dollars. When market participants expect a currency to depreciate, they will also sell fixed-interest securities denominated in that currency. Hence the rise in US interest rates.

The stock market 'crash' turned out not to have serious macroeconomic repercussions either in the United States or abroad, where stock prices had also fallen. US stock prices recovered and surpassed their 1987 peak in late 1989.

The economy continued to expand briskly during Ronald Reagan's final years in office. George Bush was less fortunate. The economy slowed sharply in the fourth quarter of 1989. After a moderate rebound, economic activity turned down in the summer of 1990 and declined 1.4 per cent through the first quarter of 1991. This was followed by a sluggish and uncertain recovery – the slowest since the Second World War. As a result, by the summer of 1992, during the election campaign, real GDP was only 5.2 per cent above the level just before Bush became president. And unemployment had risen from 5.3 to 7.5 per cent. These were the main reasons for the plunge in Bush's popularity from its extraordinarily high level after the war against Iraq and it contributed to Clinton's victory over Bush at the polls in November 1992.

Bush took a step toward containing the budget deficit. His administration negotiated with the Congress a large cut in the deficit from what it would have been by imposing ceilings on spending, higher tax rates on upper incomes and new excise taxes.

President Clinton's main accomplishment in domestic economic policy in his first year was to present and persuade Congress to adopt a deficit reduction package, involving higher taxes mainly on upper-income groups and ceilings on expenditures. Those measures along with fairly vigorous growth in the economy resulted in a decline in the budget deficit from $255 billion in fiscal year 1993 to $22 billion in 1997. For fiscal year 1998 a budget surplus – more than $60 billion – was being forecast by the Congressional Budget Office in the summer of 1998.

During Mr Clinton's second term the rate of unemployment decreased to its lowest point in two decades while inflation in 1997 fell to the levels of the early 1960s. In these circumstances, American stock prices rose even more spectacularly than in 1982–7. From 1990 to the end of 1997, the Dow Jones industrial average almost tripled. From December 1997 to its peak in November 1998 that average rose an additional 18 per cent but then it fell off, along with the stock prices of most other countries.

Balance of Payments and Exchange Rates

While interest rates came down from their elevated levels of 1980–1, real interest rates remained unusually high in the 1980s. If we measure real interest rates as inflation-adjusted rates, subtracting the rate of consumer price inflation within each year from the rate of interest, we find that the real rate on three-month Treasury bills was, on average, 3.7 per cent in 1983–9 compared with 1.4 per cent in the 1960s and a negative 1.3 per cent in the 1970s; similarly, the real rate on 10-year US government bonds was 4.9 per cent in 1983–9, compared with 2 per cent in 1961–9 and near zero in 1971–9.

With real interest rates relatively high and the budget deficit continuing to swell, the dollar appreciated further in 1983 and 1984, and turned down only in early 1985. The result was a growing deficit on current account.

We shall use virtually no equations in this book. But one equation – really an identity – helps to portray the relationship between domestic macroeconomic variables and the balance of payments:

$$(I - S) + (G - T) = (M - X)$$

where I is gross private domestic investment, S is gross private domestic saving (of businesses and households), G is total government spending, T is total tax revenue, M is imports of goods and services, and X is exports of goods and services. Thus, $(G - T)$ is the budget deficit (or surplus if T exceeds G) and $(M - X)$ is the current-account deficit (or surplus if X is greater than M). What the relationship tells us, basically, is that if a country is a net dissaver – because its investment outruns its saving, including net government saving via a budget deficit or surplus – it borrows saving from abroad in the form of a net capital inflow that finances a current-account deficit. Similarly, if a country is a net saver, it makes those savings available to the rest of the world by means of net capital outflow and a current-account surplus.

In the United States after 1982, $(I - S)$ increased as business investment and residential construction advanced and private saving declined. Moreover, as noted, $(G - T)$ rose. The inevitable result was a growing current-account deficit.

At the same time, the dollar was appreciating. Differing explanations for the rising dollar were advanced, depending upon ideology or theoretical preconception. Some members, or defenders, of the Reagan administration argued that the admirable policies pursued by the United States, especially the tax cuts enacted in 1981, were influencing investors abroad to place their funds in the United States. Others leaned on interest-rate differences. Still others saw the explanation in terms of expectations about interest rates as the US economy was likely to recover ahead of Europe and Japan.

By February 1985, the dollar's average value relative to the currencies of ten industrial countries had gained no less than 81 per cent. In real terms, taking account of price movements in the various countries, the appreciation amounted to 72 per cent. As the Bank for International Settlements (BIS) observed: 'There is no parallel for this phenomenon of an ever strengthening currency based on ever increasing capital inflows with the current account steadily deteriorating.'[2]

In Chapter 6 we consider the repercussions abroad and internationally-coordinated actions to deal with exchange rates. The effects of the dollar's appreciation on the US economy were mixed. Export growth was very slow as American producers lost market share in many countries. On the other hand, the appreciating dollar lowered the cost of imports, thereby contributing to the deceleration of inflation while also speeding up the entry of goods and services from abroad. Total imports appear to have risen about in line with GDP, but non-oil imports increased much faster than GDP while the sharp drop in the world price of oil held down growth in the total value of imports.

The combination of a growing current-account deficit and a rising dollar was rather unusual. In the past, a country moving into larger external deficit found its currency weakening. In this case, the advance of the dollar – pulled up by relatively high interest rates – was part of the mechanism by which the budget deficit and the private-saving deficiency translated themselves into the current-account deficit called for by our equation. If the dollar had not appreciated – because, say, the Federal Reserve had pursued a less restrictive monetary policy – inflation in the United States would have been greater. That would have discouraged exports and encouraged imports, thereby pushing the current account into deficit in any event. That deficit rose year by year from $11 billion in 1982 to $168 billion in 1987, when it amounted to 3 per cent of GDP.

A final burst of appreciation occurred in late 1984 and early 1985. This was regarded as a 'speculative bubble' – a rise in the market driven by speculators each of whom knew that it could not last but hoped to sell before the downturn. The dollar did turn down in February. It declined irregularly to September 1985, when it was given an additional downward push by the finance ministers and central bank governors of the five largest industrial countries (France, Germany, Japan, United Kingdom and United States) meeting at the Plaza Hotel in New York.

The dollar did not react precipitously to the Plaza agreement. Except for a brief period in 1987, the decline was orderly. My explanation at the time for the somewhat hesitant downward movement of the dollar, which was widely believed to be seriously overvalued, was that after each decline market participants were uncertain about whether the next move would be up or down. Therefore they were hesitant to take bearish positions on the dollar.

It took a while for the depreciation of the dollar to have a visible effect on the US trade balance. In testimony before Congressional committees in 1986 and 1987, a number of us carefully explained the so-called J-curve: exchange-rate changes have their effects only with a lag; the initial effect is to raise the domestic cost of imports, and until the volume of imports declines, the total value of imports increases, worsening the trade balance.

Sure enough, the trade balance did eventually respond, but only beginning in 1987. The current-account deficit reached its peak in the third quarter of 1987, more than two years after the dollar turned down. By 1992, the deficit had been reduced by two-thirds, from 3 to 0.8 per cent of GDP. It rose again thereafter, to 1.9 per cent of GDP in 1997 and 2.5 per cent in the first half of 1998.

The reversal of the dollar's steep appreciation of 1980–5 led to an impressive increase in American exports. From 1986 to 1997, the dollar value of merchandise exports almost tripled. The volume of exports rose 150 per cent while the volume of world trade increased just over 100 per cent. In other words, the share of US exports in world markets went up substantially during this period. Moreover, the increase in exports of goods and services accounted for more than 35 per cent of the growth of America's real GDP in the years from 1986 to 1997.

Thus the US economy became much more open. From 1980 to 1997, exports of goods and services in real terms rose from 7.2 to 13.4 per cent of real GDP while real imports went up from 7 to 15.4 per cent.

One of the effects of the string of current-account deficits starting in 1982 and continuing through 1998 was an alteration in the net international investment position of the United States. Up to that time, America was the foremost creditor nation – that is, its assets abroad exceeded its liabilities by an amount that was larger than the net asset position of any other country. The cumulative current-account deficit from 1982 to 1997 reached $1.6 trillion. Concurrently, the flow of private American investment abroad, mainly direct corporate investment and purchases of foreign securities – which accelerated after 1992 – came to almost $2.5 trillion. To finance the current-account deficits as well as the outflows of American capital, the United States relied on inflows of foreign capital in a variety of forms: direct and portfolio investment, purchases of US Government securities by both private investors and monetary authorities abroad, and deposits in banks in the United States. In the earlier years, acquisitions of American assets by Japanese investors attracted a lot of attention, partly because they chose some conspicuous properties. But British and Dutch holdings in the United States exceeded those of Japan.

Structural Developments

In addition to the tax reductions of 1981, a major reform of the tax system was enacted by the Congress in 1986, under the leadership of Secretary of the Treasury, James Baker. In general, the tax reform aimed at eliminating loopholes and tax preferences, broadening the tax base, and reducing tax rates – all in a 'revenue neutral' manner. Marginal tax rates for individuals and families were lowered and the number of rates was reduced from five to three: 15, 28, and 33 per cent. But various exemptions and deductions were dropped or became less generous. For corporations, the tax rate was reduced, but the investment tax credit was eliminated and depreciation allowances were made less favourable. On balance the tax reform lowered the share of personal taxes and increased that of corporations in total tax payments.

A question that has given rise to political controversy is whether the enlarged budget deficits were the result of the Reagan tax cuts or of higher government spending. Defenders of the Reagan policies point out that total Federal tax revenues did not go down as a proportion of GDP during the 1980s, but expenditures rose. What they ignore is that tax revenues would have risen were it not for the Reagan tax cuts. Reforms of the social security system undertaken in the 1970s and 1980s provided for increases in payroll taxes designed not only to finance current outlays but to create a surplus in the social security trust fund. Thus, income taxes fell and indirect taxes rose, relative to GDP, in the 1980s. The growth of expenditures, also relative to GDP, was fully accounted for by defence, health care, and interest payments on the growing Federal debt. Other civilian outlays, including grants to state and local governments, fell substantially as a share of GDP.

On top of the increase in government dissaving – in the form of budget deficits – in the 1980s, private saving declined significantly, continuing a trend that became evident in the mid-1970s. (Private saving decreased in most industrial countries.) Saving by both businesses and households fell off. The result was lower net private domestic investment in terms of GDP and a larger current-account deficit. As a by-product, the real income of Americans grew more slowly. Real per capita income after taxes rose by 1.8 per cent annually in the 1980s and 1.1 per cent in 1990–7 compared with 2.8 per cent in the 1960s. Even that lower rate of income growth owed much to the fact that an increasing proportion of the population joined the labour force. In particular, the participation rate of women rose from 51 per cent in 1979 to 57 per cent in 1989 and nearly 60 per cent in 1997.

The slowdown in the growth of Americans' incomes cannot be blamed totally on Reagan's policies. The fact is that the advance in US productivity – on which the growth of incomes ultimately depends – began to decelerate in the early 1970s. Moreover, productivity advance and economic growth also slowed in other industrial countries. But there was a pickup in productivity growth in the United States to about 2 per cent per year in 1996–7, compared with an average of 0.9 per cent in 1990–5. It remains to be seen whether that is more than a cyclical phenomenon.

There is a silver lining in this cloudy picture. While productivity in the entire non-farm business sector of the US economy rose only about 1 per cent per year in the 1980s and 1990s compared with 2.8 per cent in the 1960s, productivity growth in manufacturing did much better. Output per hour of work in manufacturing rose 3 per cent annually from 1980 to 1997, slightly more than in the 1960s and 1970s.

Related to the more rapid rise in manufacturing productivity has been a shrinkage of employment in that sector relative to total employment. In 1998 manufacturing accounted for only 15 per cent of total private non-farm jobs in the US economy, down from 36.6 per cent in 1960 and 27.4 per cent in 1980. This change has led some observers to the conclusion that output of goods has also declined as a share of total output. This is not so. The production of goods as a proportion of real GDP was slightly higher in 1997 than in 1980 or 1970.

Meanwhile employment in services increased as a proportion of total private non-agricultural employment from 87.3 per cent in 1980 to 95 per cent in 1997. In information technology, output grew twice as fast as in the rest of the economy in the five years 1993–7.

Trade union membership continued to decline, from 25 per cent of the workforce in 1980 to 14 per cent in 1997. And the unions became less militant. The number of working days lost to strikes fell to about one-tenth of what it was in the 1980s. And the unions did not press for large wage gains. Moreover, there was a change in worker diligence. In the 1970s, it was commonly believed that one should not buy a car that came off the assembly line on a Monday or a Friday because it was likely to have been sloppily put together. That was no longer true in 1998.

It is not surprising that these structural changes brought an alteration in income distribution toward greater inequality – another trend that goes back to the early 1970s but accelerated in the 1980s and 1990s. Income inequality among American families increased for a number of reasons. The demand for labour shifted toward those with more education and more advanced skills. Many additional women in higher income groups entered the labour force and their earnings rose much faster than those of women in less affluent families, whereas in the 1950s and 1960s it was women in lower income groups who entered the labour force in large numbers. Contrary to what may be commonly believed, the increase in single-parent families did not accelerate in the 1980s and explains only a little of the greater income inequality. Whether international trade and immigration have been significant factors in the increase in wage inequality has been a matter of dispute among economists. Finally, the tax system became less progressive.[3]

Another problem that came to a head in the late 1980s was the insolvency of many Federally-insured savings and loan associations, which required a 'bailout' by the government. These institutions were hurt by the sharp rise of interest rates beginning in 1979. While they held mostly fixed-rate mortgages, they had to raise the rates they paid on deposits in order to retain them. Later, after legislation gave them greater freedom to invest, many of their real estate loans went sour as the construction boom came to an end. Numerous associations became insolvent and the US Government had to pay off depositors one way or another. Part of the explanation for this débâcle was lax supervision of these institutions.

The Reagan–Bush Legacy

The principal and best known outcome of the twelve-year incumbency of Presidents Reagan and Bush was the large budget deficit of the Federal government. Despite two major efforts to do something about it – the Gramm–Rudman legislation of 1985 and the budgetary agreement of 1990, which followed President Bush's disavowal of his 'read my lips' statement pledging not to raise taxes – the outsized budget deficits persisted. As noted, early in his presidency Clinton succeeded in getting Congress to pass legislation that reduced the deficit. In 1997, under a Congress with a Republican majority, two laws were passed and signed by him pertaining to the budget. They were aimed at further reduction in the deficit over the the ensuing five years while also cutting some taxes, including estate and capital gains taxes.

Despite Ronald Reagan's contagious optimism, Americans became less hopeful than in the past. The sharp slowdown in the growth of incomes led to a distinct alteration in expectations. Whereas in the past most young adults anticipated that they would be better off than their parents, that belief waned in the 1980s. Whether the improved economic performance of the mid-1990s altered those attitudes remains to be seen.

A positive accomplishment during Reagan's presidency was the tax reform of 1986, which left the United States with a somewhat simplified and somewhat more equitable tax system.

Perhaps another aspect of the legacy is the change in the Democratic Party. Its Congressional leaders are now more pragmatic and less ideological. President Clinton is more orientated to the well-being of business enterprises than most of his Democratic predecessors. In 1997 he called for balancing the budget.

As we shall see, a similar change occurred in Britain under the Blair government. If Thatcher and Reagan were soul mates, they were also extremists in some respects. Clinton and Blair were alike in their desire to occupy the middle of the road, or the 'centre left' as Blair called it. It is not difficult to agree with conservative critics who claim that the Clinton–Blair philosophy represents 'a response or accommodation to the ideological upheavals initiated by President Ronald Reagen and Prime Minister Margaret Thatcher'.[4]

We note that the following question was posed in the late 1980s: is America in decline? Some of the developments noted above gave rise to a debate between 'declinists' and those who reject their thesis. The debate was highlighted by the publication in 1987 of Professor Paul Kennedy's *The Rise and Fall of the Great Powers*.[5] This massive book traced the evolution of empires over the centuries and attributed their decline mainly to 'imperial overstretch' or 'strategical overextension' – especially the diversion of resources from wealth creation to military purposes. Actually Kennedy's thesis, in so far as it applies to the United States, may have been rendered nugatory by the ending of the Cold War. If military rivalry, and therefore the arms race, between America and Russia is a thing of the past, what is left of Kennedy's argument? Joseph Nye and Henry Nau have written books refuting the thesis.[6]

The United States still has the highest absolute output per person in the world, just as Americans have the highest per capita income when it is properly measured, which Professor Kennedy failed to do. A study by McKinsey Global Institute compared economic performance in Germany, Japan, and the United States. Total factor productivity – the weighted average of labour and capital productivity – is higher in the United States for a number of reasons, including more intense competition, different managerial goals and government regulations and different sources of financing and relationships with banks. US enterprises depend less on bank financing and more on securities markets.[7]

The judgement seems warranted that America will not soon follow the fate of the earlier dominant powers that Kennedy regards as exemplars. Because there exists no obvious successor – as Kennedy acknowledged late in his book (pp. 534–5) – the United States is likely to remain not necessarily dominant but the most important country on the political spectrum in terms of influence over world affairs.

It is ironical that ten years after Kennedy's book appeared, the United States was being labelled as 'arrogant', and was being accused of 'triumphalism' as the lone superpower. It was said to be too powerful for its own good and for the comfort of the rest of the world and to be guilty of hubris. At the same time, the American economy was outperforming most other industrial nations in terms of its growth rate, its low unemployment, and its minimal rate of inflation. Continental Europe was suffering from high unemployment and Japan was in a state of recession about which it seemed incapable of doing anything. By comparison, the United States hardly appeared to be a country in decline.

Yet the United States was far from all-powerful in terms of influence on world events. The failure of the American Congress in the first half of 1998 to approve 'fast track negotiating authority' for the president or the US dues to the United Nations and contributions to the IMF did nothing to strengthen the country's image in the world; nor did India's and Pakistan's defiance in conducting nuclear tests in May 1998.

4.2   THE UNITED KINGDOM

The Thatcher government, which came into office in May 1979, wasted no time in introducing what Nigel (now Lord) Lawson, initially Financial Secretary to the Treasury and later Chancellor of the Exchequer, called an 'enterprise culture'. As he wrote, the new government was seeking 'not simply to remove various controls and impositions, but by so doing to change the entire culture of a nation from anti-profits, anti-business, government-dependent lassitude and defeatism, to a pro-profit, pro-business, robustly independent vigour and optimism'.[8]

In its early months the government abolished exchange controls. A year later, it lifted the regulation limiting the interest rates banks could pay on deposits (known as 'the corset'), thereby allowing banks to compete freely for interest-bearing funds

In the initial budget, introduced in June 1979 by Mrs Thatcher's first Chancellor of the Exchequer, Geoffrey Howe, income taxes were lowered and indirect taxes were raised. Specifically, the value-added tax (VAT) went up from 10–12 per cent to 15 per cent while the standard income tax was reduced from 33 to 30 per cent and the top income tax rate came down from 83 to 60 per cent (and in 1988 to

40 per cent). On balance, the budget provided for a small decrease in the deficit.

Monetary policy was tightened. In November 1979, the minimum lending rate (akin to the discount rate elsewhere) was raised by an unprecedented three percentage points, to 17 per cent. While interest rates advanced, the targeted money aggregate (M3) was exceeded, perhaps because of the removal of the corset. Meanwhile the foreign exchange value of sterling rose under the influence of high interest rates and the strong balance of payments. Oil exports exceeded oil imports beginning in 1980. The oil surplus reached a peak of £8.1 billion ($10.5 billion) in 1985.

The shift from direct to indirect taxes was designed to strengthen incentives for growth. The rationale for this and other policies bore some resemblance to the views of the supply siders in the United States. In particular, Nigel Lawson argued that growth was to be achieved by microeconomic policies, while the function of macro policies was to prevent inflation. Although Lawson publicly proclaimed this view with vigour in a lecture in 1984, in his published memoirs he states: 'In reality, the distinction may not always be quite as clear-cut as this. In certain circumstances, which history suggests do not occur very often, macroeconomic policy could also play a role in supporting economic activity.'[9]

The 1980 budget incorporated a small increase in taxes despite the budget forecast of a decline of GDP of more than 2 per cent. At the same time, the Medium-Term Financial Strategy was introduced, fathered by Nigel Lawson. It provided for a steady reduction in both monetary expansion and the budget deficit with the aim of bringing down inflation. As the strategy was originally conceived, 'a declining PSBR [public sector borrowing requirement] would enable our monetary objectives to be reached without 'excessive reliance on high interest rates'.[10] Milton Friedman is reported to have been astounded to learn that a Treasury paper gave as the main reason for tightening fiscal policy the need to exercise control of the money supply.[11]

In March 1981, a much more stringent budget was introduced. It increased indirect tax rates on items of general consumption: petrol, beer, wine, and other 'spirits', tobacco and vehicles. It also raised taxes on oil production and placed a one-time tax on bank deposits. The latter seemed inconsistent with the economic philosophy of the Thatcher government. In addition, the budget withdrew an allowance that adjusted personal income taxes for bracket creep owing to inflation. The only relief offered was a two percentage point reduction, to 12 per cent, in the Bank of England's minimum lending rate, which was then suspended. Thereafter, changes in officially-determined interest rates were measured by base rates – those on which banks base their interest charges to borrowers.

Thus the mix of fiscal and monetary policies was switched – in the opposite direction from the mix in America – as fiscal policy was tightened and monetary policy was eased.

As I wrote then: 'This is probably the first time in half a century that a major industrial country has tightened fiscal policy significantly while its output and employment were falling.'[12] Why was fiscal policy tightened? According to Lawson, the Treasury was worried about the ballooning budget deficit. The PSBR 'was running well ahead' of the target set in the previous budget. Lawson concedes that 'roughly half of the overrun could be attributed to the recession'.[13]

The budget evoked a letter to *The Times* from 364 British economists protesting the restrictive fiscal policy. Others have argued that deficit reduction was necessary in order to 'engender long-run credibility for money growth limitation' and hence for anti-inflation policy.[14]

As it happens, control over the money supply turned out not to be very effective. The target range for the growth of broad money (sterling M3) was 7–11 per cent in 1980–1 and 6–10 per cent in 1981–2, but actual expansion of this monetary aggregate was almost twice as great as the targets. Part of the explanation for the overshooting was an increase in 'intermediation' through the banks after removal of the corset. If one judges the tightness of monetary policy from interest rates and the growth of narrower monetary aggregates – not to mention what was happening to output and employment – it becomes clear that the economy was being subjected to monetary restraint.[15] Britain was not the only country that was to have difficulty in the 1980s adhering to a monetary policy based on targets for monetary aggregates.

While the complaints about the 1981 budget may have seemed justified at the time, the fact is that the economy apparently hit bottom in the first quarter of 1981 as marked by the rise of GDP by 1.8 per cent over the next four quarters. Economic growth speeded up to 3.5 per cent per year in 1983–6. As in the United States, this favourable performance after 1981 reflected in part its starting point: a rather deep recession. In 1987–8 the economy grew by almost 5 per cent per year and became overheated.

The economic recovery did not quickly reduce unemployment. It rose from $4\frac{1}{2}$ per cent in 1979 year by year to a peak of 11.8 per cent in

1986 and then fell to just under 6 per cent in 1990. On the other hand the early Thatcher policy of squeezing the economy brought a distinct deceleration of inflation. By 1983, consumer prices were rising only 4.6 per cent, compared with an average increase of 13 per cent in 1979–82. This price performance was broadly maintained until 1988, when inflation began to creep up, averaging 8.7 per cent in 1989–90.

The second half of the 1980s witnessed a boom in consumer spending and residential and commercial construction – the so-called 'bubble economy' – reflecting in part financial deregulation including the abolition of restrictions on hire purchase (instalment credit). Consumer spending was also encouraged by income tax cuts in 1987 and 1988 (when Lawson announced an income tax reform that reduced the maximum marginal rate to 40 per cent). Spending by consumers in real terms increased 6.5 per cent per year in 1986–8 in an economy that was growing 4.7 per cent per year. Expenditure on housing also rose in 1986–8. The counterpart of the spending spree was a sharp drop in personal saving as a proportion of income and a reversal of the current account from surplus to large deficit. Again we observe a similarity to events in the United States. In both countries, the reduction in income taxes, which was supposed to provide an incentive to save and invest, mainly fuelled a surge in consumer spending.

The boom in the latter part of the 1980s also owes something to the monetary policy pursued. Chancellor Lawson, dissatisfied with the various money supply targets, shifted to an exchange-rate target in early 1987 by 'shadowing the D-mark'. Lawson had for some time been recommending that Britain join the ERM, but Mrs Thatcher would not agree. Moreover, in a speech in April 1986 he expressed his misgivings about the various definitions of the money supply and went on to assert: 'In the right circumstances membership of a formal fixed exchange rate system can itself provide a very effective framework for monetary policy.'[16]

In his memoir Lawson tells us that Mrs Thatcher frequently complained about the D-mark-shadowing policy. In her memoirs, she writes: 'Extraordinarily enough, I only learned that Nigel had been shadowing the deutschmark when I was interviewed by journalists from the *Financial Times* on Friday, 20 November 1987.'[17] We may leave it to the historians to sort this one out.

The new policy aimed at keeping sterling between about 2.8 and 3 D-marks. Sterling had declined from a peak above 5 D-marks to less than 3 D-marks between early 1981 and early 1987. It began to recover strength just as the shadowing policy was adopted. As a result, that policy required heavy exchange-market intervention in the form of Bank of England purchases of foreign exchange as sterling tended to rise above 3 D-marks. Published foreign exchange reserves, measured in dollars, almost tripled from the end of 1986 to the end of 1988. While these purchases of foreign exchange were sterilised, by equal sales of government securities to the market, it is not clear what was guiding monetary policy. Interest rates were brought down substantially in 1987–8 – the base rate fell from a peak of 11 per cent in the autumn of 1986 to a low of $7\frac{1}{2}$ per cent in May 1988 (except for a brief reversal in the autumn of 1987) – as was called for by a monetary policy guided by a pegged exchange rate that was tending to rise. But the monetary aggregates increased rapidly as did the supply of credit to the economy. This credit expansion, along with cuts in income taxes in March 1988, helped finance the boom of the late 1980s.

Martin Wolf wrote in September 1992 that

> several senior officials in the Treasury and the Bank of England viewed the ERM as no more than a second-best method of running monetary policy. But Mr Lawson's erratic monetary policies convinced officials that a first-rate monetary policy – one run by themselves – would never be allowed to happen. Along with others, they concluded that monetary policy was far too important to be entrusted to politicians.[18]

The implication is that these officials preferred targeting the D-mark – in or out of the ERM – to letting the Chancellor make decisions about monetary policy. Unfortunately, Mr Wolf does not tell us what method of 'running monetary policy' the officials would have employed.

As the boom developed and the current-account deficit increased, Lawson began to raise interest rates again. Between May 1988 (when base rates were lowered at Mrs Thatcher's suggestion) and the end of the year, base rates were increased from $7\frac{1}{2}$ to 13 per cent. Sterling, which had been 'uncapped' in early 1988, rose above 3.2 D-marks in early 1989 and then declined.

In any event, the boom gave way to slow growth in 1989 and to falling GDP beginning in mid-1990, shortly before Lawson's resignation as Chancellor (about which more below). Real GDP fell more than 4 per cent from the second quarter of 1990 to the same period of 1992. With the recession came a bursting of the bubble, including declines in house prices that left many new homeowners with negative equity and threatened with repossession. And unemployment rose from its low point of 5.9 per cent in 1990 to 10.3 per cent in 1993. That is the economic condition that John Major inherited.

Balance of Payments, Exchange Rates and Monetary Policy

In its early years, the Thatcher government enjoyed a luxury denied to most of its predecessors. It did not have to worry about the balance of payments – at least not until near the end of her time as prime minister. The combination of oil exports and the recession-induced fall-off of imports produced a current-account surplus of nearly $7 billion in 1980 and $14 billion (2.7 per cent of GDP) in 1981. In 1982–5, the surplus averaged $4.5 billion per year.

Tracking movements in the exchange rate is complicated by the wide swings in the dollar against all currencies in the 1980s. While the pound changed little in terms of dollars from 1978 to 1981, its effective exchange rate – that is, its trade-weighted average value – rose almost 18 per cent; its rate in terms of the Deutschemark went up by about the same amount. As interest rates came down in 1982–5, sterling's foreign exchange value also decreased. By 1985 its D-mark value was back roughly to where it had been in 1979 (Figure 4.2).

Britain's current-account surplus disappeared in 1986 – owing in part to the sharp drop in world oil prices – and turned to a rapidly growing deficit, reaching more than $36 billion in 1989. Although the inflation rate remained relatively stable, the effective exchange rate of sterling declined 10 per cent from 1985 to 1987 and its D-mark value went down by about 23 per cent.

We have observed that Lawson's policy of shadowing the D-mark and consequently engaging in heavy intervention in foreign exchange markets was a basis for disagreement between the Prime Minister and her Chancellor of the Exchequer. She was presumably receiving advice from Sir Alan Walters, either in London or from across the Atlantic in Washington. By March 1988, the disagreement between Thatcher and Lawson was out in the open, both in the House of Commons and in the press. According to Lawson, 'It was conspicuous how, during her last three years in office, she was always eager to claim that her Ministers agreed with her, but found it extraordinarily difficult to say that she agreed with her Ministers.'[19]

Through much of Mrs Thatcher's time in office, debate about entry into the ERM raged in the inner circles of policymaking. Sir Alan

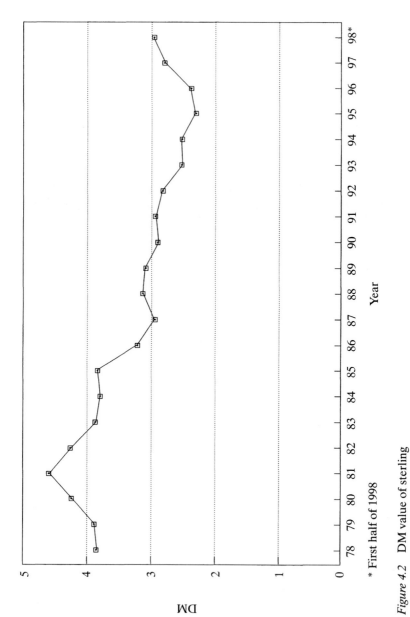

* First half of 1998

Figure 4.2 DM value of sterling

Walters's book, *Britain's Economic Renaissance*, published in 1986 with a preface dated October 1985, contains a strong criticism of the EMS. One gets the impression that, in this part of the book, Sir Alan drew on memoranda he had written for the Prime Minister. His opponents in the inner debate were Chancellor Lawson and Foreign Secretary Geoffrey Howe.

The simmering disagreement between Lawson and Walters had a dramatic denouement. On 26 October 1989, Nigel Lawson abruptly left office, stating in his letter of resignation that 'the successful conduct of economic policy is possible only if there is, and is seen to be, full agreement between the Prime Minister and Chancellor of the Exchequer. Recent events have confirmed that this essential requirement cannot be satisfied so long as Alan Walters remains your personal economic adviser'. On the same day John Major was appointed Chancellor and Walters resigned.

Mrs Thatcher is of the opinion that the Alan Walters question was merely Lawson's pretext for resigning, which she seems to believe he wished to do in any case, for reasons that she does not explain.[20]

Lawson, in addition to pushing for membership in the ERM, had proposed that the Bank of England become an independent central bank.[21] It is doubtful that Sir Alan disagreed with that proposal. What he strongly opposed was the EMS, which he had characterised in print as 'half baked'. One of his criticisms, which came to be known as the 'Walters critique', was that under the fixed exchange rates of the EMS nominal interest rates among its members would equalise so that those with higher rates of inflation would have lower real interest rates than those with less inflation. In fact, this did not happen. Short-term interest rates in Italy exceeded those in Germany by several percentage points while the lira was in the ERM.

Lawson's initial motivation for wanting Britain in the ERM was that it would impose financial discipline by forcing a restrictive monetary policy on Britain in the face of political opposition to tight money. Later, he became disenchanted with the monetary aggregates as guides to monetary policy. Geoffrey Howe, as Chancellor, rejected Lawson's recommendation concerning ERM membership partly on the basis that it might conflict with domestic monetary policy. Only when he became Foreign Secretary did Howe begin to advocate ERM membership.

The Economist for 4 November 1989 offered the view that 'Mr Lawson's resignation may one day be seen as the moment that Mrs Thatcher's term of office started to draw to its close' (p. 69).

Just under a year later Mrs Thatcher reluctantly agreed to British entry to the ERM. Many of us believed, and wrote, that this was done at too high an exchange rate (2.95 D-marks) and recalled that Winston Churchill, as Chancellor of the Exchequer, had restored Britain's pre-war exchange-rate parity in 1925, leading Keynes to attack the move in an article entitled 'The Economic Consequences of Mr Churchill'. The consequence of Mrs Thatcher's decision became evident in September 1992, when Britain was forced to drop out of the ERM. Over the next six weeks sterling depreciated against the D-mark by almost 15 per cent.

A month after the decision to join the ERM, Mrs Thatcher resigned. Her standing with the public had been eroded not only by the Lawson–Walters episode and her views about Britain's role in Europe, but, more importantly, by her insistence on the adoption of a poll tax, which Nigel Lawson identifies as 'the greatest single political blunder of the Thatcher years'. This regressive form of taxation, which was euphemistically dubbed a 'community charge', was substituted for the local property tax on residences. It was highly unpopular.

Structural Developments

Privatisation – a term that came into much more common use during the Thatcher era – was pursued both in the field of residential housing and nationalised industry.

Publicly-owned rental housing was sold to occupants with the aid of mortgage interest relief. From 1979 to 1989 the proportion of houses that were owner-occupied increased from 55 to 67 per cent.

The privatisation of nationalised industries took the form of sales to the public either of shares in those companies or of the physical assets. Among the companies privatised, in whole or in part, were many in the energy field (oil and gas), airlines, automobiles (Jaguar and Rolls-Royce), steel, and telecommunications.

The total proceeds from the sale of shares and physical assets came to £61 billion in the years 1979–90. These receipts financed almost 60 per cent of the fiscal deficit. The number of shareowners in Britain rose from 2 million in 1979 to 12 million in 1989 and the public sector's share in the nation's capital stock fell from 44 to 31 per cent.

Some of the privatised companies were natural monopolies – such as public utilities. The case for their privatisation was problematical. In some industries, a procedure for regulation was established. *The Economist* saw fit to comment as follows on the process:

> It was once the popular mainspring of Thatcherism, but privatisation now threatens to become a political liability ... Public unease about privatisation has been growing for months, and needs no encouragement from Labour. Few people are persuaded that water and electricity should be sold, and the extravagant efforts of the advertising industry have served only to reinforce their doubts.
>
> This is a pity. Privatisation has been a powerful force for good in Margaret Thatcher's Britain. The sale since 1979 of 54 state-owned companies into the private sector has been a remarkable feat of political will, in the face of hostile vested interests.[22]

The combination of privatisation, deregulation, legislation to curb the power of trade unions, and an overvalued exchange rate led to a pickup in productivity growth, especially in manufacturing. Output per worker increased at a rate of 2.4 per cent per year in 1980–8, compared with 1.5 per cent in the 1970s. In manufacturing, output per worker advanced 4.6 per cent annually in the 1980s as against 1.5 per cent in the previous decade. 'Overmanning' was cut back, but at a cost, perhaps inevitable: unemployment averaged more than 10 per cent in 1980–7.

As might be expected, the changes in taxation during the Thatcher years led, as in the United States, to a relative decrease in the weight of income taxes and a corresponding rise in indirect tax revenues. As a proportion of total taxes collected, income taxes declined from 33 per cent in 1978 to 26.5 per cent in 1989. Also, as in the United States, income distribution became more unequal.

The Thatcher Legacy

Mrs Thatcher's growing unpopularity led to what some have called a 'palace coup' by the powers that be in her party and to her resignation in November 1990, the longest-serving prime minister in this century. Somewhat earlier *The Economist* summed up her legacy as follows:

> Mrs Thatcher's departure might be good for Britain. Some of the challenges facing the country are ones on which she is ill-equipped

to give a lead. She is instinctively unhappy with the thought of spending a lot more on education, particularly at secondary schools. She is temperamentally opposed to some of the things the government ought to do to revive the inner cities, because she has persuaded herself that most local government is bad government.

... Mrs Thatcher's achievement – and it has been a great one – has been to articulate a few simple but necessary rules for British politics, when all around her were speaking in the conditional. The rules include a commitment to an open, market economy; a recognition that wealth creation is more important than redistribution, because without it there is precious little to distribute; a clear-eyed understanding that the world is a risky place, where military defences remain necessary; a determination to challenge the corruption of vested interests; perhaps above all, the incessant repetition that people must bear the consequences of their actions.[23]

We have also observed that the Thatcher revolution left Britain's economy less 'overmanned' and therefore more productive, less subject to governmental controls and more responsive to the price system, less dominated by trade unions and less nationalised.

But it also has to be said that macroeconomic policy left something to be desired. Although inflation was brought down by 1987 to its lowest level in two decades, it was reignited by the boom of the late 1980s, reaching 9.5 per cent in 1990. The current-account deficit also increased markedly. The boom gave way inevitably to recession.

Finally, as in the case of Reagan's America, the Thatcher revolution had a profound effect on the terms of political debate as reflected in the positions taken by the opposition party. Britain's Labour Party has become much less Socialist and much more accepting of the market mechanism.

Although Margaret Thatcher deserves credit for this change, it is useful to recall that its seeds existed long before she came along. As far back as 1951 Denis (now Lord) Healey, later to become Defence Minister and Chancellor of the Exchequer in Labour governments, wrote these words (in an obituary article on Ernest Bevin):

The Labour Party may hope to carry the Welfare State and planning further than the Tories, but for a long time physical and psychological factors will fix rigid limits. Further 'soaking the rich' will no longer benefit the poor to any noticeable extent. Further nationalisation no longer attracts more than a tiny fringe of the Labour

Party itself; it positively repels the electorate as a whole. Even among Labour economists there is a growing revolt against physical controls in favour of the price mechanism. A policy based on class war cannot have a wide appeal when the difference between the classes is so small as Labour has made it.[24]

Britain after Thatcher

John Major inherited an economy in recession and suffering from a high rate of inflation. While the inflation rate came down in 1991–2, unemployment rose to $10\frac{1}{2}$ per cent of the labour force at the end of 1992. And, of course, the foreign exchange trauma of September 1992 (next chapter) was still haunting the government.

Although a recovery started in mid-1992, unemployment decreased only slowly and Major's popularity rating, like that of Bush, Mitterrand, and Kohl, fell to a low level after his party won a surprising victory in a general election in April 1992. Britain was not a happy place. Anthony Sampson was quoted as saying 'Britain is going through a period of self-examination and self-doubt and self-humiliation that is greater now than at any time I can remember over the last 30 years'.[25] Maybe so. But compared with most of the countries in continental Europe, the UK economy performed rather well. Output rose, on average, by 2.9 per cent per year in 1993–7, compared with 1.8 per cent for the EU as a whole. Unemployment was roughly halved over the same period, while it remained high at more than 11 per cent in the entire EU.

Despite the economic improvement, the Conservative Party lost the election of May 1997 by a wide margin, as Tony Blair's 'New Labour' Party achieved the largest parliamentary majority in modern British history. The new government's Chancellor of the Exchequer, Gordon Brown, called for 'long-termism' in economic policy in which business can flourish. That requires, he said, price stability and moving beyond the old dogmas of the past to 'tackle the underlying weakness of the British economy – low investment, skill shortages and inadequate infrastructure'. His first budget, presented on 17 March 1998, proposed elimination of the deficit by the year 2000. In this and other ways, the Blair and Clinton governments resembled each other and both differed, in basic philosophy, not only from the opposition party but from earlier leaders of their own parties.

During a visit to London, newly-elected South Korean President Kim Dae-jung perceptively characterised Tony Blair as 'a born politician who is able to harmonize ideals and realities. While retaining the fundamentals of the Labour party, he has been absorbing the positive aspects of Margaret Thatcher's political heritage.'[26]

In general, the British economy appears rather different from what it was in 1979. Apart from the structural changes, such as privatisation of industry and housing, that prevail, inflation is back down again. There is little labour unrest and wages are increasing only moderately. Productivity is rising somewhat faster in the overall economy than in the 1970s and much faster in manufacturing. What was called the 'British disease' is not very evident.

5 Adjusting to Shocks in France, Germany and Japan

Each in its own way, France, Germany and Japan have had to make substantial adjustments in economic policy and political orientation in the years since 1980. France shifted away from Mitterrand's socialist electoral programme of 1981 towards the policies of Thatcher and Reagan. Germany had to adjust to the economic shock of unification and absorption of the former East Germany. Japan became a major capital exporter but in the late 1980s went on a speculative spree at home that gave way in the 1990s to its most severe recession since before the Second World War.

5.1 FRANCE

François Mitterrand was born in 1916 in the Cognac region of France to a relatively prosperous family that was conservative, religious and nationalistic. He studied law and political science. Nothing in his background or early life pointed to his assumption of the leadership of the Socialist Party in the 1970s.

Mitterrand served in the French army and was wounded and taken prisoner by the Germans in 1940. After two failed attempts, he escaped and became a civil servant in the Vichy regime. Apparently, he was an admirer of Marshal Pétain. He later joined the Resistance. This led him into politics in the post-war period and to his first ministerial post: Overseas Territories in the government of René Pleven in 1950–1. He held eleven ministerial positions under the Fourth Republic.

Mitterrand opposed de Gaulle's return to power in 1958 and lost his seat in the National Assembly. After some time in the Senate he was returned as a deputy in 1962 and joined the opposition to de Gaulle. He ran against de Gaulle in the presidential election of 1965, leading a centre–left coalition including the Communists.

In 1971 he participated in the regeneration of the Socialist Party and was chosen as its First Secretary. His rhetoric then became more 'socialist', even revolutionary – calling, among other things, for 'the appropriation of the great means of production'. As Guy Mollet, the former Socialist prime minister, put it, 'M. Mitterrand has learned to speak socialist'.[1]

He lost the election of 1974, by a narrow margin, to Valéry Giscard d'Estaing. Finally, in 1981, he led the left-wing coalition to victory.

Having based its election campaign heavily on the need to reduce unemployment, the Mitterrand government, on entering office in May 1981, increased the budget deficit it inherited from 29 billion to 52 billion francs by raising family allowances, housing subsidies, aid to industry including capital contributions to nationalised industries, and by enlarging public employment. In addition, the minimum wage was immediately increased by 10 per cent and from June 1981 to March 1983 by 38 per cent.

The first fully-fledged budget under the new government – prepared by the young Budget Minister, Laurent Fabius – was aimed at economic recovery. Two features are noteworthy from our point of view. The budget has been described as Keynesian: an effort to encourage economic expansion by adding to aggregate demand through fiscal policy. The second feature is that, in hindsight, France appeared to be 'going it alone' with expansionary measures while some of its neighbours were pursuing contractionary – or at best neutral – policies. Yet, in July 1981, the OECD was forecasting that the industrial countries would show a growth rate of GDP of 2 per cent in 1982, whereas there turned out to be a contraction of 0.4 per cent. Expecting other economies to expand, the French policymakers did not deliberately 'go it alone'.

In any event, the budget for 1982 called for a 27 per cent increase in expenditures and a deficit of 95 billion francs or 2.6 per cent of GDP. The budget also included some tax increases presented as a means of financing the battle against unemployment but aimed, in addition, at 'taxing the rich'. The tax on individual incomes was raised and a ceiling was placed on family exemptions above certain levels of income. What incited the greatest outcry was a new tax on wealth. Above 3 million francs (about $450 000 in 1982), an annual tax between 0.5 and 1.5 per cent was levied. Works of art were exempt for fear that they would be exported to escape the tax. This 'tax on large fortunes', which Mitterrand had proposed in his election campaign, brought in 3 billion francs in 1982 as only half of the estimated 200 000 eligible taxpayers made declarations of their wealth above the taxed minimum.

While François Mitterrand and Ronald Reagan differed greatly in economic philosophy, both adopted what looked like expansionary Keynesian policies – via deliberate increases in budget deficits – in the midst of recession in 1981–2, although Reagan's programme went under the title of 'supply-side' economics. In addition to stimulating demand, Mitterrand's actions increased unit labour costs. Less than five months after the new government took office, the franc was subject to its first devaluation in the EMS – by 3 per cent while the D-mark went up by 5.5 per cent.

Meanwhile the new government's nationalisation law found its way through the parliament. It involved the public takeover, with compensation of stockholders, of five industrial groups, 39 additional banks (several major banks had been nationalised immediately after the Second World War under General de Gaulle's first government), and two financial institutions. Added were two large steel companies, a maker of military aircraft, and a conglomerate that produced armaments, computers, and a variety of other products. After the nationalisations of 1982, state-owned firms were responsible for one-fourth of value-added in industry, about 10 per cent of total employment, and 80 per cent of banking activity.

A result of the shift in macroeconomic policy was that the French economy grew by 2.5 per cent in 1982 as domestic demand rose by 3.5 per cent, while many other industrial countries were undergoing contractions in demand and output. Other results were an acceleration of inflation in France to nearly 12 per cent and a more than doubling of the current-account deficit to $12.1 billion in 1982. The latter change together with capital flight led to a reduction in the foreign exchange reserves by one-fifth in 1981 and an additional one-fourth in 1982.

In light of these developments, the government began to reconsider its economic policies in the spring of 1982. It turned toward the views of Finance Minister Jacques Delors, who had for some time argued for a 'pause' in the pace of Socialist reforms. Then the party in power did badly in the cantonal elections of March 1982. A plan for an abrupt policy change was worked out by the Prime Minister's office and officials in Delors' Treasury. Shortly after the seven-nation economic summit meeting that Mitterrand hosted at Versailles in early June, he held his second large press conference at the Elysée. He spoke in very general terms about the economic difficulties and, in a new departure, stressed the need to reconstitute savings, develop risk capital, give priority to investment, control the budget deficit and combat inflation. For the first time, he put the battle against inflation on the same footing as the fight against unemployment.

What motivated Mitterrand to accept Prime Minister Mauroy's recommended turnaround was the prospect that 'the left' would fail again as it had under Leon Blum in France in 1936 and under Harold Wilson in Britain in 1964–7. It would fail partly because France could not successfully pursue an expansionary policy when the other major countries were mainly concerned with inflation and were therefore in a deflationary mode. Mitterrand learned this at the Versailles summit if he did not already know it.

President Mitterrand left the specifics of the new policy to be made public by Mauroy, but only after an early June weekend meeting of European finance ministers and central bank governors at Brussels had agreed on another devaluation of the French franc, by $5\frac{3}{4}$ per cent, and another revaluation of the Deutschmark, by $4\frac{1}{4}$ per cent.

With the objective of reducing inflation in 1983 to 8 per cent, Mauroy announced that, accompanying the latest franc devaluation, wages and prices would be frozen for four months and the budget deficit would be limited to 3 per cent of GDP. In a vote of confidence on these measures in the National Assembly, the Communists supported the government.

Thus France turned to '*rigueur*' in order to deal with its high rate of inflation and menacing external deficit. The decision was based, in large part, on the realisation by the government that it existed in a world of interdependence. As Favier and Martin-Roland put it, both Mauroy and Mitterrand were motivated by the necessity to change policy if they were to 'endure'. To endure they had to show that they knew how to lead, to manage.

On 1 November 1982 the wage and price freeze came to an end but the government succeeded in getting the unions to accept, or at least tolerate, an end to the indexing of wages to prices. This historic change was made possible by the participation of four Communist ministers in the government.

Even so, inflation in France was higher than in many other industrial countries. The trade deficit was large and France's foreign exchange reserves were running low. In the early months of 1983, debate went on within the government concerning the foreign exchange problem. The alternatives were either to drop out of the EMS or to tighten the screws on the economy once again with a further dose of rigour. But as the debate proceeded, it became clear that these were not realistic alternatives. Dropping out of the EMS would lead to a brusque decline of the franc on foreign exchange markets, which in turn would raise the domestic cost of imports. To support the franc, either interest rates would have to be hiked steeply – which would be a form of rigour – or France would have to adopt highly restrictive import controls, which would run counter to its EC obligations.

Another weekend meeting at Brussels, 19–20 March 1983, resulted in France's third devaluation in less than two years. The franc went down an additional $2\frac{1}{2}$ per cent and the D-mark was revalued by $5\frac{1}{2}$ per cent. Then Mitterrand addressed the nation. He defended the decision to remain in the EMS and stressed that France must now do battle against unemployment, inflation, and the trade deficit. The decision to remain in the EMS was widely interpreted as historic: France confirmed its commitment to the European Community.

Once again, Mitterrand left it to Prime Minister Mauroy to announce the details of the new economic programme. The measures, aimed mainly at reducing the trade deficit, included, among others, a further 20 billion franc cut in the budget deficit by means of new taxes, 'forced saving' in the form of advance payments of income and wealth taxes, and a decrease in foreign exchange outlays via a limitation on travel allowances for French tourists going abroad. It was estimated that the new measures would lower GDP growth by 2 per cent.

Some of these decisions were hard for the Communist ministers to swallow, and they began to distance themselves from the government while continuing to support it in the parliament.

Thus France moved from rigour to austerity. This was reinforced by the budget for 1984 prepared in Delors's ministry and characterised as the most stringent since the Liberation. It was proposed that receipts rise by 8.4 per cent while outlays would increase by only 6.3 per cent.

Public agitation against rising taxes became evident in the summer of 1983. Mitterrand shocked his ministers in September by announcing that this tendency would be reversed beginning in 1985. What worried Mitterrand, as always, were the politics. The French Socialists were becoming the party of high taxes while the right, as represented by Thatcher and Reagan abroad and Jacques Chirac at home, favored tax reduction.

While Mitterrand's rhetoric was designed to keep a distance between his economic policies and those of Thatcher and Reagan, in practice he shifted economic policy in the liberal direction. Income tax rates and social contributions were reduced in the budget for 1985. Tax revenues, which had risen from 38.5 per cent of GDP in 1970 to 42.7 per cent in 1979, reached a peak of 47.6 per cent in 1985 before falling slightly.

As the result of the budgetary decisions of 1982 and 1983, French fiscal policy had became more restrictive. According to the OECD's measure of the cyclically-adjusted budget balance, the budget moved towards restraint by 1.1 per cent of potential GDP between 1983 and 1985.

Economic growth remained sluggish in 1983–4, averaging only 1 per cent per year, but picked up in the following years. The unemployment rate continued to creep up, reaching 9.7 per cent in 1984, and peaking, in the 1980s, at 10.5 per cent in 1987. (It rose higher in the 1990s.) But the rate of inflation came down from 13.4 per cent in 1981 to 5.8 per cent in 1985 and only 2.7 per cent in 1986 when both the dollar and the oil price declined. And the balance of payments improved greatly. The current-account deficit virtually disappeared by 1985. In 1986 there was a surplus of $2.4 billion. With this improvement in the external position, the franc was revalued (by 2 per cent) along with the D-mark and other ERM currencies against the lira in July 1985.

The continued rise of unemployment was the result not only of slow growth but also of another basic reform aimed at industrial modernisation: ending subsidies to inefficient firms and helping those sectors on the frontier of technology. There followed massive lay-offs in a number of industries, particularly steel and coal, and numerous demonstrations by unemployed workers. One is reminded of the policies of Margaret Thatcher.

In July 1984 Mauroy was succeeded by Fabius, who, at just under 38, became the youngest prime minister in the history of Republican France. The four Communist ministers left the government, and Pierre Bérégovoy became finance minister when Jacques Delors assumed the presidency of the European Commission.

Fabius's role was to continue to reconcile his Socialist government with the French business community by emphasising 'the importance of profit, and of individual or private initiative as motors of investment and therefore of the creation of employment'. His new finance minister pursued deregulation by abolishing quantitative credit controls and liberalising financial and foreign exchange markets.

First Cohabitation – 1986–8

The legislative elections of March 1986 gave a bare majority to the rightist parties in the National Assembly and required Mitterrand to appoint a prime minister of a different party from his own. He chose Jacques Chirac, and this led to a period of 'cohabitation' for the first time in the Fifth Republic under the constitution that Charles de Gaulle had fashioned.

The Socialists lost their majority even though, as Favier and Martin-Roland put it, they 'had succeeded where one least expected it. Disinflation, de-indexation [of wages], recovery of profit margins of enterprises, industrial modernisation, and, on the plane of behaviour, a reduction in the ideological antagonism between labour and capital.'[2]

One of the early actions of the Chirac government (7 April 1986) was to devalue the franc by 3 per cent in the EMS, while the D-mark was revalued by the same amount. The aim was to encourage exports, but Mitterrand advised against it and the Socialists in the National Assembly were also critical. That turned out to be the last overt French devaluation in the EMS until its near demise in the summer of 1993.

There was considerable political disagreement between Chirac and Mitterrand. A law was passed authorising privatisation, and the government proceeded to sell shares in a number of large firms. The plan was to privatise 65 enterprises in five years. In 18 months, 40 per cent of the programme was accomplished. After the stock market decline of October 1987, the privatisation effort was suspended.

The Chirac government also repealed the tax on large fortunes and reduced the top marginal tax rate from 65 to 58 per cent.

Another Socialist Prime Minister

In the presidential elections of April–May 1988, François Mitterrand defeated Jacques Chirac by a comfortable margin. Though not required to do so, Chirac immediately submitted his resignation as prime minister and Mitterrand named as his successor Michel Rocard, a Socialist with a strong leaning toward free markets. The growth rate averaged 4.4 per cent in 1988–9 and unemployment declined somewhat from its peak of 10.5 per cent in 1987 to 8.9 per cent in 1990 (and then rose again).

Beginning in 1991, France felt the impact of German reunification. Exports accelerated but interest rates had to be raised. Meanwhile France's adherence to the ERM strengthened. The notion of the stability of the French franc relative to the D-mark – the *franc fort* – became increasingly important as a matter of national policy. The byword was 'credibility'. It was measured by the premium of French short-term interest rates over comparable German rates. Inflation and interest rates tended to converge with those in Germany in the latter part of the 1980s. In 1989 consumer price inflation in France was 3.4 per cent compared with 2.9 per cent in Germany. The interest rate gap – both short- and long-term – had narrowed to 2 per cent in 1989 as compared with about 6 per cent in 1982 and 4.7 per cent in 1985. In 1991, inflation in France, at 3.2 per cent, was below that in Germany for the first time in living memory, and French short-term interest rates were only 0.4 per cent above German rates (Figure 5.1).

By the summer of 1992, the interest-rate gap was even smaller. But in September the ERM was badly shaken. Britain and Italy had to drop out and Spain and Portugal had to devalue. France maintained its D-mark parity, but at the cost of a sharp rise in short-term interest rates and heavy intervention in foreign exchange markets.

The *franc fort* policy symbolised the transformation that had occurred in French economic policy and performance since François Mitterrand assumed the Presidency of the Republic in 1981. Inflation was historically low. While the economy had slowed, France was growing faster than many of its trade partners. Its balance-of-payments deficit was relatively small. The negatives were a high rate of unemployment (10.5 per cent) – made somewhat less painful by a generous system of unemployment compensation – and the need to maintain lofty interest rates to protect the franc in the ERM.

The aims of the *franc fort* were set forth by Jean-Claude Trichet, then Directeur du Tresor in the Ministry of Finance, in a note to Finance Minister Bérégovoy dated 10 April 1992:

> Our grand objective is to pursue a policy of controlling inflation with the aims – ambitious but which are the only ones that our country is able to adopt today – firstly to maintain in France inflation lower than Germany's, secondly – as a consequence of the first objective – to see to it that the franc would appear progressively as having a potential of revaluation against the deutsche mark, and thirdly – as a consequence of the second objective – to reduce and then reverse the 'risk premium' between the franc and the deutsche mark and therefore to obtain in time long-term interest rates lower in France than in Germany.[3]

As for structural developments, the privatisations of the Chirac period were succeeded by a policy of 'neither privatisation nor nationalisation' as enunciated by Mitterrand in 1988. Some partial

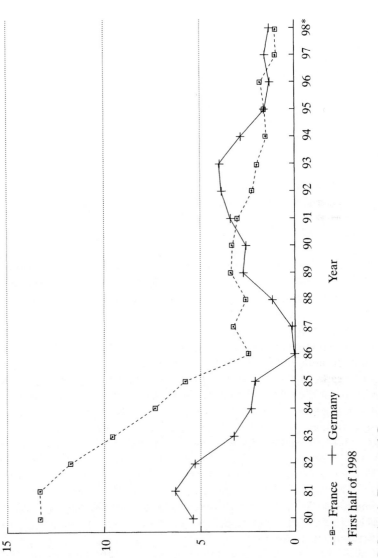

Figure 5.1   Inflation in France and Germany

privatisations took place – for example, Volvo was permitted to acquire a 20 per cent share in Renault, a state-owned company, and Mitterrand announced that he now favoured partial privatisations if they resulted in increased investment or employment. Ironically, one of the motivations for the government's more liberal policy regarding privatisation was that it brought revenue to the Treasury. President Mitterrand may have looked across the Channel at what Mrs Thatcher was doing in this respect.

Second Period of Cohabitation

In the parliamentary elections of March 1993, the Socialists suffered a crushing defeat and a second period of cohabitation began, with Edouard Balladur as prime minister. High unemployment was generally cited as the major reason for the election outcome.

Balladur's first budget attempted to cut the deficit by reducing expenditures and raising taxes. He soon realised that this was an error and launched a 'Balladur bond' in the amount of 110 billion francs to combat unemployment. He also undertook a large privatisation programme, starting with the chemical firm Rhone Poulenc and Banque Nationale de Paris, bringing revenue to the treasury.

Unemployment continued to rise and in July speculation against the franc began in foreign exchange markets. It was based not on a belief that the franc had become overvalued relative to the D-mark but that the government and the Bank of France would have to agree to lower interest rates in order to deal with the unemployment. As is brought out in the next chapter, the upshot was a decision to increase margins in the EMS to ±15 per cent. As it turned out, France used very little of this scope to let the franc depreciate. It stuck to the *franc fort* policy. Meanwhile unemployment rose above 12 per cent in 1994 and, except for 1995, remained at or above that figure into the spring of 1998.

Mitterrand's second term ended in May 1995. He had nudged France further away from the 'exceptionalism' of its earlier history. He managed to preside over France's transformation despite the fact – as later revealed – that he suffered from prostate cancer through his entire 14 years in the Elysée.

Claude Imbert has observed that just as de Gaulle had 'applied his prestige and historic authority to the much needed liquidation of long-standing national traditions' – colonialism and the French right's resistance to change – his main opponent, François Mitterrand, later ended the exile of the French left, 'which had channelled itself away into a Marxist ideological ghetto'.[4] That helped to pave the way for Lionel Jospin's election victory in 1997.

One of the many ways in which the change in France may be illustrated was in the language of Mitterrand. In 1981–2, he frequently employed the word 'socialism' to justify his policies. In the late 1980s and 1990s, that word was no longer heard from him.

Mitterrand was responsible for other changes. Paris has been somewhat altered: the Louvre has a glass pyramid entrance designed by I. M. Pei and a new Richelieu wing (formerly occupied by the finance ministry); at La Défense a monumental arch has been constructed in alignment with the Louvre, the Place de la Concorde, and the Arc de Triomphe; a modern new opera house exists at the Place de la Bastille; and a new, very modern, national library has been built along the Seine.

In a three-way presidential campaign in 1995, Jacques Chirac, then Mayor of Paris, defeated Balladur and Socialist candidate Jospin. Chirac chose Alain Juppé as prime minister. With unemployment rising, his performance was less than impressive. As the popularity of the government deteriorated, Chirac decided to call early elections in May 1997. To his surprise and possibly humiliation, the Socialists, with Communist support, won a majority in the National Assembly and Jospin took over as prime minister in another cohabitation.

As viewed in 1997 and the autumn of 1998, the French economy looked healthy except for the high unemployment rate – even though it had fallen below 12 per cent. Economic growth had accelerated to 3 per cent in the year ending June 1998 and inflation – around 1 per cent – was lower than Germany's. The current account was in surplus and the franc was strong.

Jospin's election campaign had included a pledge to create 700 000 jobs for young workers and to cut the work week to 35 hours. In office, with Jacques Delors' daughter, Martine Aubrey, as labour minister, he promised to redeem that pledge by the year 2000. Whether that would come to pass remained to be seen. Jospin also restarted privatisation.

Jospin's 'low-key, collegial style is a novelty in France' wrote *Washington Post* correspondent Anne Swardson.[5] According to political science professor Olivier Duhamel, 'He has profoundly changed the way we govern ... He has broken with the monarchial tradition ... that continued from Louis XIV to ... Mitterrand.'[6] And – not unimportant – he has a sense of humour. There are predictions that he will be the next president of the Republic.

5.2   GERMANY

Less space is devoted to Germany (and Japan) than to the United States, Britain, and France not because they are less important but because they underwent less of a transformation. In the case of Germany the big metamorphosis came only in 1990 with the reunification of East and West Germany.

An international agreement back in 1978 had a lasting effect on German attitudes about economic policy. Faced with sluggish economic growth and a large current-account surplus, the German government under Chancellor Helmut Schmidt agreed to adopt a more stimulative budget policy at the annual economic summit meeting, held in Bonn in July 1978. Included were a cut in taxes and an increase in expenditures with a combined effect equivalent to 1 per cent of Germany's GNP. A number of other countries took similar action while the United States agreed to pursue a more restrictive fiscal policy and to deregulate the price of oil and adopt other measures to reduce its oil imports.

In 1979–81, inflation in Germany worsened and the current account moved into deficit. This led a number of observers to criticise, and blame, the coordinated agreement at the summit. The fact is that the heads of government who met in 1978 could not possibly have foreseen the fall of the Shah of Iran a year later. That is what set off the second oil shock and imposed inflation and balance-of-payments deficits on all oil-importing countries. But the German view of the effects of the Bonn agreement was to influence German policymakers in the 1980s and beyond, reinforcing their distaste for 'artificial' measures aimed at stimulating the economy when it was operating well below capacity.

Germany's GDP increased only 1 per cent in 1980 and was flat in 1981, while unemployment rose slightly. In 1982, output declined and unemployment jumped almost 2 percentage points to 6.4 per cent.

When Helmut Kohl took over the Chancellorship in October 1982, Schmidt's government had already reversed Germany's budget policy from its stance of 1978–9. The 1982 budget called for a compression of expenditures and a reduction of the budget deficit in the face of a sluggish economy. In this and other ways the change of government in Germany, in contrast with what happened in Britain and the United States, did not involve a sharp break with earlier policies.

The recovery from the 1982 recession was anaemic. GDP growth averaged only 2.1 per cent per year in 1983–7. In other European countries, economic expansion was somewhat more rapid. But Germany's inflation subsided significantly, from 5.2 per cent in 1982 to near zero in 1987.

With demand expanding more slowly than in its main trading partners and with a lower inflation rate, Germany's exports outpaced imports and the current account of the balance of payments moved toward a much larger surplus – from less than 1 per cent of GDP in 1983 to a peak of 4.8 per cent in 1989.

The Kohl government intensified the process of fiscal consolidation initiated under Helmut Schmidt. The structural budget deficit of all levels of government combined was almost eliminated by 1985. While this may have had beneficial long-run effects in encouraging investment, it must have been an important factor in holding down the growth of the economy.

But there were other views on this question. The sluggishness of the economy led to the notion among some German economists that Europe in general and Germany in particular was suffering from a hardening of the economic arteries. Herbert Giersch, former head of the Kiel Institute and well-known internationally, appears to have coined the term 'Eurosclerosis'. What he had in mind was that real wages were too high, unemployment compensation too generous, and labour laws too restrictive to encourage new hiring and to permit adequate mobility of labour. This inflexibility impeded employment and growth, according to Giersch and others who agreed with him. That view became more general in Europe in later years although it then focused more on unemployment than on general economic growth.

The German economy continued on a slow growth path through 1987 but growth picked up to 3.7 per cent in 1988. That followed a shift in fiscal policy from restraint to stimulus beginning in 1986. Probably more important was the increase in population owing to immigration. From 1985 to 1991, West Germany's population rose 3.6 per cent after having declined by almost 1 per cent in the previous five years.

The immigrants consisted of three groups: East Germans, ethnic Germans from the Soviet Union and Eastern Europe and people from elsewhere – mainly the former Yugoslavia, Romania, Bulgaria, and Turkey – seeking asylum. The German constitution contained both a 'law of return' for ethnic Germans and a law of asylum. It is estimated that more than 800 000 people immigrated in 1989, legally or otherwise. The economic effect in West Germany showed up in two ways:

an acceleration of spending on housing and consumer goods but also a slow decrease in unemployment despite a faster rise in employment.

The Berlin Wall came down on 9 November 1989. It was a joyous event even though that particular date is infamous in German history: the Nazi rampage against Jews – *Kristallnacht* – occurred on 9 November 1938.

Events moved rapidly thereafter. Immigration from East Germany (the German Democratic Republic – GDR) accelerated to an estimated 2000 per day early in 1990. In the GDR output was falling and the quality of life was being affected by the departure of professionals, including medical doctors, and skilled workers. It was estimated that nearly 4 per cent of the GDR labour force left in 1989 and more than twice that many were likely to move in 1990.

In the words of Kurt Biedenkopf, minister-president of Saxony in eastern Germany:

actual unity was achieved the minute the Wall was opened and the government in East Berlin allowed its population – its up-to-then incarcerated population – to move freely into the West. This opening of the Wall represented de facto unity because West Germany had never recognized the citizenship of East Germany, so when the Wall opened, everyone in East Germany became a German citizen. They could cross the border and ask for a passport. They could cross the border and enjoy all the rights bestowed on German citizens by the constitution, by social legislation, by the legal order. And they did. In fact, they, not politics, determined the speed of unification.[7]

Thus Chancellor Kohl felt an urgent need to stem the inflow of people. That explains the hasty announcement in February 1990 of the intention to form a currency union with the GDR. In April the governments of East and West Germany agreed on an economic and monetary union, to be established by the summer. Against the advice of the Bundesbank, the Kohl government decided on a conversion rate of east marks into D-marks at one-to-one for wages and salaries and for bank accounts up to certain levels. On the very day of the announcement, the President of the Bundesbank, Karl-Otto Poehl, was in East Berlin conferring with his GDR counterpart and agreeing with him that early monetary unification was not on the cards. The Kohl government overrode the objections of the Bundesbank because it was anxious to give East Germans a motivation to remain at home while aspiring to the living standard existing in the west. It is clear that political considerations prevailed over economic good sense in the management of the unification process.

Monetary unification took place on 1 July 1990. The D-mark became the currency of the GDR and the Bundesbank became its central bank. On 3 October in an atmosphere of euphoria, the two countries were unified politically. The GDR ceased to exist. The euphoria did not last long.

Industrial production in east Germany plunged by about two-thirds from mid-1990 to the spring of 1991 and unemployment rose from about 1 per cent of the labour force to 15 per cent in the summer of 1991. Unemployment continued to increase steadily, reaching more than 21 per cent at the end of 1997. In early 1998, it finally turned down.

In general, unification exposed eastern Germany to both a demand shock and a supply shock. Consumers switched their purchases from goods made in the east to previously unavailable products from the west. The most conspicuous example was the shunning of the Trabant – a car made in eastern Germany – in favour of the wide array of German and non-German cars that could be bought in the western part of the country. East German products could not compete in the west in terms of quality and design. On top of that, there was a collapse of exports to Eastern Europe and the former Soviet Union (while west Germany's exports to those market's rose). The supply shock was based on sharply rising labour costs as wages in eastern Germany – less than one-third those in the west – went up rapidly after unification. These wage hikes were encouraged by the trade unions in west Germany, which were concerned about a migration of industry to the east attracted by lower labour costs. While wages in the east rose steeply, productivity there was only one-third of west Germany's output per person. Thus producers in the east suffered a severe squeeze on their costs. For these reasons industrial production and GDP plunged in the east.

Meanwhile, efforts were made to deal with state enterprises in eastern Germany. A trust fund agency (*Treuhandanstalt*) took over more than 12 000 industrial firms. Its task was to privatise, restructure or close down these enterprises. Many of them were 'loss-making', had very poor environmental standards, were burdened with heavy debts or had unclear property rights.

Initially unification brought depression to eastern Germany and prosperity to western Germany. In the latter, GDP growth, which had been 3.6 per cent in 1989, picked up to 5.7 per cent in 1990, as the result of a cut in income taxes at the beginning of the year and the shift of east German consumer and investment spending to the west after monetary unification. Much of the latter spending was financed out of transfers from the central and state government budgets in west Germany, which shifted strongly into deficit. Seven years after unification, during which the transfers amounted to about DM 1 trillion, they still weighed heavily on central and state government budgets.

The acceleration in demand in the west pushed up the rate of inflation, from 1.3 per cent in 1988 to 3.6 per cent in 1991 and 5.1 per cent in 1992, high by German standards. The Bundesbank responded by steadily tightening its policy. Short-term interest rates in Germany rose from 4 per cent in 1987 to a peak of 9.4 per cent in 1992.

The mix of fiscal and monetary policies – a large budget deficit and tight money – was similar to what prevailed in the United States in the first half of the 1980s. And some of the effects were also similar. In particular, there developed upward pressure on the D-mark and the large current-account surplus disappeared, giving way to a deficit. The D-mark appreciated further in 1992 and 1993 when crises in the EMS led to depreciations of other currencies.

In effect, the additional resources being absorbed by east Germany, and largely financed through government budgets in west Germany, came from Germany's trade partners as their exports to it increased sharply. If east Germany were still a separate country, west Germany's current account would have looked very different, since shipments of consumer and capital goods to the east would have counted as exports.

The rapid growth in west Germany gave way to a downturn in mid-1992 under the influence of high interest rates and declining orders, both domestic and foreign, to German industry. Unemployment rose from 6.2 per cent in 1990 to a peak of 11.8 per cent in the fourth quarter of 1997. Output growth picked up in 1996–7, led initially by exports, as the D-mark depreciated relative to the dollar.

In eastern Germany a construction boom helped to turn the economy around. Output rose almost 6 per cent in 1993 and 15 per cent in 1994. The growth rate slowed after that. With high labour costs, among other problems, unemployment above 20 per cent – about twice the rate in western Germany in early 1998 – was mainly structural. Wages in the east were lower than in the west but productivity was even further behind. According to the Bundesbank, wage costs per unit of output were one fourth higher in east Germany in 1996.[8] While economic conditions improved in the east, a wide gulf remained between the two parts of the country. It is clear that the costs – social and cultural as well as economic and financial – and time duration of the unification process were underestimated in 1990.

As Günter Grass expressed it:

> Many people from the East hoped to join the West with their own face, their own experiences. But the West was coming like colonial masters, treating them like children. It was a shock for many. They were astonished. There is no longer a wall or an iron curtain, but Germany is divided socially and economically. There are Germans first and second class. I'm afraid this will take longer than the wall to fix.[9]

Thus, as compared with 1980, Germany is a very different country, politically and economically. It was, and may still be, the strongest economy in Europe. But it is burdened with high unemployment and with the problems of transforming and supporting its eastern provinces.

5.3   JAPAN

'Japan is indeed the object-lesson of national efficiency, and happy is the country that learns it.' These words were written in 1905 by a British prime minister, Lord Rosebery.[10] Their peacetime validity was demonstrated to the west only after the Second World War, when Japan's economic performance was phenomenal. Apart from what the economic statistics show, consumers in the United States and elsewhere became familiar with Japan's efficiency as they eagerly bought Japanese automobiles and television sets, then VCRs and compact disc players, and more recently personal computers as well. While Japan became known throughout the world as a major exporter, it is surprising to note that its economy is only slightly more open than the US economy. Japanese merchandise exports and imports in the 1980s were 10.3 per cent of its GDP. The comparable figure for the United States was 7.7 per cent. In contrast, Germany's trade was about one-fourth of its total output.

The Japanese economy had grown very rapidly in the 1950s and 1960s, roughly twice as fast as other industrial countries. It was a country of high saving and high investment. The differential in growth rates narrowed considerably in the 1970s, when Japan was affected by the first oil shock. In addition, by then Japan had caught up with other industrial countries technologically and could no longer increase productivity rapidly simply by importing know-how. The deceleration of growth was a reflection mainly of a slower advance of productivity rather than of unutilised resources. The unemployment rate – remarkably low in Japan, partly because of life-time employment and partly because the statistics do not cover part-time workers – was 2 per cent in 1980, reached a peak of 2.8 per cent in 1986 and declined to 2.1 per cent in 1990. As the economy slowed again and then stagnated in the 1990s, unemployment rose above 4 per cent in 1998.

In the years after 1973, Japan developed a big budget deficit relative to its GNP. That deficit was second in size only to Italy's among the seven largest industrial countries. Government debt held by the public grew twelve-fold between 1973 and 1979. As a consequence, the powerful Ministry of Finance (MOF) came to the judgement that Japan should, at all costs, avoid budget deficits and, if possible, achieve surpluses so as to reduce the outstanding government debt. Japan weathered the second oil shock, in 1979–80, with much less inflation and economic slowdown than most other countries. An opportunity thus presented itself to cut back the budget deficit, which was done year by year beginning in 1980. The general government deficit fell from 4.8 per cent of GDP in 1979 to 0.8 per cent in 1985 and moved into surplus in 1987–92. As is discussed in the next chapter, one result was the emergence of a large current-account surplus in the 1980s. Before 1980, that surplus, at its peak in 1978, was about $17 billion, or 1.7 per cent of GDP. In the 1980s, the current-account surplus grew steadily from $4.8 billion in 1981 to $84 billion, or 3.5 per cent of GDP, in 1987. Japan's export volume increased 44 per cent in real terms in 1980–5 while the volume of its imports went up only 10 per cent.

The large external surplus subjected Japan to criticism from abroad regarding its macroeconomic policies, its trade practices, its retail distribution system and its inter-corporate relations. It was suggested that Japan should take steps to expand domestic demand and thereby use more of its saving at home. This was said to be especially desirable in view of the prospect that the yen would appreciate as the dollar came down from the high levels it moved to in the first half of the 1980s. Japan was charged with discriminating in various ways against imports. Rice imports were banned. Public works contracts were said to exclude foreign bidders. Its distribution system was hard for foreign producers to break into. And the *keiretsu* arrangements – horizontal and vertical relationships among companies in production and distribution – were also said to discriminate against imports.

Proposals for macroeconomic reform garnered additional support in Japan from the publication in April 1986 of the Mayekawa report – by an advisory group headed by former Bank of Japan Governor Haroo Mayekawa – addressed to Prime Minister Yasuhiro Nakasone. That report, and a follow-up in 1987, assembled a number of long-standing proposals aimed at reorientating Japan's use of resources towards the satisfaction of pressing domestic needs, including residential housing, public works, and increased leisure. The report gave added impetus to the idea of stimulating domestic demand in Japan.

The Mayekawa report bore some fruit in 1987, following a year of GDP growth of only 2.9 per cent. Finance Minister Kiichi Miyazawa proposed a supplementary budget to which the figure of 6 trillion yen was attached. That figure greatly exaggerated the programme's impact on the economy. In fact, fiscal policy became more restrictive in the following two years. Nevertheless, domestic demand, which had increased 3.6 per cent per year in 1984–6, accelerated to 5.8 per cent annually in 1987–90.

The result was that Japan outdid the United Kingdom in generating a 'bubble economy' – a speculative boom in stocks and real estate. What brought it on?

As in Britain, much of the answer lies in monetary policy. The Bank of Japan's discount rate was reduced in steps from 5 per cent in 1985 to 2.5 per cent in 1987 and market rates, both short- and long-term, fell substantially. The yield on long-term government bonds came down from 6 per cent in 1985 to 3 per cent in the spring of 1987. The narrow money supply, which had increased 3.2 per cent per year in 1983–5, rose by more than 8 per cent per year in 1986–8. The easing of monetary policy, perhaps excessively, has been attributed in part to Japan's effort to support the Louvre agreement (next chapter) by preventing the yen from appreciating further relative to the dollar.

In addition to monetary policy, financial deregulation played a role in promoting the boom. Liberalisation of the financial system began in the 1970s but was speeded up in the 1980s, partly in response to prodding by the US Treasury. But the worldwide increase in capital mobility, based in part on the development of new financial instruments, made deregulation imperative if Japanese financial institutions were to compete with their counterparts abroad. Interest rates were freed from governmental ceilings, banks were permitted to attract additional types of deposits, and firms, which had earlier been largely confined to commercial banks for loans, found it possible to borrow at home in securities markets and abroad from banks and securities markets.[11]

In these circumstances, stock prices in Japan skyrocketed. From 1982 to the peak level at the end of 1989, the Nikkei average rose more than fivefold, while the Dow Jones average in New York tripled. The very high price–earnings ratio, and low dividend yield, made equity financing very inexpensive for Japanese business enterprises. The rapid advance in stock prices also created large capital gains for individual stockholders, for corporations (which hold much of each others' stocks), and for banks.

Furthermore, the yen appreciated sharply, rising from 260 per dollar in February 1985 to 126 per dollar at the end of 1988. This 'yen shock' (*endaka* in Japanese) stimulated investment aimed at upgrading products so that they could compete at the higher exchange rate. It also made assets abroad look inexpensive to Japanese investors.

All these factors stimulated the 'animal spirits' of Japanese corporations and led to a substantial increase in domestic investment spending, which rose, in real terms, by 42 per cent from 1986 to 1990 while real GDP went up by 21 per cent.

To the speculative rise in stock prices was added an even greater boom in the prices of real estate in the second half of the 1980s. By 1989, the total value of real estate in Japan was estimated by a Japanese government agency to have a value four times the value of all the property in the United States, which has an area 25 times that of Japan.[12]

The Japanese seemed to have discovered a perpetual motion machine for their economy. The increase in the prices of real estate and equities led to a substantial expansion of bank capital, which enabled banks to lend more to borrowers who pledged their holdings of real estate as collateral; the borrowers used part of the funds from new loans to buy more equities and real estate. Household spending increased in response to the growth in personal wealth. The household saving rate, which had averaged 16.6 per cent of disposable income in 1980–6, fell to 13 per cent in the next five years. This, plus the availability of cheap finance, encouraged business investment spending.

The bubble mentality made a large part of the Japanese population feel rich. They responded by spending on plant and equipment, new

houses, impressionist art, expensive imported automobiles and jew-
ellery, and on the acquisition abroad of businesses, office buildings,
golf courses, hotels, and estates in Hawaii and California. In Japan
more than 160 golf courses were built between 1989 and 1991. The
price of memberships 'range from a few million yen up to the
Y250 million range' (about $2 million).[13]

As was inevitable, the bubble imploded. The Bank of Japan began
to raise its discount rate in May 1989. The Tokyo stock market, which
had quickly shrugged off the sharp drop in stocks in the United States
and elsewhere in October 1987, reached a peak at the end of 1989. By
early 1993 stock prices in Tokyo had fallen more than 50 per cent, and
were being supported at that level through purchases by government
pension funds and savings institutions. Share prices recovered somewhat in the next three years but fell again in 1997 and 1998. Land
prices, which are estimated to have tripled between 1986 and 1991,
declined by more than 60 per cent in the next five years. Commercial
property values in Tokyo were reported to be 80 per cent below their
1991 peak in June 1998.[14]

With the collapse of the speculative bubble, the real economy of
Japan entered a long period of stagnation and then recession.
Consumers felt much less wealthy as the values of their stocks and real
estate declined and they cut back on their spending.

Businesses found it much more costly to raise capital and they
reduced their investment outlays for this reason as well as because
they had excess capacity created in the earlier investment boom. The
result was that industrial production was $8\frac{1}{2}$ per cent lower in mid-
1998 than in 1991. Business profits decreased, new commercial
buildings remained empty.

Japanese banks were left with a large volume of bad debts – estimated at $600 billion, equal to about 16 per cent of Japan's GDP –
and holdings of stock that had fallen steeply in value. Their capital
was severely impaired and they struggled to restore or maintain the
Basle capital adequacy ratio of 8 per cent of assets by restricting new
loans so as not to add to their assets. Some banks failed. The problem
was compared with the 1980s crisis in the US savings and loan associations but was much more serious. Thus credit became scarce even
though the economy was stagnant. Bank loans to the private sector
increased only 2.4 per cent in the five years to the end of 1997.

In these conditions, the government enacted several stimulus pack-
ages, but their effects on overall economic activity were not lasting.
Real GDP rose by less than one per cent per year in 1992–5 and then

increased 3.9 per cent in 1996. That pickup in growth led the government to announce an increase in the national consumption tax from 3 to 5 per cent beginning in April 1997 along with other fiscal tightening measures. The result was an anticipatory spurt of buying by consumers in the first quarter of 1997 but then a fall-off. The economy contracted in late 1997 and was headed for another fall in 1998. That was the result not only of weak spending by consumers but also tight credit to small and medium-sized enterprises, as the banks held back their lending. At the same time exports fell off as Japan's Asian neighbours suffered economic and financial crises.

In these circumstances, the government announced in December 1997 a tax reduction equivalent to $15 billion, which was widely regarded as totally inadequate. In 1998 Japan was under strong pressure from other Group of Seven leaders to adopt more stimulative policies and to deal with its banking problems.

In April 1998 Prime Minister Hashimoto announced a fiscal stimulus package in the amount of 16 trillion (equivalent in value to about $128 billion). It was enacted in June but, according to Adam Posen, the effective stimulus was only 60 per cent of the amount announced.[15]

The Hashimoto government resigned in July 1998 after the defeat of the Liberal Democratic Party in upper-house elections. The successor government, under Prime Minister Keizo Obuchi, was initially paralysed by factional disputes but finally, in October, a bill was passed aimed at solving the banking problem. Whether it would be effective was uncertain, as was the future performance of the economy in the absence of more effective fiscal stimulus.

Balance of Payments and Exchange Rates

While the dollar appreciated sharply relative to many currencies in the first half of the 1980s, it moved rather little against the yen. In fact the yen's effective exchange rate (its trade-weighted average value) moved up from 1980 to 1985 as other non-dollar currencies depreciated much more than the yen. Nevertheless, as noted, Japan's current-account surplus increased strongly in 1981–7. It then fell by more than half during the bubble but rose again after 1990.

The effective exchange rate of the yen continued to appreciate in the first half of the 1990s, reaching a peak in 1995, when the dollar was at a low point. Then, as the economy weakened, short-term interest rates declined below one per cent and the Asian crisis had its effects, the yen depreciated, falling as low as 135 per dollar in late September 1998.

The current-account surplus both required and facilitated Japan's role as a major supplier of capital to other countries, especially the United States. Actually, outflows of long-term capital exceeded the current-account surplus from 1981 to 1990. The difference was made up by inflows of short-term capital as Japanese banks and others borrowed abroad.

Japan might have become a major exporter of capital, acquiring assets in the United States and elsewhere, even if it had not developed a substantial current-account surplus. After all, the United States continued to undertake direct foreign investment abroad in the 1980s, even though it had a deficit in its current account. It did so by borrowing abroad in other forms.

We may identify as another significant transformation in the 1980s Japan's emergence as the world's largest exporter of capital. Japanese direct investment abroad rose from little more than $2 billion in 1980 to $48 billion in 1990 and included not only manufacturing plants but also real estate and financial services in North America, Europe, and East Asia. Particularly noteworthy are 'transplants' – Japanese automobile factories established in the United States – stimulated in large part by 'voluntary export restrictions' applied by Japan on exports from the homeland. After the bubble burst, direct investment flows fell off to less than $14 billion in 1993 and then rose gradually to $26 billion in 1997.

Portfolio investment – purchases abroad of bonds and, to a smaller extent, stocks – increased from $3.75 billion in 1980 to $113 billion in 1989. It declined in the next few years but rose again in 1994–7 as Japan's long-term interest rates went down. At less than 2 per cent, those rates enabled the Japanese government 'to borrow more cheaply than any other government in recorded history'.[16]

The result was that foreign assets owned by Japanese investors increased by a multiple of more than 17 from 1980 to 1997, when they amounted to $2.7 trillion. Over the same period, their external liabilities also increased, largely in the form of borrowing from banks abroad. In effect, Japan became an international financial intermediary, borrowing short-term and acquiring long-term assets.

For a while, these developments aroused fears in some quarters in the United States, to which much of the capital went. There were adverse reactions to the acquisitions of properties, whether conspicuous ones like the Rockefeller Center or residential properties in Hawaii or motion picture companies. And fears were expressed that the US Treasury was too dependent on Japanese investors for the sale of its securities to finance the budget deficit. These fears turned out to be unjustified.

The Political and Economic Outlook

In the midst of the period of stagnation, a political crisis came to a head in the late spring of 1993. The Liberal Democratic Party had been wracked by a series of scandals over the years. Prime Minister Kiichi Miyazawa, who had taken office in 1991, was unable to deliver on a pledge to enact legislation on political reform. A no-confidence vote led to the fall of his government in June and to elections in which the LDP lost its majority after 38 years as the ruling party. The opposition was motivated by a wish not only for electoral reform to eliminate payoffs from business to politicians and to move to a one-representative-per-constituency system – but also to accelerate deregulation of the economy. It was aimed at what is called in Japan the 'iron triangle' – the power relationship among politicians, large corporations and bureaucrats. Bureaucrats, not a pejorative term in Japan, have over the years had enormous power in running ministries. The reformers want to deliver that power back to ministers. But ministers are dependent on the bureaucrats for information because they do not have a staff of their own.

Morihiro Hosokawa, a former journalist and former governor of an affluent prefecture on Kyushu, was chosen by the seven-party coalition as prime minister. At the age of 55, he became the second youngest head of government since the Second World War. In November a commission appointed by Hosokawa and headed by the chairman of the *Keidanren*, Japan's main business federation, proposed the elimination or relaxation of 475 government regulations. According to a *New York Times* correspondent in Tokyo, the commission

> proposed everything from making it simpler to open large department stores and liquor shops to encouraging housing construction and easing quotas on fish imports. It called for creation of Japan's first product liability law and something that would mark a minor revolution in a country that permits dozens of cartels – strict application of the anti-monopoly laws.[17]

Hosokawa had to resign in April 1994, and was succeeded briefly by Tsutomu Hata and in June 1994 by the first socialist since the 1940s,

Tomiichi Murayama. When Murayama resigned in January 1996, Ryutaro Hashimoto of the LDP took over. In an election in October 1996, the LDP regained a bare majority.

Hashimoto pledged to carry on with deregulation including a 'big bang' in the financial field over a five-year period ending in 2001. The 'big bang' – a term taken from London's deregulation in the 1980s – was to cover foreign exchange, securities markets, the insurance industry, and holding companies, among other reforms.[18] But as noted, Hashimoto was succeeded by Obuchi in July 1998 and the political outlook did not inspire confidence.

In the autumn of 1998, the economic outlook was far from favourable. The economy had contracted in the nine months ending June 1998 and the Asian crisis could only slow it further. The yen had depreciated against the dollar until October 1998, thereby aggravating the crisis in other Asian countries. The banking system was in trouble. The economy was characterised as 'operating rather like a twin-engined aircraft with only one engine fully working'.[19] Beyond that macroeconomic weakness, Japan was badly in need of structural reform, as noted earlier.

For the longer run, the low birth rate and the 'aging of Japan' create problems not unfamiliar to other countries but probably more acute in Japan. That long-run prospect has a significant influence on policymakers and helps to explain some of the short-run macroeconomic policy mistakes.

6 Economic Interactions and Economic Integration

The 1980s and early 1990s saw a continuation of the trend toward growing international economic interdependence that has been evident since the end of the Second World War. One manifestation of this trend is the increase in world trade relative to world output. Even more striking was the augmentation of financial interdependence – a more recent phenomenon than the growth of trade. In the 1970s and especially in the 1980s international capital flows among industrial countries increased by large amounts. In the 1990s, such flows went also to developing countries and countries in transition – emerging markets.

The decade of the 1980s began with interactions that were less than happy, given the high rates of inflation in 1980–1 spurred mainly by the sharp rise in the price of oil. In the seven largest industrial countries, consumer prices rose 12.7 per cent in 1980. They all tightened their monetary policies and several of them also moved toward more restrictive fiscal policies. The result was that the combined GDP of the Group of Seven slowed in 1980 and fell 0.3 per cent in 1982.

It is a reasonable supposition that in tackling the inflation problem the policymakers of each of the major countries looked inward and did not take account of the effect on their exports of the restrictive policies pursued in the other countries. This shows up in imports: the volume of imports of the Seven shrank 4.2 per cent in 1980–2. Since most of their trade is with each other, their exports slackened in 1981 and fell in 1982. This made the recession more severe than anyone expected. In other words, what happened was a failure of policy coordination among the major countries.[1]

6.1 INTERNATIONAL PAYMENTS IMBALANCES

As observed in Chapter 4, US budgetary policy shifted abruptly in 1982 under Ronald Reagan. The budget deficit, abstracting from the effects of recession in 1981–2 and recovery thereafter, quintupled as a percentage of GDP from 1981 to 1986, reaching 3.5 per cent of GDP.

Meanwhile, Germany and Japan were trying to reduce their budget deficits and succeeding.

Although the US policy mix would by itself have tended to produce a deficit in the current account of the American balance of payments, the policies of Germany and Japan also contributed to that outcome. According to our equation on p. 30 the shift in the budget deficits of Germany and Japan would have moved those countries toward current-account surpluses in any event. The combination of policies pursued by the three countries led to outsized current-account imbalances, as may be seen in Table 6.1.

A straightforward way to interpret these developments is as follows. The United States in the 1980s experienced a shortfall of saving as the government dissaved (in the form of a growing budget deficit) and private saving by households and businesses also fell off. This created the need to import saving from abroad, which took the form of a current-account deficit and was financed by net purchases of American securities and other types of lending and investing in the United States by foreign residents.

In Germany and Japan, governments increased saving (by way of diminishing budget deficits) and this, in combination with private saving and investment, led them to export the excess saving in the form of current-account surpluses. These surpluses were financed by outward flows of capital undertaken by German and Japanese individuals and businesses either directly or through financial institutions.

Another interpretation can be given to these events – one that might seem too favourable to the United States. Germany and Japan were determined to reduce their budget deficits in the 1980s. They were able to achieve that aim without unduly depressing their

Table 6.1   Current-account balances of United States, Germany and Japan
($ billions)

	1980	1983	1987	1990	1992	1997
United States	2.2	−44.2	−168.1	−91.6	−51.4	−155.2
Germany	−13.3	4.6	46.4	48.3	−19.1	−2.8
Japan	−10.8	20.8	84.4	44.1	112.6	94.4

Source: IMF, *International Financial Statistics*; US Department of Commerce.

economies in part because the United States was following the reverse policy. The growing export surpluses largely offset in the case of Japan and more than offset in the case of Germany the contractionary effect of the reduction in their budget deficits.

The appreciation of the dollar and the corresponding depreciation of the yen and D-mark in the first half of the 1980s were the instruments that helped to create the payments imbalances and the international transfer of savings. But, as noted in Chapter 4, these external imbalances would have appeared even if, somehow or other, exchange rates had been held steady. To hold the dollar down the Federal Reserve would have had to relax its monetary policy significantly, permitting lower interest rates. The result would have been higher inflation in the United States. That would have discouraged American exports and attracted imports. Similarly, if the yen and D-mark had not depreciated, Japan and Germany would have had lower rates of inflation, which would have tended to produce current-account surpluses. In other words, the validity of our equation $[(I - S) + (G - T) = (M - X)]$ does not depend on exchange-rate movements. It holds true under any exchange-rate regime.

Thus more by accident than design the three countries pursued complementary policies that created sizeable payments imbalances. By historical standards, these imbalances – the current-account deficit of the United States and the surpluses of Germany and Japan – were of record magnitude in the 1980s. That this was possible is related to the enormous increase in the mobility of capital that had occurred. In earlier years, it would have been assumed that a budget deficit of the magnitude of that in the United States in the mid-1980s would have the effect of crowding out domestic investment. It was taken for granted that for each country gross saving and gross investment were closely correlated. A well-known study by Professor Martin Feldstein and a colleague, published in 1980, supported that assumption.[2] But later studies tended to refute it.[3]

In any event, the large payments imbalances among the three industrial countries shrank temporarily towards the end of the 1980s. During its boom, Japan's imports rose sharply and its external surplus declined. Germany's current account moved into deficit in 1991 under the impact of unification. The US deficit fell. Later in the 1990s, the Japanese and US imbalances increased again as Japan's imports shrank owing to its recession, while the strong US economy brought with it a faster growth of imports. Once again the enlarged imbalances were easily financed by private capital.

Another significant aspect of the transformation of the world economy is that nations can now tolerate, perhaps even enjoy, large divergences between gross domestic saving and domestic investment since lenders and investors in other countries are ready and willing to finance them. This may be the revival of an old rather than the appearance of a new phenomenon. The United States in the nineteenth century sustained a significant margin of investment over saving thanks to inflows of capital from Europe, especially England.[4] In more recent years it has almost been a defining characteristic of developing countries that they receive capital from abroad, enabling them to invest more than their own saving would allow.

6.2   ENHANCED MOBILITY OF CAPITAL

The greater ability of nations to sustain an excess of investment over saving is one aspect of another significant alteration in the international landscape: the greatly enhanced mobility of capital across national borders. That change began in the 1970s, became more evident in the 1980s, and even more so in the 1990s. Among the factors accounting for it were financial deregulation, the dismantling of exchange controls, and the revolution in computer technology and telecommunications. New information now moves around the world instantaneously and investors and lenders are virtually as familiar with economic, financial and political conditions in other countries as with those at home. And trading can take place on a 24-hour basis.

Moreover the computer has made possible the creation of new financial instruments – such as options, interest-rate swaps, and exchange-rate swaps, known as derivatives – that facilitate the international movement of funds. An increasing proportion of this movement was in the form of purchases and sales of securities, both short and long-term. The word that appeared in the 1980s was 'securitisation' and the international activities of securities firms grew rapidly. It became possible and quite common, for example, for an American corporation to issue bonds denominated in a foreign currency, say Japanese yen, in London and to swap the proceeds back into dollars while protecting itself against the risk of an appreciation of the yen by a transaction in the forward market and an interest rate swap. Another example: trading of futures contracts on German government bonds (*Bunds*) is dominated by London rather than Frankfurt.[5]

A measure of the increase in capital mobility may be seen in the rise of gross capital outflows from 14 industrial countries – mostly to each other – from about $65 billion per year in 1975–9 to about $460 billion in 1989. Gross annual foreign purchases and sales of US Treasury bonds and notes each increased from about $40 billion in 1979 to $2 trillion in 1991 while gross foreign purchases of US stocks rose from $22 billion to $200 billion. Average daily foreign exchange transactions in London grew from $184 billion in 1989 to $464 billion in 1995. In New York, the increase was from $115 billion to $244 billion.

In the early 1990s another form of capital mobility made its appearance: greatly enlarged private flows to developing countries (Table 6.2). Direct investment quintupled from 1990 to 1997 and purchases of developing-country securities increased by a much larger multiple; there appeared emerging market funds through which investors in industrial countries bought shares of stock in developing countries. Lending by commercial banks revived in the 1990s.

Partly as cause and partly as effect, the growth rate of developing countries sped up from an average of 4.3 per cent per year in the 1980s to 5.9 per cent in 1990–7. At the same time, the aggregate current-account deficit of developing countries (not including Hong Kong, Korea, Singapore and Taiwan) increased from $24 billion in 1990 to $61.8 billion in 1997. The foreign exchange reserves of developing countries (plus the four cited in the previous sentence) rose

Table 6.2   Private capital flows to developing countries
($ billions)

	1990	1997*
Direct investment	23.7	120.4
Portfolio equity	3.2	32.5
Bonds	0.1	53.8
Bank loans	3.8	41.1
Other	11.1	8.3
Total	*41.9*	*256.1*

*Preliminary
Source: World Bank, *Global Development Finance 1998*, p. 3.

from about $200 billion at the end of 1989 to almost $730 billion in mid-1998.

These phenomena not only brought benefits to the recipient countries but also provided a stimulus to the growth of industrial nations as their exports increased more rapidly. In effect the developing world was acting as a locomotive for the global economy.

Along with the benefits, the enlarged flow of capital, especially mobile capital in the form of securities transactions, created the possibility of crises in the recipient countries, as occurred in Mexico in 1994–5 and in Asia in 1997–8.

6.3 EXCHANGE-RATE POLICIES

As the dollar rose in the first part of the 1980s, complaints were heard from abroad about the inflationary effects of rising import costs. This was especially so in France. The policy stance of the Reagan administration against exchange market intervention no doubt contributed to the widespread expectation among market participants that the dollar would continue to strengthen.

The speculative bubble of late 1984 and early 1985 shook but did not alter the policy of non-intervention. But, under the influence of a letter from Margaret Thatcher to Ronald Reagan, Secretary Regan signed on to a Group of Five communiqué in January 1985 stating that greater exchange-rate stability was desirable and that they would undertake coordinated intervention 'when to do so would be helpful'.

As it turned out, the dollar peaked in February 1985 and declined irregularly during the following six months.

In early 1985 Donald Regan and James Baker – Chief of Staff in the White House – switched jobs. Baker brought Richard Darman with him as Deputy Secretary of the Treasury. The Baker–Darman team was to reverse three of the policies pursued by the Regan–Sprinkel Treasury. One concerned intervention in foreign exchange markets.

Baker took the initiative to convene a meeting of the Group of Five finance ministers and central bank governors (soon expanded to the Group of Seven with the addition of Canada and Italy) at the Plaza Hotel in New York in September 1985. They surprised the world by announcing that exchange rates should better reflect fundamental economic conditions and that 'some further orderly appreciation of the main non-dollar currencies against the dollar is desirable. They stand ready to cooperate more closely to encourage this when to do so would be helpful'. In the words of Nigel Lawson,

> for the first time in many years, the Finance Ministers of the major nations had genuinely got their act together, had reached an agreement of substance, and were all speaking about it in much the same terms. This gave a new credibility to the idea of international financial cooperation in general and to the G5 (and its successor) in particular.[6]

It is no coincidence that this fundamental shift in policy came after James Baker took over as Secretary of the Treasury in the United States. Donald Regan's interest in exchange rates was minimal, judging from the book he wrote after leaving office.[7] Its index includes not one mention about the dollar, exchange rates, the balance of payments, the Group of Five, or any related subject. Baker was more pragmatic and more attuned to current policy problems. His motivation for promoting the Plaza agreement was quite clear. He saw the danger of protectionism in the US Congress if imports continued to surge and exports continued to languish. He hoped to head it off with a declining dollar.

The announcement effect of the G-5 statement along with concerted intervention and a temporary increase in Japan's interest rates served to lower the dollar's value. Between February 1985 and the end of December 1986, the dollar depreciated by about 40 per cent against the yen and the D-mark. In late October 1986, the American and Japanese finance ministers announced their agreement that the dollar need not depreciate further against the yen. In return the Bank of Japan cut its discount rate. The explanation for this Baker–Miyazawa agreement appears to be that Baker was concerned that further appreciation of the yen would weaken the Japanese economy, whose exports had levelled off in real terms. What was needed was a pause in the dollar's depreciation in order to give some breathing space to Japan to implement domestic macroeconomic measures to offset the reduction in its external surplus. This reasoning was to apply to Germany and other European countries as well. Baker had been irritating his fellow ministers of finance in Europe and Japan by calling publicly for more expansionary policies in those countries and even threatening them with steeper declines in the dollar if they did not act.[8]

The Baker–Miyazawa agreement was a prelude to a broader one among the major countries, to be concluded in February 1987, after a further sharp decline of the dollar in terms of both the yen and the D-mark.

Even before this, Baker and Darman had apparently decided that the dollar had depreciated enough for the time being. They were no doubt encouraged in this judgement by Paul Volcker, who had for some time been hinting publicly that he was not in favour of additional dollar depreciation. As the only man in US history to have participated in two devaluations of the dollar (in 1971 and 1973), Volcker was entitled to this judgement. What worried him were 'the potentially disturbing consequences of further dollar declines on confidence, on inflation, and potentially on economic growth itself'.[9]

The G-6 (Italy absented itself to protest its exclusion from a preparatory meeting) met at the French Finance Ministry – still at that time in its palatial quarters in the Louvre and now in a late twentieth-century structure at Bercy in the eastern part of Paris – and announced that

> the substantial exchange rate changes since the Plaza Agreement will increasingly contribute to reducing external imbalances and have now brought their currencies within ranges broadly consistent with underlying economic fundamentals. Further substantial exchange rate shifts among their currencies could damage growth and adjustment prospects in their countries.

While France's finance minister, Edouard Balladur, hoped to get an accord on a system of target zones at this meeting (French officials have never been comfortable with flexible exchange rates) the unpublished agreements were hazy on the central rates that would be aimed at and the ranges for fluctuation around them. The central rates were close to those in the markets at the time of the meeting. An inner range of $\pm 2\frac{1}{2}$ per cent was for discretionary intervention and an outer range of ± 5 per cent was to determine mandatory intervention; yet the margins were characterised as 'soft', presumably because Bundesbank President Karl-Otto Poehl did not want to be required to undertake exchange-market intervention. According to Toyoo Gyohten, then Vice Minister in Japan's Finance Ministry, 'There was no clear and firm agreement ... The exchange rate discussion took place over dinner, while all the participants were quite busy cutting their meat and sipping their wine'.[10]

Within weeks after the Louvre meeting, the yen rose well above its Louvre rate. Market participants apparently were not impressed by the ministerial declaration of February or its strong reaffirmation at a subsequent meeting in Washington in April. In that month, the yen was 'rebased' from its Louvre central rate of 153.5 yen per dollar to 146 – an appreciation of 5 per cent.

Central banks were intervening in foreign exchange markets in an effort to keep exchange rates within the agreed margins. For 1987 as a whole, Japan's foreign exchange reserves rose by $38 billion and Germany's by $27 billion; the reported reserves of the United States fell by $4 billion. It has been estimated that total intervention purchases of dollars amounted to $117 billion in 1987 – a year in which the US current-account deficit amounted to $163 billion.[11]

The market expectation of additional dollar depreciation, and additional yen and D-mark appreciation, naturally led to rising interest rates on dollar securities, particularly rates on long-term obligations. Between March and mid-October 1987, the yield on 10-year US government bonds rose from $7\frac{1}{4}$ to 10 per cent, reflecting the combined expectations of a worsening of inflation and dollar depreciation. As noted in Chapter 4, the increase in American interest rates helped to trigger the stock market crash in October 1987.

6.4   US BALANCE OF PAYMENTS

The growing current-account deficits of the United States in the 1980s led some observers to question whether the financing would continue to be forthcoming. The deficits through 1985 were covered almost entirely by private capital flows to the United States from abroad. In fact, the deficits were overfinanced by private funds since Americans were lending and investing abroad.

As it turned out, 1987 was a major exception to the generalisation that private capital was financing the US deficits. In that year, central banks, intervening in foreign exchange markets, acquired enough dollars to cover most of the American deficit. Precisely how large that fraction was is hard to know, since some of the dollars so acquired by central banks were placed not in banks or securities in the United States but elsewhere – in the so-called Euromarkets. Thus they did not show up in US balance-of-payments statistics as liabilities to official institutions.

What happened in 1987 generated concerns that the financing of continuing US deficits could lead to a crisis as investors became reluctant to add to their dollar portfolios. Even before that, in December 1985, the Institute for International Economics published Stephen Marris's *Deficits and the Dollar*, which predicted a 'hard landing' not only for the dollar but for the US economy, with harmful effects on other countries.[12] Marris's reasoning was that the US deficit was so large and interest obligations on its debt were growing so fast that even if the dollar were to depreciate quite a bit more, the deficit would not be cured. This would lead to a drying up of the foreign financing of the deficit. As that happened the dollar would plummet and American interest rates would shoot up, creating a recession in the United States that would drag down the economies of many other countries, both industrial and developing.

It is clear that Marris's fears were unfounded. The dollar did fall quite sharply in 1987; its trade-weighted average value dropped by 18 per cent. But the US current-account deficit declined substantially after 1987, and the dollar rose in the second half of 1988 and in much of 1989. In 1989, the Federal Reserve and other central banks sold dollars to moderate its upswing.

A study carried out at the Bank for International Settlements showed that, despite the string of US external deficits in the 1980s, the share of dollars in the total private financial asset holdings in other industrial countries was modest – only 3.8 per cent in 1988. There was ample scope for these holdings to grow.[13]

They did grow in subsequent years and by amounts that exceeded the American current-account deficits. The cumulative US current-account deficit in 1990–7 amounted to about $760 billion while cumulative inflows of private capital to the United States came to $2.3 trillion. Over the same period, official holdings of dollars in the United States grew by about $450 billion, much of it representing increasing reserves of developing countries that were the recipients of private capital inflows.

6.5   EUROPEAN INTEGRATION

The EC moved toward greater unity, even if in fits and starts. The EMS evolved and a Europe 'without frontiers' came into being. These developments revived the idea of European Economic and Monetary Union (EMU).[14]

European Monetary System

The EMS underwent seven exchange-rate realignments in the first four years after it was established in March 1979. These devaluations and revaluations compensated for divergences in rates of inflation among the seven countries that were members of the exchange-rate mechanism (ERM). In 1979–82 consumer prices rose 5.3 per cent per year in Germany, only slightly more in the Netherlands and Belgium, but over 12 per cent in France, and 18 per cent in Italy. Rates of inflation narrowed progressively in the next few years. By 1989, inflation ranged from 1.1 per cent in the Netherlands to 6.3 per cent in Italy. With this narrowing, interest rates also tended to converge.

After a realignment in January 1987, central exchange rates in the ERM remained unchanged until September 1992. In that interval, the belief developed that the ERM had become a fixed-rate system. As noted in Chapter 5, France's rate of inflation converged with and then fell below that of Germany, and the interest-rate differential between the two countries became very small. That was taken as an indicator of the credibility of the fixed exchange-rate relationship between the D-mark and the franc – the *franc fort*. Belgium, Luxembourg, and the Netherlands were in a similar position relative to Germany. At the same time, there were, as Horst Ungerer has written, 'perceptions that the system was "asymmetric" because of the dominant rate of the Deutsche mark'.[15] These views evolved further towards aspiration for a common currency as proposed in the Delors Report of 1989 and embodied in the Maastricht Treaty of 1990 (see below).

The seven original members of the ERM were joined by Spain in 1989, the United Kingdom in 1990, and Portugal in 1992 – all three adopting the wide band of 6 per cent around their central exchange rates rather than the narrow band of $2\frac{1}{4}$ cent. These three countries as well as Italy had higher rates of inflation than Germany and France and, as we observed earlier, Britain probably joined the ERM at too elevated an exchange rate. Burdens were imposed on the system by the steep rise in German interest rates, which the other ERM members had to stay with or exceed even when economic activity began to slow down in 1991.

The result was a brusque blow to the idea that exchange rates among ERM countries could remain fixed. Speculation developed in the ERM in the summer of 1992 after a referendum in Denmark rejected the Maastricht Treaty. At the same time the dollar declined relative to the D-mark in the foreign exchange markets, following a cut in the Federal Reserve discount rate and an increase in the Bundesbank's rate. Upward pressure on the German currency made it more difficult for other ERM members to keep their exchange rates in line with the D-mark. In August, both the pound sterling and the

Italian lira fell to their lower margins, requiring heavy central bank support in the markets. Meanwhile the approach of the French referendum on Maastricht, scheduled for 20 September, added additional uncertainty to the idea of a common currency and therefore to the fixity of ERM exchange rates.

In early September the Finnish markka, weakened by the economic turmoil in the former USSR, was permitted to float downward. This put pressure on the Swedish krona – though not a member of the EC, its currency was pegged to the D-mark – and the Bank of Sweden raised its marginal lending rate first to 25 per cent, then to 75 per cent, and ultimately to 500 per cent although the economy was in recession. This action struck some observers as the ultimate absurdity in the obsession with maintaining fixed exchange rates. In November Sweden was forced to let the krona float down.

On 14 September the Bundesbank lowered two of its rates by one quarter percentage point and the Italian lira was devalued in the ERM by 7 per cent. Two days later sterling, after heavy exchange-market intervention to support it, dropped out of the ERM. The next day Italy followed. Spain and Portugal later devalued. The French referendum approved the Maastricht Treaty by a small margin and the French franc held its D-mark parity but only at the cost of heavy intervention and a sharp but temporary hike in interest rates.

In the summer of 1993, another foreign exchange crisis led to the suspension of what was left of the fixed-rate ERM. That crisis was not the result of overvalued exchange rates. Rather it reflected the fact that membership in the ERM required France, in the face of rising unemployment, to maintain interest rates at the high level determined by the Bundesbank. In fact, France's real short-term rates were three times those in Germany given its lower inflation rate and its somewhat higher interest rates. Its unemployment, at 11.6 per cent, was above that in Germany and had become an acute political issue. The overwhelming defeat of the Socialist Party in the elections of March 1993 was widely attributed to the high level of unemployment.

The crisis was triggered by the Bundesbank's decision at its pre-summer recess meeting of 29 July not to lower its discount rate along with its Lombard rate. The foreign exchange markets then moved heavily against the French franc along with most other ERM currencies, presumably on the grounds that France needed to reduce its interest rates in order to cope with unemployment. If it did so in the absence of a similar reduction by Germany, that would weaken the franc. The Bank of France and the Bundesbank intervened in the markets heavily. This led to a weekend meeting in Brussels at which it was finally decided to widen the ERM margins to 15 per cent on either side of central rates. The large amount of leeway was chosen 'to discourage potential speculators from targeting specific currencies by raising the exchange risk'.[16]

The judgement seems clear that it had been premature to regard the ERM as a fixed-rate arrangement. Even if Germany's interest rates had not risen so steeply, the currencies of some ERM countries were bound to become overvalued, given that their rates of inflation were significantly above that of Germany. Moreover, the economies of the ERM members did not move together. Those that weakened were not able to use monetary policy to encourage economic recovery. And, as we shall see, the Maastricht Treaty put a yoke on fiscal policy.

In a speech in Washington during the crisis in September 1992, Margaret (now Baroness) Thatcher, criticising the fetish with fixed exchange rates in Europe, quipped that politicians and bankers who are pushing for a single currency in Europe treat the exchange rate 'as a virility symbol – and I must say that, for myself, I never felt the need for a virility symbol'.[17]

Europe 1992

In any event, the convergence that was occurring in the EMS encouraged other steps towards greater integration in the EC. In February 1986 the Single European Act was signed, providing for what became known as 'Europe 1992' or the free movement of persons, goods, services, and capital among the twelve member countries of the EC. (Greece joined in 1981 and Spain and Portugal in 1986.) It also became known as 'Europe without frontiers', 'the internal market' and 'the single market'. Most of its provisions came into force by 1 January 1993.

A study sponsored by the European Commission – the Cecchini report – on the effects of Europe 1992 estimated that the EC would gain significantly in terms of output and employment as the result of eliminating border formalities, technical regulations applying to cross-border trade, barriers to market entry, as well as from the economies of scale in a market of 320 million people. If supported by appropriate macroeconomic policies, these effects would translate into sizeable increases in GDP, ranging from 4 to more than 6 per cent over the levels that would have otherwise prevailed.[18]

These are static or one-time effects of the formation of the single market. There could also be dynamic or continuing effects, which would show up as higher growth rates for the members of the EC. A study by Richard Baldwin produced 'back of the envelope' estimates of a permanent rise in the annual EC rate of growth amounting to between one quarter and one percentage point. Even at the lower end of this range the results would be significant over time. Apart from his numerical estimates, Baldwin's main point was that the cumulative effects of Europe 92 over time would be much larger than the one-time jump in GDP estimated in the Cecchini Report.[19]

The elimination of remaining exchange and capital controls, freeing capital movements, occurred in eight of the member states in July 1990. (Spain, Portugal, Greece, and Ireland were given until 1993 to comply.) This helps to explain the large speculative capital flows in 1992 and 1993, which led to the disruption of the ERM.

European Monetary Union

The planned evolution toward a European Community that would be unified economically stimulated the idea that there should also be a common currency and a single central bank – what came to be called an Economic and Monetary Union (EMU) in Europe. Although, as noted, the notion had spread that the ERM was a system of fixed exchange rates, even permanently fixed rates in the EC were not regarded as an alternative to a common currency. The reason was that the credibility of such fixed exchange rates could not be assured as long as individual nations had the possibility of realigning their currencies in the ERM. That, in turn, could undermine the single market.

Most ERM countries had given up the autonomy of monetary policy, instead linking their interest rates to those in Germany. That is why the ERM was also known as a 'D-mark zone'. A desire to share in the formulation of monetary policy was another motivation. In the ERM France's monetary policy was, in effect, decided in Frankfurt by the Bundesbank. In an EMU France would be represented on the governing council of the European central bank and would therefore have a say in its monetary policy decisions.[20] Thus a single currency and a single monetary policy, administered by a single central bank, came to be regarded by its proponents as a natural complement to the Single European Act. It was thought that the full benefits of a unified economic area would be reaped only if the individuals and businesses in that area did not have to exchange currencies in order to undertake transactions across national borders or to face uncertainty about future exchange rates.

Enthusiasts for EMU also had strong political motivations, as discussed below.

This was not the first time the idea of an economic and monetary union was broached in the EC. The Werner Committee report of 1970 proposed a progressive move to such a union by 1980, but the international monetary turbulence of the 1970s – the oil shock of 1974–5 and the move to floating exchange rates – made it a dead letter. The spirit of the Werner Report was revived when the EMS was established. In June 1988 the European Council (the heads of government of the 12 countries) organised a committee of central bank governors and other experts, chaired by Commission President Jacques Delors, to examine the possibility of forming an economic and monetary union. The report of the Delors Committee was submitted in April 1989, calling for a three-stage move to EMU, in which there would be irrevocably fixed exchange rates or, preferably, a single currency, and a single European central bank. The report also called for coordination of fiscal policies among members of EMU and 'binding rules' limiting budget deficits and the means of financing them. The Delors Report embodied the principle of 'subsidiarity' – a term originally used in papal encyclicals to indicate that social problems should be dealt with at the most immediate or local level consistent with solution. In the EMU context it is designed to limit the functions of higher levels of government (the Council of Ministers, the EC Commission, the European Parliament) to what is essential, making them subsidiary to the governments of the member states or conceivably even lower levels of government.

The European Council (heads of state and government) accepted the Delors Report and decided that its first stage would begin in mid-1990.

Meeting at Maastricht in the Netherlands in December 1991, the Council adopted amendments to the Treaty of Rome (which established the European Economic Community) that were to be put to a vote in each of the member countries. In broad terms, the Maastricht Treaty provided for evolution to EMU in three stages. Union could have eventuated by the end of 1996 if a majority of the member states had met the stipulated conditions but it would begin in any event by January 1999.

The agreement provided for a European central bank and for the eventual substitution of a common currency, later dubbed the *euro*, for the present currencies of the individual nations. It also incorporated 'convergence criteria' that would determine whether and which countries qualified for membership in EMU. These criteria involved the rate of inflation (no higher than 1.5 per cent above the average of the three countries with the lowest inflation rates), long-term interest rates (no higher than 2 per cent above the three low inflation countries), stable exchange rates (no realignments in the past two years), and 'a sustainable government financial position' (a general government deficit less than 3 per cent of GDP and a gross government debt less than 60 per cent of GDP).

These convergence criteria were the subject of much discussion and criticism in the economics literature.[21] One criticism was that the efforts of EC – and after 1994, EU – nations to fulfil the criteria imparted a 'deflationary bias' to the European economy. The slowdown in some countries and recession in others in 1992–3 was being aggravated by efforts to curb budget deficits. However desirable that may be in the medium term – and such deficits were bloated in a number of EC countries – to do so in a recession tended to aggravate the downturn or discourage recovery. It would have made more sense, in economic terms, to have formulated the budgetary convergence criterion in terms of structural – cyclically-adjusted – budget deficits.

For the period after EMU is in effect, German Finance Minister Theo Waigel had proposed a stability pact designed to limit budget deficits and to penalise EMU member states that exceeded the limits of 1 per cent of GDP in normal times and 3 per cent in recessions. It was not acceptable to other members. At the Dublin meeting of the European Council in December 1996, a compromise was reached – the Stability and Growth Pact. It provides for discretion as well as rules. A deficit above 3 per cent will not be penalised if GDP falls by 2 per cent or more. If the decline in GDP is between 0.75 and 2 per cent, whether or not a penalty is imposed will be subject to political decision of the Council.

With monetary policy and exchange-rate policy no longer available to individual member states of EMU, fiscal policy would be the only instrument left to deal with country-specific shocks – that is, events such as German unification that have non-uniform impacts on the members of the EMU. The need for greater flexibility of fiscal policy was pointed out in a report by the deputies of the finance ministers and central bank governors of the Group of Ten (the ten largest industrial countries) as follows:

The political ability of countries to accept such constraints ['a pegged exchange rate regime'] in favour of a credible exchange rate commitment depends crucially on the effectiveness of their individual and collective efforts to maintain internal macroeconomic stability without monetary policy autonomy. These efforts are likely to be more successful in economies with relatively flexible wages and prices, low structural rigidities, and countercyclical fiscal stabilisers that are relatively effective and well-disciplined. Establishing effective mechanisms in these respects is necessary for countries to reap the full benefits from maintaining stable exchange rates.[22]

Comparisons have been made with the United States. Although the individual states do not conduct countercyclical fiscal policy, the Federal government's tax and transfer system partially compensates regions of the country that experience a fall of income. It has been estimated that when a state goes into recession at least 28 per cent of each dollar of income decline is offset by either lower tax payments to Washington or additional receipts (mainly unemployment compensation) from the Federal government.[23] The EU budget is and will continue to be much smaller, relatively and absolutely, than that of the Federal government in the United States. Hence that type of offsetting would be much less significant in EMU. This prediction about the size of the central budget of the future EMU rests on the principle of subsidiarity.

In May 1998, it was agreed that EMU would come into effect on 1 January 1999 with 11 members (all 15 EU countries except Denmark, Greece, Sweden and the United Kingdom). The European Central Bank (ECB) came into existence with Wim Duisenberg as president. He, along with a vice president and four others, constitute the Executive Board of the Bank. The 11 national central banks are to be associated with the ECB as the European System of Central Banks (ESCB), similar in structure to both the German and American central banking systems.

What role the euro would play internationally was the subject of much interest and much conjecture. In particular, to what extent would it displace the dollar (i) as a reserve currency held by monetary authorities around the world and (ii) as a private means of payment, store of value, and unit of account?[24]

Economic integration in Europe has come a long way and is very likely to continue. Apart from the economic rationale for increasing the degree of integration of the European nations, and enlarging EMU membership in the future to include not only other Western European nations but also some countries in Eastern Europe, there are strong political motivations drawing these countries closer together. As Charles Bean puts it,

> neither the costs nor the benefits of monetary union are in principle as great as critics and advocates respectively have made out. In fact, from a purely economic perspective, it seems to me something of a storm in a teacup. Why then has so much fuss been made over it? I think the answer is primarily political ... A separate currency is an important symbol of nationhood, while a common currency is an equally potent symbol of a shared political destiny.[25]

To be more explicit about it, the French government is strongly wedded to EMU because it is a way of embracing Germany, keeping it in the Western European camp and discouraging future adventurism. The German government under Helmut Kohl shared this view; as Ungerer wrote: 'Germany – as a geographically, politically, and historically exposed country – has since the end of World War II consistently placed the greatest importance on economic as well as political integration as a means to be firmly anchored in Europe and the Western world.'[26]

6.6   INTEGRATION IN NORTH AMERICA

The North American Free Trade Agreement (NAFTA), signed in December 1992 among the United States, Canada, and Mexico, 'is the most comprehensive free trade pact (short of a common market) ever negotiated between regional trading partners, and the first reciprocal free trade pact between a developing country and industrial countries'.[27] It incorporates much of the already-existing Canada–United States free trade agreement, extending to Mexico the obligation to liberalise trade and investment. In general, tariff barriers and most non-tariff barriers on trade among the three countries will be eliminated over a period of 10 to 15 years. The free trade area could gradually spread to other countries in the Western Hemisphere.

6.7   CONCLUSION

It is clear that economic and financial integration has intensified both on a global and a regional basis. The world is becoming smaller, in the sense that nations have a greater impact on each other when a change takes place in their economies. That calls for increased cooperation, if not coordination, in policymaking.

7 The Elements of Economic Reform: Eastern Europe

At the end of the Second World War, the Soviet Union's Red Army occupied the countries of Eastern and Central Europe (henceforth referred to as Eastern Europe). Stalinist regimes, both political and economic, were established in Albania, Bulgaria, Hungary, Poland and Romania, as well as in East Germany. In 1948 Czechoslovakia came under full Communist control but in the same year Yugoslavia, under Josip Broz Tito, broke with the Soviet Union and followed its own socialist road; in later years this included 'self-management' of enterprises and much less central planning than elsewhere in the region.

Uprisings against Stalinism in Hungary in 1956 and in Czechoslovakia in 1968 were put down by Soviet troops on the basis of what came to be known as the Brezhnev doctrine, which proclaimed that a threat to socialism in any one country was regarded as a matter of concern to all socialist countries and justified intervention. Nevertheless, Hungary, while hewing to the Moscow line in foreign policy in the years that followed, was able to undertake economic reforms, including the introduction of some market mechanisms. In the early part of the 1980s Poland moved partially away from central planning. On the other hand, Romania under the iron fist of Nicolae Ceauşescu pursued an independent foreign policy but its economic regime was based on central planning and forced industrialisation of what had been a rich agricultural country. What did central planning involve?

7.1 CENTRAL PLANNING

The system of central planning, in the USSR and Eastern Europe, was based on directives from governmental ministries regarding the allocation of resources by state-owned enterprises. These enterprises accounted for a high proportion of industrial production and, except in Poland, for most agricultural production. The share of the

95

state sector in value added in commercial and industrial activities ranged from 65 per cent in Hungary to 82 per cent in Poland and 97 per cent in Czechoslovakia.[1] Both the inputs (raw materials and capital goods) and the outputs of enterprises were dictated by the plan. Prices played a very small part in this process: workers could choose among available jobs on the basis of wages paid and consumers could respond to the prices of the goods they found in the shops.

The plans emphasised heavy industry, large firms and specialised production. In most product lines, fewer firms than in the west were responsible for total output. Part of the motivation for this concentration was to simplify the task of planners in allocating resources.

Prices had little relation to world prices – energy, food and rents were subsidised for households. State-owned enterprises that were able to earn profits under the price system provided the government with tax revenue. Those that could not cover their costs were either subsidised or supplied with inexpensive credit. In the language of economists, these firms were subject to a 'soft budget constraint'; that is, in contrast to firms in a market economy, they were not required to alter or close down operations when they were unprofitable. In most of these countries foreign trade was primarily conducted by state trading organisations and differences between foreign and domestic prices were compensated for by taxes or subsidies.

The excess spending by enterprises combined with deficits in government budgets tended to generate inflation, which was held down – repressed – by price controls. Where that happened, households accumulated large amounts of liquid assets in the form of currency or deposits that they would have been prepared to spend if attractive goods had been available – a condition known as a monetary overhang.

Despite these shortcomings, the system of central planning produced reasonably rapid rates of growth in the first two or three decades, if the available statistics are to be believed, and they are known to be deficient. According to economist Angus Maddison, GDP growth in Bulgaria, Czechoslovakia, East Germany, Hungary, Poland, and Romania was rather close to that in 16 OECD countries in 1950–65 and 1965–80. But in the 1980s, growth slowed much more in the centrally-planned economies than in the OECD area, as may be seen in Figure 7.1.[2]

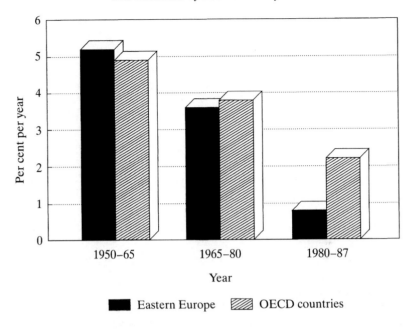

Figure 7.1   Growth in Eastern Europe and OECD

What explains the slowdown? In part, the Eastern European nations were affected by economic and financial conditions abroad. Energy prices rose, though less than in world markets. High interest rates in the west in the early 1980s were also a factor, since the Eastern European countries had begun to borrow in western financial markets in the 1970s and some of them became heavily indebted. More generally, what applies to the Soviet Union is probably true also for Eastern Europe: a command economy finds it difficult to keep up with a rapidly changing technological frontier.[3] Even when growth rates were more satisfactory, the quality of output was inferior.

The system became increasingly inefficient, but it provided stable prices, full employment, and a relatively equal distribution of incomes, to which the populations of centrally-planned economies became accustomed. As reform began, it is understandable that people reacted negatively to open inflation or unemployment or seeing their neighbours become rich.

7.2   THE PROCESS OF TRANSITION TO A MARKET
ECONOMY

The introduction of *glasnost* and *perestroika* in the USSR by Mikhail
Gorbachev, who became general secretary of the Communist Party of
the Soviet Union in March 1985, provided a more congenial atmosphere for reform in Eastern Europe. In effect, the Brezhnev doctrine
was permitted to lapse.

With the breaching of the Berlin Wall in November 1989, political
revolution spread through Eastern Europe (except for Albania, where
the change occurred only in 1991). The era of one-party Communist
rule came to an end. Until that happened, basic economic reform
could not occur since it was not consistent with Communist ideology,
as became evident in the Soviet Union under Gorbachev (to be
covered in Chapter 8).

The political revolutions in Eastern Europe were accompanied by a
desire to break away from Soviet hegemony, to move closer to Western
Europe, and to make the transition to market economies. Eventual
membership in the European Community (now European Union),
with its political and economic implications, became the goal.

In some countries the process of political and economic reform was
spurred by outstanding leaders. In Czechoslovakia's 'velvet revolution'
Václav Havel was a symbol of freedom and Václav Klaus, a strong
believer in free markets whose idol was Margaret Thatcher, did much
to shape the economic reform. Lech Walesa became Poland's demo-
cratically-elected president. Leszek Balcerowicz, Deputy Prime
Minister for Economy from September 1989 to October 1991 (and
again from September 1997) bravely applied stringent macroeconomic
policies and put Poland ahead of most of its neighbours on the road to
economic reform.

Economic reform – making the transition to a market economy – is
a difficult process for which, as noted earlier, there is no precedent
and no blueprint. It has been compared by many, including Lech
Walesa, to converting a fish soup back into a fish.

David Lipton and Jeffrey Sachs, who were advisers to Solidarity in
Poland, put it this way:

> Even with a consensus on the ultimate aims of reform, the tactical
> difficulties of creating a market economy are profound. Fundamental
> social, political, and economic changes must be carried out in the
> context of a deep and worsening economic crisis, inexperience in

managing a market economy, fragile political institutions, the residual pressures of the communist power structure throughout society, the reemergence of historical enmities, and often very deep ethnic fissures.[4]

Moreover, the process imposed painful costs on numerous groups in society as the result of unemployment, open inflation, and the high cost of consumer goods. The initial euphoria at liberation gave way to a realisation that the transition was bound to take time, as we have already noted in the case of east Germany.

Underlying the various changes required by the transition to a market economy is the withdrawal of governments from detailed decision-making, introduction of a system of incentives on the part of managers and workers – incentives to produce more efficiently, to respond to market signals, to innovate and to undertake reconversion aimed at changing the composition of output so as to supply products for which a demand exists at home or abroad.

The transition to a market economy involves three categories of reform:

(1) Macroeconomic stabilisation via fiscal and monetary policies designed to reduce inflation and inflation expectations once prices are liberalised;

(2) Institution building to put in place the necessary features of a market economy: property rights, a system of commercial and bankruptcy law and an efficient accounting system; a banking and payments system, non-bank lenders and financial markets that can provide the financial lubrication needed in a market economy; a properly functioning central bank in place of 'monobanks' that mainly finance government deficits and state-owned enterprises on the basis of central plans; anti-monopoly regulation; introduction of a tax system that does not rely solely on the earnings of state enterprises; the creation of a social safety net, especially unemployment insurance and possibly a labour-intensive public works programme;

(3) Structural reforms starting with the elimination of price controls and subsidies so that prices can perform their function of influencing the distribution of demand and supply and so that, given the exchange rate, prices are in line with those in world markets; the downsizing, restructuring, or closing of 'loss-making' enterprises, including the so-called industrial dinosaurs; the

establishment of markets and market-type relationships among firms; privatisation and a system of corporate governance that provides incentives for efficiency on the part of managers; the liberalisation of foreign trade and, when possible, the establishment of currency convertibility.

The various reforms are interrelated. They are all necessary. A major question has to do with the order in which they are carried out – what has been called the sequencing of reforms. Some aspects of sequencing are clear, but it is not possible to map out the entire process in advance. Moreover, it differed from country to country depending on its history, traditions and political situation.

In the words of Václav Klaus, former Prime Minister of the Czech Republic:

I like to compare the transformation process with chess playing. When we want to play chess, we must know how to play. We must know how to move various pieces on the chessboard. We must know the basic opening strategies. But it's not possible to know the situation on the chessboard after the fifteenth or twenty-fifth move.[5]

Still, some priorities can be set forth. Macroeconomic stabilisation has to come early, along with price liberalisation and the elimination of most subsidies on consumer goods. Inflation, open or repressed, existed in most of the eastern countries. In Poland, consumer prices rose on average by more than 30 per cent per year in 1980–8. In Hungary the inflation rate was 8 per cent per year over the same period. In the other countries inflation was repressed, showing up in shortages of goods, queues at shops and a large monetary overhang.

The other aspects of reform – establishing the institutions of a market economy and restructuring inefficient enterprises – clearly take time.

A question around which controversy prevailed was whether to employ a rapid approach – otherwise known as 'big bang' or 'shock therapy' (the latter being an 'emotionally-loaded' and biased term[6]) – or a gradual approach to the introduction of reforms. The big bang approach was adopted for price liberalisation and macroeconomic stabilisation in Poland, Czechoslovakia, Bulgaria, and Romania, while Hungary pursued a policy of gradualism. The result in the former countries was a burst of inflation and then a subsidence. This steep rise of prices was regarded as an effective means of absorbing the monetary overhang. Consumer price inflation in Poland was almost

250 per cent in 1989 and more than 500 per cent in 1990 before tapering off to 20 per cent in 1996 and less than 16 per cent in 1997. Romania's inflation rate continued to accelerate through 1993, partly because a rapid depreciation of its exchange rate raised the cost of imports; after it diminished to just over 30 per cent in 1995, inflation picked up again, exceeding 150 per cent in 1997. Czechoslovakia managed the transition to a relatively free price system with a much smaller rise of prices. Bulgaria suffered a sharp increase in the inflation rate – to more than 300 per cent at the end of 1996. In July 1997 it adopted a currency board and its consumer prices rose just over 20 per cent in the first half of 1998.

In general, sellers now have to compete much more than in the past in quality and price for the consumer's attention and the consumer has a wider choice than under central planning. But, as is noted below, there remain some non-competitive elements in the transition economies.

Perhaps inevitably, the beginning of reform was accompanied by sharp drops in output, as is shown in Table 7.1. Poland's economy turned up again in 1992 and was joined by the Czech Republic and Romania in 1993. Only in 1994 were all five of the depicted countries growing. The level of output estimated for 1997 – as measured – remained below the 1989 level in all Eastern European countries (including those not shown in the table) with the exception of Poland, which was, after Ireland and Turkey, the fastest-growing country in Europe in 1995–7. A weighted average of the GDPs of the Eastern

Table 7.1 Output changes in Eastern Europe (per cent per year)

	1991	*1992*	*1993*	*1994*	*1995*	*1996*	*1997*	*1998**
Bulgaria	–11.7	–7.2	–1.5	1.8	2.1	–10.9	–6.9	5.5
Czech Republic**	–11.5	–3.3	0.6	3.2	6.4	3.9	1.0	1.0
Hungary	–11.9	–3.1	–0.6	2.9	1.5	1.3	4.4	5.2
Poland	–7.0	2.6	3.8	5.2	7.0	6.1	6.9	5.8
Romania	–12.9	–8.7	1.5	3.9	7.1	3.9	–6.6	–4.0

*Projection. **Czechoslovakia before 1993.
Sources: EBRD, *Transition report 1997*; IMF, *World Economic Outlook*, October 1998.

European and Baltic states was 5 per cent below the 1989 level in 1997 and projected to be 1 per cent below in 1998.[7]

As the IMF has pointed out, 'official statistics almost certainly overstate the contraction – and, in some countries, understate the recent expansion – because they do not fully reflect the growth of new private enterprises or the informal sector'. Data tend to be collected only from large state-owned enterprises. New enterprises and the informal sector do not always get counted.[8]

Accompanying the output declines were substantial increases in unemployment. From near zero in 1989 unemployment rose by 1993 to more than 16 per cent in Poland and Bulgaria, 13 per cent in Hungary, 10 per cent in Romania, and 3.5 per cent in the Czech Republic. By 1997, it had come down in Poland (to 10.5 per cent), in Bulgaria (13.7 per cent), in Hungary (10.4 per cent), and in Romania (7.0 per cent). In the Czech Republic, as is brought out below, unemployment started to rise again beginning in late 1996. There also existed, and perhaps still exists, a sizeable amount of hidden unemployment as non-viable state-owned enterprises continue to provide jobs, financing themselves with credit. There may also be some hidden employment reflecting moonlighting and jobs in private establishments that are not picked up in the statistics.

A significant part of the decline in GDP in these countries was the result not of their economic reform measures but of the disruption of trade with the USSR. That trade was carried out under the Council for Mutual Economic Assistance (CMEA). The pattern of trade under CMEA had involved exports of manufactured goods, including armaments and some agricultural products, from Eastern Europe to the Soviet Union in exchange for raw materials, natural gas and oil at subsidised prices. Exports and imports among the former Soviet Union and the Eastern European nations, including east Germany, is estimated to have fallen by 50 per cent in 1991, when this trade reverted to world market prices and payment in convertible currencies. The sharp rise in the prices of energy imports from the former Soviet Union had a depressing effect on enterprises in Eastern Europe. Moreover, chaos in the former Soviet Union led to a sharp contraction of its imports – which many state enterprises in Eastern Europe were accustomed to supplying. Another part of the output decline resulted from shortages of raw materials and energy previously imported from the Soviet Union. In other words, disruption of CMEA trade had both a demand and a supply effect on Eastern Europe.

7.3 PROGRESS AND PROBLEMS OF REFORM

In general, macroeconomic stabilisation, price liberalisation and the opening of economies to foreign trade came quickly. Structural reform measures were adopted at a slower pace. Part of the explanation for the recessions in the early 1990s was that central planning had been abolished but the institutions of a market economy were not yet fully in place.

The problem of responding to market incentives is especially acute in the case of the large state-owned enterprises. Movement away from socialist planning involves two types of ownership change: the springing up of new private firms and dealing with state-owned enterprises either by privatising them – intact or broken into parts – or closing them down.

The huge state-owned industrial dinosaurs in heavy industry, including armaments, were a major problem. They had to shrink in size and some had to disappear since they could not compete in quality or price in a competitive system where new firms are created using up-to-date technology and imports are free to enter. But mass unemployment posed clear political dangers and that slowed the process of liquidating or privatising state-owned enterprises. Meanwhile the dinosaurs were kept going with bank credits.

Privatisation

According to Scott Thomas, economist in the US aid mission to Poland, privatisation:

> originally meant sale or liquidation of productive assets. The concept has broadened considerably in usage, especially in the context of post-Communist economies. It can mean selling the business and leasing the land and fixed assets. It can mean leasing the business, too. It can mean selling, leasing or giving away some or all of the assets in the enterprise concerned to management and workers. It can mean retaining government ownership of a large minority interest. It can mean stripping away viable assets for sale or giveaway, and leaving behind for the state nonviable assets, along with non-performing loans and other liabilities. It can mean giving to all adult citizens, for free or for a nominal fee, vouchers that can be used to bid for shares in public factories. It can mean hiring foreigners to run holding companies charged with administering public

factories in blind trusts for those citizen-owners. It can mean providing public loans and grants to state-owned enterprises for investments that will 'prepare' them for sale, or to write business plans for the same purpose. It can mean all of these things, and still include the sale of some factories to the highest bidders. In practice, with respect to the larger enterprises, it almost never has meant liquidation.[9]

What is left out of this recitation is the sale to foreign investors. Foreign direct investment in Eastern Europe and the Baltic states rose from $3.8 billion in 1994 to a projected $9.9 billion in 1997.[10] Given the limited amount of capital in the hands of residents of Eastern European countries, a major alternative is to allow foreign investors to buy into state-owned enterprises. But there are obvious political limits to this option. In Hungary numerous enterprises that make consumer goods are now largely owned by foreign multinational companies. This has aroused some resentment and lessened public enthusiasm for privatisation. In Poland workers have demonstrated against a proposed sale of a majority of shares in a state-owned cement company to a Belgian firm. A poll among state-sector industrial workers revealed that half oppose privatisation and only 3 per cent approve of foreign ownership.[11]

Another privatisation technique is the distribution to the public of vouchers that carry the right to bid for shares – 'ingenious and unconventional mass privatisation programmes designed to help create capitalism without capital' as described by Anthony Robinson in the *Financial Times*.[12] This method was utilised in what are now the Czech and Slovak Republics in 1992 as a means of accomplishing a rapid transfer of some state-owned enterprises into private hands. In the process, hundreds of private investment funds, akin to pension funds or mutual funds in the west, were established through which a majority of citizens surrendered their vouchers and obtained shares (which became tradable on the Prague stock exchange in 1993). The assumption was that the investment funds would act to oversee the activities of the enterprise managers in a way that enhances efficiency and productivity, including restructuring or downsizing of the privatised firms. But the funds, which are controlled by state-owned banks, are said to 'siphon off profits from good companies and prop up bad ones with loans'.[13] In addition to outright fraud such as 'self-enrichment of the managers',[14] the investment funds apparently did little to improve corporate governance and management. These deficiencies, along with a foreign exchange crisis, led in 1997 to the resignation of prime minister Václav Klaus, who had earlier been regarded as a hero in his strong push for free markets. Unfortunately, those markets were unregulated.[15] In 1998, a law was enacted requiring the investment funds to become open-ended so that their shares will be valued at net asset value (NAV). The problem was described as follows by Jari Spicka, head of the financial markets department of the finance ministry: 'Voucher privatisation resulted in a freezing of the structure of ownership. The funds are bad owners. Our companies must be restructured but the funds do not have the expertise to do this and they're not able to provide additional capital.'[16]

It is clear that even if privatisation is a necessary condition, it is not a sufficient condition for producing efficient, market-orientated firms. The mere transfer of ownership from the state to private shareholders does not accomplish a restructuring and conversion of enterprises to a condition where they are viable in a market economy, nor does it establish a competitive environment.[17]

The foreign exchange crisis in the Czech Republic in 1997 led to a sharp increase in interest rates and an abrupt slowdown in economic growth from 3.9 per cent in 1996 to 0.1 per cent in 1997.

In Poland, privatisation was pursued slowly and by a variety of paths. 'Internal privatisation' has been the principal method: the existing management and workers have been allowed to buy, to lease, to take over, or to sell the assets of the enterprises. The last of these practices, known as asset stripping, can lead to the demise of the enterprise but it does accomplish some privatisation. In any event, the system permitted a significant rise of productivity in manufacturing and rapid growth in industrial production. A voucher-based mass privatisation programme was later adopted and completed in 1997.

Privatisation in Hungary has not involved vouchers and the distribution of shares. Rather, firms are sold directly by the government to foreign or domestic investors, sometimes to existing management – this is known as self-privatisation or spontaneous privatisation.

According to the European Bank for Reconstruction and Development, in early 1998 privatisation was nearing completion in the Czech Republic, Estonia, Hungary and the Slovak Republic. Yet 'the first phase of liberalisation and privatisation has left out many politically and socially "sensitive" (often structurally weak) sectors. Postponed adjustment in these sectors – for instance agriculture (and downstream processing and marketing), steel, shipyards, mining and power – is becoming an increasingly visible drain on resources.'[18]

The process of dealing with state-owned enterprises has clearly not been completed. Meanwhile two other forms of ownership change – the creation of new private firms, referred to as greenfield investment, and the privatisation of small businesses, mostly in trade and services – go on apace. The greenfield investments are taking place largely in consumer goods and services, including hotels – that is, sectors neglected by central plans that focused on heavy industry.

More generally, the share of GDP produced in the private sector has increased but the estimates vary. According to a compilation by the European Bank for Reconstruction and Development, the proportion was almost 75 per cent in the Czech Republic at the end of 1996, but that includes many enterprises in which the state continues to hold a share. In Hungary, the private share was about 75 per cent and in Poland, 65 per cent.[19]

7.4   TRADE AND INVESTMENT WITH THE WEST

While trade among CMEA countries fell sharply after 1990, some of the Eastern European countries were able to increase their exports elsewhere, especially to western Europe. Poland's exports to all industrial countries rose 160 per cent, in dollar value, from 1989 to 1997 while its total exports increased by 74 per cent. Hungary raised its exports to industrial countries by 275 per cent over the same period.

Meanwhile capital inflows increased. It is estimated that net private flows (direct investment, portfolio debt and equity flows, bank loans and trade finance) to six Eastern European countries plus Russia increased from $3 billion in 1991 to more than $45 billion in 1997.[20]

The Czech Republic was on the receiving end of large capital inflows in 1995–6 under a pegged exchange rate. That complicated its monetary policy. Inflation worsened and the current-account deficit swelled to more than 8 per cent of GDP in 1996. In the spring of 1997, a managed float was adopted.

On the other hand, capital inflow to Poland increased in the first two months of 1998 despite the crisis in other emerging markets.

There is a connection between new direct investment in Eastern Europe and trade policy in the west. If investors fear that western markets will not be open to exports from the east, they will hesitate to open new or acquire existing plants there.

7.5 THE OUTLOOK

In 1998 the countries of Eastern Europe were on an upward growth path and their inflation rates had come down. Most of them had moved to current-account convertibility as they reintegrated into the world economy. The first category of reform referred to above is being achieved in most countries. And some aspects of institution building and structural reform have occurred.

Still, the institutional and structural reform aspects of the transformation will take a while to complete. Financial systems and capital markets need further development, along with prudential oversight. On the structural side, privatisation has proceeded on a broad scale but it has further to go. In some countries competition needs to be encouraged and corporate governance needs improvement.

In other words, what the IMF calls 'second generation' reform requirements remain to be carried out, not only in Eastern Europe but certainly also in Russia and the other CIS countries (next chapter).[21]

Such reforms will be essential for those countries of Eastern Europe – especially the Czech Republic, Hungary and Poland – that hope to join the EU early in the twenty-first century.

One should not mistake the trees for the forest. The main point is that what were basically undemocratic countries with command economies in 1980 now have mostly popularly-elected regimes that have made significant progress on the road to market economies.

8 Chaos and Reform in the Soviet Union and Russia

When Mikhail Gorbachev came to power in March 1985, he was presiding over a large economy, rich in resources but also inefficient and isolated from the world economy. In the 1960s the USSR produced *Sputnik* and Khrushchev boasted that the Soviet economy would 'bury' the west. In the 1970s the Soviet Union had to import large amounts of grain. In the 1980s its growth rate slowed and dissatisfaction with its economic performance began to be openly expressed. The inadequacies of central planning described in the previous chapter applied, of course, to the Soviet Union, from which central planning was exported to Eastern Europe.

Soviet statistics are of doubtful validity. But even when refined by western scholars they show rates of growth of more than 5 per cent per year in the quarter century ending in the mid-1950s, despite the severe destruction of the Second World War. The country was industrialised and millions of peasants were drawn away from agriculture into factories, where they enjoyed rising standards of living.[1]

That spurt of centrally-planned industrialisation and growth was achieved under Stalin by brutal methods in which human rights were ignored and the environment was despoiled. Nevertheless it permitted the Soviet Union to become a military superpower and to have influence throughout the world. In later years, particularly in the 1970s and 1980s, the growth rate slowed markedly. In Gorbachev's words:

> At some stage – this became particularly clear in the latter half of the seventies – something happened that was at first sight inexplicable. The country began to lose momentum. Economic failures became more frequent. Difficulties began to accumulate and deteriorate, and unresolved problems to multiply. Elements of what we call stagnation and other phenomena alien to socialism began to appear in the life of society. A kind of 'braking mechanism' affecting social and economic development formed. And all this happened at a time when scientific and technological revolution opened up new prospects for economic and social progress.

He went on to state: 'In the last fifteen years the national income growth rates had declined by more than a half and by the beginning of the 1980s had fallen to a level close to economic stagnation.'[2]

There were several reasons for the slowdown. Growth had depended much more on increasing inputs – labour and capital equipment – than on rising productivity. Additions to the labour force were made possible in part by steady advances in the participation of women. By the early 1970s, 85 per cent of adult women were in the work force, compared with 60 per cent in the United States. Growth of the labour force tapered off in the 1970s and employment growth slowed. Similarly, plant and equipment investment could not keep expanding rapidly without impinging unduly on the availability of consumer goods. The growth of both gross and net investment declined sharply between 1970 and 1985.[3] And, of course, military expenditures were a burden, accounting for a higher proportion of GDP in the USSR than in the United States.

Meanwhile productivity gains did not compensate for these changes that began to limit economic growth. Total factor productivity – output per unit of labour and capital – increased only one-half per cent per year in 1950–73 compared with 3.35 per cent in OECD countries and 1.73 per cent in developing countries. In 1973–84, total factor productivity declined 1.4 per cent annually in the Soviet Union while it rose by 1.28 per cent per year in the OECD nations.[4] One explanation is that as technology became more complex (though it lagged far behind that in the industrial countries), the system of central planning was less and less capable of efficiently allocating physical inputs and outputs of individual enterprises. Another is that neither managers nor workers had the incentive to increase efficiency.

Furthermore the concentration of production in one or a few plants was inefficient since it meant that a shortfall of output in one enterprise had a big effect on the enterprises it supplied.

Apparently the command economy was capable of industrialising but was ill-suited to the management of an industrialised economy.

The poor economic performance can also be attributed to a passive and dependent workforce. In both industry and agriculture the incentive system discouraged individual effort and pride of workmanship. Kyril Tidmarsh, former Moscow correspondent of *The Times* of London, wrote that working-class professionalism was discouraged by 'the leveling of wages and the narrowing of differentials, regardless of skills or output'. Moreover 'undesirable "dirty" jobs eventually had to be remunerated with inappropriately high pay'. The result was that low-skilled workers 'thus became higher paid while the high skilled saw their pay decline'. This was of course a perverse incentive:

> Every operation in industry had a quantitative labor 'norm' that workers had to fulfill for basic pay. Productivity above the norm was sometimes rewarded. It was well known, however, that dramatic or continuing norm-beating would lead to an upward revision of the work goal. For decades, therefore, the system encouraged workers to produce below potential.[5]

As a result of all this, the Soviet economy was a shortage economy. Consumers were accustomed to standing in lines and even to paying bribes to secure favourable treatment from salespeople in shops.

The quality of the goods produced was also unsatisfactory in the eyes of Soviet consumers. Despite shortages, consumers were refusing to buy some goods in the 1980s. In addition, many products, including computers and communications equipment, were technologically obsolete.

The unsatisfactory performance of the economy was openly discussed by Yuri Andropov during his brief tenure as General Secretary of the Communist Party beginning in November 1982 and ending with his death in February 1984. In a speech in 1983, he 'lamented that the quality of many consumer goods – including TVs, radios, cameras, and watches – was so low that they simply could not be sold and instead sat in warehouses'.[6]

On the other hand, the Soviet system provided its citizens with full employment, stable prices and what they regarded as an equitable distribution of income. Economic reform was bound to clash with these cherished features of the system.

8.1 *GLASNOST* AND *PERESTROIKA*

Mikhail Gorbachev, trained in the law at Moscow State University, spent 20 years as a local politician in Stavropol in southern Russia where he was born. His southern accent was at times the butt of jokes in Moscow, to which he was called in 1978 to be in charge of agriculture for the Communist Party. He was made a full member of the Politburo in 1980. In March 1985, he became the youngest general secretary of the Party in the history of the Soviet Union. He immediately projected a new style of leadership, in sharp contrast to his predecessors. He displayed vigour, a smiling countenance, an attractive and stylish wife, and a willingness to mingle with the populace. It is reported that in nominating Gorbachev to be general secretary, Andrei Gromyko said that 'this man has a nice smile, but he has got iron teeth'.[7]

Shortly before he became general secretary, Gorbachev used the term 'radical reform' – startling in the Soviet context – to signal his intentions.

In addition to economic reform (on which more below), Gorbachev's early moves included *glasnost* – greater openness and self-criticism in society, accountability of public officials, and an end to censorship. *Glasnost* also carried the demythologising of Stalin much further than Khrushchev had ever done. At the Moscow airport in the autumn of 1988, I was startled to see a donation box for the victims of Stalin, into which departing travellers were invited to deposit their left-over roubles.

Glasnost also included a shift in attitudes towards the outside world. A 'world view' was adopted with respect to ecology and international economic relations. Soviet officials began to admit their interdependence with other countries and to think about joining international economic institutions such as the GATT and the International Monetary Fund and World Bank. The change in viewpoint can be illustrated by a personal recollection. In the late 1970s the Soviet Ambassador to the United States, Anatolii Dobrynin, was invited to The Brookings Institution for lunch. During the discussion I started to put a question to him with the words 'In this interdependent world...'. He interrupted and, wagging a finger at me, said 'Soviet Union not interdependent.'

In Gorbachev's philosophy *glasnost* was closely linked to *perestroika* – economic restructuring – since the latter required public participation and backing in the face of entrenched opposition by the bureaucracy.

Gorbachev also pursued the anti-alcohol campaign started by Andropov. Involving a reduction in the production of alcohol, shorter hours for liquor stores, and a rise in the legal drinking age, it was aimed at increasing productivity as well as at improving the quality of life. It became the subject of both jokes and bitter complaints and did not last long, in part perhaps because it resulted in a loss of revenues to the government and an enlarged budget deficit.

Economic reform was Gorbachev's first priority. That is what *perestroika* was all about. He stressed the need for an 'acceleration' of economic development: a more rapid rate of growth of the economy and a distinct improvement in the quality of output, though it was probably naïve to expect this combination of outcomes to be realised.

Among the means he pressed for were modernisation of machinery and equipment and a wage policy that raised the incomes of those with higher skills. As it turned out, the increase in investment combined with the budget deficit resulted in a pickup in inflation.

Reform moved ahead in 1987 with a decision that appeared to eliminate centrally-determined annual plans and to give state enterprises operational autonomy, including self-financing, but subject to rewards or penalties depending on their performance. Yet state orders still covered 90 per cent of industrial output in 1988, and Gorbachev and his colleagues in the Kremlin continued to hold ministries responsible for the quality of output in their sectors. Firms were given more freedom to set their prices and wages and both rose more rapidly in 1988–9. Another reform was the authorisation of private and cooperative enterprises in the supply of consumer goods and services, but employees of state enterprises could not be hired full-time in these activities. By the end of 1990, 245 000 cooperatives were in existence employing more than 5 per cent of the labour force and accounting for almost 7 per cent of GNP.[8]

A major political reform was proposed by Gorbachev in 1988 and was implemented in 1989: the separation of the functions of the Communist Party and the government. The Party would give up its economic responsibilities. A real parliament – the Congress of People's Deputies – would be created and it in turn would elect a smaller full-time Supreme Soviet. In 1990 Gorbachev was elected president by the Congress. A constitutional amendment provided for the popular election of the president beginning in 1995.

The late Ed Hewett noted – in the penultimate paragraph of his book, *Reforming the Soviet Economy*, published in 1988 – that every Soviet leader since Stalin had tried in his own way to reform the system. Gorbachev

> seems to be a different kind of leader ... But he is also the product of the old system. He has been educated by it and is a politician who has succeeded by working the system. His approach reflects the continuity of his background: in part it is a refutation of the past and in part it is a recasting of past policies. Those links to the past bring with them the weaknesses of past approaches.[9]

In the view of Anders Åslund: 'To Gorbachev, reforms were a means to an end rather than an end in themselves. His aim was to reinforce and revitalize the USSR so that it could maintain its superpower status – a status threatened by its stagnant economy and the arms race with the United States.'[10]

8.2   CRISIS AND BREAK-UP

As is evident from the quotations from Gorbachev, Hewett and Åslund above, the Gorbachev economic reforms did not go very far. The central planning bureaucracy in Moscow was reduced in size and authority. State enterprises were given more autonomy but there was no system of market prices to provide signals and guide their decisions. A striking example: the output of a heavy machine-building factory in the Urals, which employed 50 000 workers in the 1980s, measured its output in terms of tons of machinery, whether the products were machines, oil drilling equipment, bulldozers, or washing machines.[11]

Furthermore competition was virtually non-existent either domestically or from imports. In fact, many of the state enterprises were monopolies. Also there was no macroeconomic policy. The budget deficit increased in the second half of the 1980s as revenues from alcohol and oil exports declined while expenditures for investment and defence increased. And too much money was being created by the central bank.

The result was stagflation: the USSR experienced a 4 per cent decline in GDP in 1990 as manufacturing production, agricultural output and oil extraction dropped. Prices, though still legally controlled, rose faster as enterprises exploited their monopoly powers and followed a long-standing practice of shifting production to ostensibly new products for which they were entitled to raise prices. Shortages and hoarding of goods became more acute and that in turn led enterprise managers to hoard stocks of raw materials. Also the monetary overhang grew as consumers found themselves with even larger amounts of unwanted roubles.

In these conditions, public dissatisfaction increased, encouraged no doubt by knowledge of what was happening in Eastern Europe in 1989. Strikes occurred – a virtually unprecedented event in Soviet history.

Numerous comprehensive reform plans were put forward with much publicity but were not accepted by the leadership. Some partial reform decrees were promulgated but were not always implemented. Boris Yeltsin, an ex-member of the Politburo who was to become president of the Russian Republic in 1991 in a historic free election, emerged as a strong advocate of economic reform and gathered around him the most able economists anxious for reform. At a Communist Party Congress in July 1990 he dramatically turned in his party membership card. Meanwhile Gorbachev tried to take a middle road between reformers and conservatives. At the same time various republics, especially but not only those in the Baltics, were clamouring for, and in some cases seizing, greater autonomy from Moscow. They issued declarations of sovereignty and began to sign economic co-operation agreements with each other.

The economic and political fragmentation was highlighted by the resignation in December 1990 of Foreign Minister Eduard Shevardnadze, who warned of the possible approach of a 'dictatorship' but that 'the future belongs to democracy and freedom'.

Output in the Soviet Union declined again in 1991, by 5 per cent. Among the reasons were a shortage of imported supplies owing to the scarcity of foreign exchange and the collapse of trade with Eastern Europe.

The wholesale price system was liberalised at the beginning of 1991 with a view to improving incentives. Some retail prices were also raised. In April there was a major reform of retail prices, which raised them on average by 60 per cent. For the year 1991 as a whole retail prices almost doubled as compared with 1990.

In the spring of 1991, Gorbachev and the leaders of nine of the fifteen republics agreed on a new Union treaty that gave additional powers to the republics and allowed the other six (Armenia, Estonia, Georgia, Latvia, Lithuania, and Moldavia) to decide for themselves whether to sign the new treaty. The treaty, which was strongly opposed by conservatives in Moscow, was scheduled to be signed on 20 August 1991.

As history records, a coup was attempted on 19 August by Gorbachev's vice president, Gennady Yanayev, and seven other officials who had been appointed by Gorbachev. They announced that Gorbachev, who was on vacation in the Crimea, could not carry on his duties owing to ill health and they were assuming power and declaring a state of emergency. Tanks rumbled into Moscow. The coup leaders held a press conference that was covered by CNN and people all over the world were able to observe their grim nervousness and insecurity.

Large numbers of Muscovites gathered in the streets to oppose the coup and Boris Yeltsin, in a memorable act, stood atop a tank in front a government building – the so-called White House – to denounce the coup as 'reactionary' and 'anticonstitutional'. On the next day 50 000 people assembled at the same place, where they were addressed by Shevardnadze. Similar demonstrations took place in other cities.

On the international front the coup was supported by Saddam Hussein, Muammar Qaddafi, and Fidel Castro.[12]

The coup – or *putsch,* as it is often called in Russia – was opposed by Russia's defence minister, a retired general, who advised the troops not to follow the commands of the coup leaders. Gorbachev, whose communications with Moscow and elsewhere had been cut off, returned to Moscow with a Russian delegation sent by Yeltsin. Soon the coup leaders were arrested.

On his return to Moscow Gorbachev, at a press conference, proclaimed his loyalty to the Communist Party while calling himself a true believer in the socialist idea. This and the coup itself were among the catalysts that sealed his fate and led to the dissolution of the Soviet Union and the independence of the republics. Public opinion swung to Yeltsin and other republican leaders. On 23 August the activities of the Russian Communist Party were suspended by decree. The next day Gorbachev resigned as its general secretary and dissolved its Central Committee. That put an end to the era of Bolshevism that began in 1917. Later that autumn the Constitutional Court of Russia ruled, after a lengthy trial, that the Communist Party was illegal as a national entity but that communists could meet at a local level. Among the 13 judges on the court, 12 were former members of the Communist Party. In the words of Georgi Arbatov, 'the *coup d'état* became the Party's *coup de grâce*'.[13]

As David Remnick, former *Washington Post* correspondent in Moscow, wrote, 'Russia faced a great historical moment, an elected president occupying the Kremlin for the first time in the thousand-year history of Russia, the hammer and sickle gone from the flagpole, the regime and empire dissolved.'[14]

In December 1991 the republics, other than those in the Baltics, agreed to form the Commonwealth of Independent States (CIS). This ended the Soviet Union. Gorbachev resigned as president on Christmas Day.

His resignation speech, addressed to 'Dear Compatriots, fellow citizens' noted that the country has

plenty of everything: land, oil and gas, other natural riches, and God gave us lots of intelligence and talent. Yet we lived much worse than developed countries, and kept falling farther and farther behind them.

The reason for this could already be seen [when he found himself at the head of state]. The society was suffocating in the vise of the bureaucratic-command system, doomed to serve ideology and bear the terrible burden of the arms race.

The process of renovating the country and of making radical changes in the world community turned out to be far more complicated than could have been anticipated. However, what has been done ought to be given its due. This society has acquired freedom, liberated itself politically and spiritually – and this is the foremost achievement, which we haven't fully understood yet because we have not yet learned how to use freedom.[15]

Mikhail Gorbachev will go down in history for having transformed what was the Soviet Union in many ways: moving it away from the totalitarian ideology and practices that dominated all of his predecessors; abandoning the notion of a class struggle at home and an arms race abroad; opening the society to free speech and a free press, tolerating dissent, encouraging freedom of religion, emigration and political freedom generally, including contested elections; withdrawing Soviet troops from Afghanistan; changing foreign policy, especially relations with the other superpower, the United States; liberating Eastern Europe and allowing it to go its own way; and starting the process of economic reform, even if he failed to pursue it adequately.[16]

In the words of the American journalist Robert Kaiser:

In the end Gorbachev did resemble the man he liked to compare himself to. Like Lenin, Gorbachev was a missionary figure who led a crusade to a new Russia. He had the personality of a missionary: zealous, utterly self-confident, solemn to a fault. His determination to turn away from the past and start afresh was his greatest strength. In this he succeeded. But his zealotry and his self-confidence were confining; he could begin the process of reinventing his country, but at the critical moment he could not reinvent himself.[17]

8.3   RUSSIA

It is not possible to cover developments in all 15 of the republics of the former Soviet Union. We shall focus on Russia. The Russian Federation is the largest country in the world in area spread over 11 time zones and the sixth largest in population (about 150 million).

It consists of 16 autonomous republics, 5 autonomous regions, and 10 autonomous 'national regions'. There are also Russians in the other republics. For example, more than half the population of Alma-Ata in Kazakhstan and Bishkek in Kyrgyzstan are ethnic Russians, as are one-third of the people in the capitals of Tajikistan and Turkmenistan.

Boris Yeltsin, the president of the Russian Federation, was born in 1931 in Sverdlovsk (now Yekaterinburg) in the Ural mountains. He attended the Urals Polytechnic Institute and then worked as a construction engineer in his home area until 1968, when he became a Party functionary, serving on the Sverdlovsk District Central Committee. Shortly after Gorbachev took office as general secretary, he brought Yeltsin to Moscow to head the Central Committee's construction department. He was named a candidate member of the Politburo in 1986 and also first secretary of the Moscow City Party Committee, a position in which he became very popular with Muscovites. In October 1987 at a plenum of the Central Committee Yeltsin criticised the leadership for the slow pace of reform and in February 1988 he was expelled from the Politburo. In 1989 he was elected to the Congress of People's Deputies from Moscow with 89 per cent of the votes. As noted earlier, he was elected president of the Russian Republic in 1991 and re-elected in 1996.

It has been written that under

Stalin's regime a maverick such as Boris Yeltsin would have been shot; under Khrushchev he would have been jailed; and under Brezhnev he would have been sent to an insane asylum. Because of the transformation that Gorbachev engineered in Soviet politics, Yeltsin was able to arise again and challenge his one-time patron.[18]

Yeltsin was characterised in 1993 as 'a deeply ambiguous figure: by turns courageous and backsliding, clear and muddled, uncompromising and hesitant. Yet his gut instinct for a more liberally inclined Russia has not deserted him and his shaky popularity remains higher than that of any contender.'[19] That judgement appeared questionable in 1998.

Chaos and Reform and More Chaos

Yeltsin inherited an economy whose output had fallen, with a large budget deficit, heavy external debts and meagre foreign exchange reserves. Oil production, its largest earner of hard currency, had dropped drastically. And little structural reform had been accomplished.

With Yegor Gaidar as a deputy prime minister, some aspects of economic reform proceeded more rapidly in Russia in 1992. It began with the deregulation of most prices before a macroeconomic stabilisation policy had been put in place. Thus prices soared in 1992 except for those that remained under control, including energy and rents. Oil prices were raised but remained well under the level of world prices. From December 1991 to December 1992 consumer prices rose 2500 per cent. Inflation began to subside in 1993 and declined year by year thereafter, until the autumn of 1998. Whatever its other effects, the hyperinflation put an end to rationing and soaked up the monetary overhang.

The steep rate of inflation in the early 1990s was attributable to the outsized budget deficit – more than 20 per cent of GDP in 1992 – and the credit-creating activities of the central bank. In both cases the funds were used to subsidise state-owned enterprises. This was in effect a form of unemployment insurance on a large scale. The subsidies and credits to loss- making state-owned enterprises enabled them to meet their payrolls. The alternative would have been massive unemployment, with possible serious political repercussions. Another reason for the inflation was that Russia was lending large amounts of roubles to other republics, enabling them to buy Russian goods.

Inflation along with the general political and economic uncertainty led to capital flight. Everyone who could do so exchanged roubles for foreign currencies, mainly dollars. Thus the rouble's exchange rates depreciated rapidly, raising the domestic cost of imports. Consequently some imports were subsidised, adding to the budget deficit.

Most of the other republics of the CIS were still using the rouble and the inflation in Russia necessarily spread to them to the extent that they were not creating their own inflations. They too had to liberalise their prices and let them go up. Otherwise their output would have been siphoned off to Russia, attracted by its higher prices.

President Yeltsin's early reform measures met strong opposition from his vice president and in the Congress of People's Deputies from both former communists and members of what is called, ironically enough, the military- industrial complex (for those too young to remember or with short memories, a term coined by President Eisenhower shortly before he left office). In September 1993 Yeltsin ordered the parliament disbanded, calling for new elections. This led to another crisis when the parliament resisted and attempted a coup by first trying to take over a television station. Yeltsin secured the support of the military leaders who proceeded to shell the very same White House where he defied the revolutionists of 1991. Yeltsin prevailed and elections in December approved a new constitution but also sent a large number of nationalists, former communists and anti-reformers to the new Duma, the lower house of parliament.

Toward the end of January 1994 economic reform appeared to be in retreat as Prime Minister Chernomyrdin formed a new government saying that the time for 'market romanticism' was over.'[20] He proposed dealing with inflation, which worsened during the period of political turmoil, by non-monetary means, which sounded like price controls. Two of the principal reformers in the previous government, Yegor Gaidar and Boris Fyodorov, refused to participate in the new one. And two chief foreign advisers to the government, Anders Åslund of Sweden and Jeffrey Sachs of the United States, were asked to step aside.

The prospects for reform appeared dim. Yet in the first months of 1994 Chernomyrdin pursued an anti-inflationary budget policy and encouraged continued privatisation. Inflation fell to a monthly rate of 5 per cent by July. But the relative stability did not last and in October there occurred a foreign exchange crisis as the rouble plummeted. That in turn led to a political crisis and the government survived a confidence vote in the Duma in late October. As Anders Åslund put it: 'That an exchange crisis could almost bring the government down shows that Russia had really become a market economy.'[21]

Nevertheless, measured output declined more steeply in 1994 – by 12.6 per cent. Consumer price inflation subsided from the rates of the two previous years but still amounted to more than 200 per cent in the 12 months to December 1994. Russia's general government budget deficit was brought down after 1992 to 5.8 per cent of GDP in 1995 after which it increased again in 1996 and 1997 as tax receipts fell off. In the words of an IMF analysis: 'In 1997, the federal government collected less than 12 per cent of GDP in revenue, about 30 per cent less than what was targeted in the budget.'[22]

As was widely observed, the public, including enterprises, were in arrears in paying taxes and the government was in arrears in paying wages to government employees. Enterprises were even more in arrears than the government in the payment of wages. But labour mobility is low since enterprises provide various social services for their employees.

With the reduction in the budget deficit – although it remained too high – and a much more effective monetary policy by the Central Bank of Russia, the rate of inflation also decreased year by year to $5\frac{1}{2}$ per cent in the 12 months ending July 1998. In these circumstances, the government redenominated the rouble on 31 December 1997, lopping three zeros off. The exchange rate was just above 8000 per dollar at that time. In early 1998, it was about 6 per dollar. By October, it had depreciated to 14.5 per dollar.

For the first time in seven years, and perhaps longer, real GDP rose slightly in 1997. Industrial production went up almost 2 per cent.

Interest rates came down with the rate of inflation until the autumn of 1997, when the outbreak of the crisis in Asia sent them up again and sent stock prices down along with stock markets in most other countries. The Treasury bill rate had decreased to about 18 per cent in July 1997 but then rose again. These were additional indications that Russia had been reintegrated into the world economy and world financial system. As an 'emerging market' it was also affected by the 'Asian flu'. Actually the reintegration became evident earlier as foreign investors bought shares on the Russian stock market, helping to push share prices up sharply in 1996 and the first half of 1997. Foreign direct investment came in at $2 billion per year in 1995 and 1996 and was projected at $3.9 billion in 1997.[23] Also the Russian government as well as municipalities and corporations issued Eurobonds in London.

The negative aspect of these developments was that the high interest rates discouraged domestic investment and GDP fell slightly in the first half of 1998. The government was having difficulty financing the budget deficit and capital was fleeing the rouble, leading to extremely high interest rates.

Meanwhile, Yeltsin sacked Chernomyrdin in March 1998 – reportedly because of the latter's presidential ambitions – and replaced him with the young reformer Sergei Kiriyenko. He did not prevail and the re-appointment of Chernomyrdin was turned down by the parliament. Finally, in September, Yeltsin named former foreign minister Yevgeny Primakov as prime minister and he in turn brought some former Soviet officials back into the government and Soviet-era central bank governor Gerashchenko back to the that post.

In the autumn of 1998, Russia was in a condition of severe uncertainty both economically and politically.

Privatisation and Industry Reform

The institutional and structural categories of economic reform, identified in Chapter 7, have been implemented to a significant extent but still have a way to go.

A privatisation programme was pursued vigorously under Anatoly Chubais. In late 1992 vouchers were issued to every man, woman and child in Russia – a programme similar to that introduced in the former Czechoslovakia. Predictably workers and managers as well as 'conservative' politicians, including former President Gorbachev, were critical of this action. The vouchers were eligible for exchange at auctions for shares in enterprises put up for privatisation. The vouchers could also be bought and sold by the citizenry and by investors from abroad. A substantial portion of the shares – either 40 per cent or 51 per cent – could be acquired by the employees and managers; if they chose a majority of the shares, they paid more heavily.

The motivation behind this scheme was not only the obvious economic one – improving the efficiency of the enterprises by introducing the incentives associated with the profit motive – but also political: to give the public a stake in private enterprise and make the reform process irreversible.

The voucher-based mass privatisation programme was completed in mid-1994 and was followed by cash-based privatisation involving auctions or tenders. One of its aims was to bring revenue to the budget. All in all, the number of wholly-owned state enterprises was reduced from more than 200 000 in 1992 to 88 000 at the end of 1996; additional firms were privatised in 1997. As a result, about 70 per cent of GDP was accounted for by the private sector in mid-1997.[24]

But the process created problems. A system of 'shares for loans', first proposed by a consortium of large Moscow banks, provided for bank credits to the government collateralised by shares in enterprises and auctions designed to assure competition among the lenders. When the credits were not repaid, the banks were able to hold on to the shares and the system became 'a focal point of enormous controversy'. A handful of banks were able to acquire enterprises at low prices and to become the nuclei for industrial conglomerates headed by so-called 'oligarchs'.[25] The system was characterised by David Remnick as 'surely the biggest land grab in the history of the world'.[26]

While thousands of enterprises have been privatised, corporate governance leaves a lot to be desired and restructuring has not gone far enough. A mere change of the ultimate owners from the state to citizens does not by itself assure significant improvement in the quality of management, productivity and hence the quantity and quality of output of large enterprises. According to the EBRD's transition report in 1997:

> Enterprise restructuring has hitherto been achieved mainly through changes in the product mix, shedding of labour through attrition, expanded use of unpaid leave or reduced hours. Deeper restructuring in the form of factory shutdowns, changes in management, major reorganisations and modernisation is at a very early stage and is constrained by, among other factors, limited access to investment resources. Recent evidence suggests that roughly 25 per cent of the medium-sized and large companies are engaged in serious restructuring... About half of the medium-sized and large companies have not as yet undertaken any meaningful restructuring.[27]

Russia has been characterised as having a 'virtual economy' by Clifford Gaddy and Barry Ickes.[28] They argue that very little reform had been achieved in the industrial sector which does not 'add value' but survives on the basis of underpriced raw materials, low wages, and low taxes, if these payments are made at all.

Meanwhile, a few so-called capitalist tycoons ('oligarchs') in banking and other fields have achieved enormous wealth and power. They are reminiscent of the railroad 'robber barons' in the United States in the nineteenth century. Referred to as 'the bankers' they supported Yeltsin's re-election but were in conflict with the reforming deputy prime ministers, Chubais and Nemtsov.

8.4   THE OUTLOOK

Privatisation – in both senses: new firms being organised and old ones moving into private ownership – is under way. Some enterprises that made armaments are turning out consumer goods such as washing machines. Structural and institutional reform are creeping forward. A start has been made on allowing citizens to buy and sell farm land.

As reform moved ahead haltingly, it was accompanied by some of the excrescences of a free, non-totalitarian society. Crime is rampant and a 'mafia' exists. Corruption and bribery were present under the old system but they are apparently more blatant now. Those individuals who have become rich, legally or illegally, ride around in Mercedes or BMWs while pensioners have difficulty making ends meet. The difference between the rich and the poor is greater than at any time since before the Communist revolution. Ironically many of the *nouveau riche* are former Communist Party *apparatchiks*.

Yet, Russia is now a democracy with free elections and a free press. It has joined the world economy and financial system. That is evidenced not only by its vulnerability to the financial crisis in Asia but by the prospect that a crisis in Russia could shake the western European economies. The financial crisis in Russia could also undermine democracy there.[29] Although Russia has progressed in economic reform, the political and economic outlook was highly uncertain in the autumn of 1998.

9 From Mao Zedong to Zhu Rongji: Economic Reform in China

China's experience with economic reform has been very different from that of the countries in transition. In fact, the IMF classifies China as a developing country, not one in transition. Politically China has not yet moved towards democracy. It remains a Communist one-party state. Its late 'paramount leader', Deng Xiaoping, spoke of his death as going to an appointment with Karl Marx. But his successor, Jiang Zemin, has used the term 'socialist democracy' and personal freedom appears to have increased somewhat.

China, with the largest population and the third largest area of the countries of the world, is more decentralised – politically and economically – than Russia and the nations of Eastern Europe. That has allowed for local initiatives and experiments that, if successful, can spread elsewhere. Substantial economic reforms have been adopted but on a gradual basis. There has been no shock therapy. Nor had there been a significant amount of privatisation of state-owned enterprises, at least until 1998. But new private firms have come into existence. A substantial part of China's output is produced by entities that operate according to market principles. As *The Economist* has written:

> Plunges do not appeal to the Chinese, who call their method of reform 'crossing the river by feeling the stones underfoot.' As early as the mid-1980s, Chinese economists were arguing that quick wholesale reform has the same defect as central planning: it requires the government to take too many big decisions on questions, such as the right sequence of reform or the right way to privatise, that it knows too little about. Far better to experiment cautiously, letting different regions and different companies try different things. If they work, extend them, If not, bury them.[1]

China's reform has been based on marketisation rather than privatisation. And it has differed from region to region. The coastal provinces – notably Guangdong – have developed rapidly on the basis of Deng Xiaoping's 'open door' policy. This has authorised joint ventures with foreign capital, much of it from Hong Kong. The interior provinces have moved ahead on the basis of saving in the local agricultural sector, which made possible the formation and growth of town and village enterprises (TVEs).

As a World Bank study put it: 'China's unique attempt to complete two transitions at once – from a command to a market economy and from a rural to an urban society – is without historical precedent.'[2]

China has avoided the drastic declines in output that have afflicted all the countries in transition. In fact, its growth performance has been astonishing, even when official data are modified by Angus Maddison (see below, page 134). In 1993–4 the government was trying to cope with an overheated economy that grew by about 13 per cent, according to official data. In late 1997, inflation was down to about 1 per cent and the economy grew by almost 9 per cent. But economic activity weakened in early 1998 as China was affected by the crisis in other Asian countries. At the same time, some serious structural problems emerged – problems not unfamiliar in the countries in transition.

The country that Napoleon is said to have called a 'sleeping giant' has awakened.

9.1 PRE-REFORM DEVELOPMENTS

Mao Zedong led the Chinese Communist revolution, which came to fruition in 1949. Under his direction China carried out a major and bloody land reform in which landlords were killed and peasants took over ownership of properties that they had formerly leased. Later, agriculture was collectivised, industry was nationalised and heavy industry was encouraged as China adopted the Soviet system of central planning, advised by thousands of Soviet technicians. Central planning was relaxed somewhat but continued in force even after the split with the Soviet Union in the late 1950s.

In 1957 Mao initiated the Great Leap Forward, which involved establishing peoples communes in the countryside and abolishing private plots. The average commune consisted of 5000 households. The peasants were mobilised to build roads, dams and irrigation networks. The next year a programme of local steelmaking was launched in the communes and elsewhere: many hundreds of thousands of small furnaces were built throughout the country but inadequate provision was made for supplying the raw materials needed and the steel proved to be mostly useless. The programme was a total failure and was soon abandoned but only after agricultural production plummeted because of the diversion of peasant labour from its usual activities. The result was a famine in which 20 to 30 million people died from starvation or malnutrition. China's GDP, which had doubled from 1950 to 1958, fell by almost one-fourth in the next three years.

Mao believed in permanent revolution and continuous class struggle. According to the late eminent China scholar, John K. Fairbank, he took on the self-image of an emperor when he instigated the Cultural Revolution in 1966.[3] It was aimed at intellectuals and 'revisionists' in the Communist Party (CCP) who were accused of taking the 'capitalist road'. Universities and secondary schools were closed and students, carrying little red books containing the 'thoughts' of Chairman Mao, were mobilised as Red Guards, first attacking their university presidents and professors. Then they went on a rampage destroying libraries, recordings of European classical music, works of art and other trappings of 'bourgeois life'. Intellectuals, artists and musicians were humiliated, persecuted, and sometimes killed or led to commit suicide to avoid beatings. Others were sent to rural areas where they were required to do degrading work. Many officials of the CCP were ousted from office. Among the absurdities perpetrated during that period, vehicles in Shanghai were told to advance at red lights and stop at green lights, as the Red Guards reasoned that the revolutionary colour should not be associated with coming to a halt. When the country was close to civil war the Red Guards were disbanded.

It is estimated that a million people were killed during the Cultural Revolution and many times more were victimised. 'Central to it all was the assumption of conspiracy – "hidden enemies and traitors" among the intellectuals within the CCP.'[4]

Despite all the turmoil, China made economic progress under Mao, who died in 1976. The growth rate from 1952 to 1978 was respectable – around 6 per cent per year according to official data and 4.4 per cent according to Maddison. But, as in the Soviet Union, Chinese economic growth in the 1960s and 1970s was the result almost entirely of increased investment and employment. Productivity advanced very little as the Great Leap Forward and Cultural Revolution created economic chaos. But more than that was involved. According to Fairbank, the 'dead end of involution – growth of product without development of greater productivity per person – that had held the Chinese farmer back for centuries still held him back in 1950–1978'.[5]

Nevertheless, as China expert Harry Harding has noted, China created an industrial base, 'exploded its own nuclear bomb, launched earth satellites, built primitive computers, and synthesised insulin'.[6]

9.2 THE REFORMERS

The foregoing events provided fertile ground for Deng Xiaoping's initiation of economic reform. The people were ready for a change, both in the countryside and in the cities. Moreover, although China's economic performance had been favourable as compared with other centrally-planned economies, it lagged far behind its East Asian neighbours, the 'four little dragons': Hong Kong, South Korea, Singapore and Taiwan. This widening gap also motivated China's reformers.

Not long after Mao's death, Deng Xiaoping was restored to his position as vice-chairman of the CCP and vice-premier. He became the leader of a group in China's power structure that was critical of the Cultural Revolution and favoured a more pragmatic approach to policymaking, particularly economic reform. Under Deng, China also turned outward in foreign policy, normalising relations with the United States and sending 10 000 academics and technicians to study there.

Deng Xiaoping was born in 1904 in Sichuan province in central China. Like Mao, he grew up in rural China in a well-to-do family and received a better education than the average farm boy. In 1920 Deng sailed for France with an uncle, where he worked in factories and became a communist. In 1926 he studied for several months in Moscow on his way back to China. After working in the Shanghai Communist underground for a few years, he was sent to Guangxi province to organise the peasants into a military force in order to try to capture Canton and other large cities from Chiang Kai-shek's Kuomintang. Thus his military career began. He later became a military commander, organising his troops from scratch and learning tactics and strategy along the way. Eventually he came to direct field armies of hundreds of thousands of soldiers.

After the revolution, Mao made Deng the proconsul, in effect, of southwestern China. His task was to build the area into an independent economic entity as a defence against the possibility of an American nuclear attack on eastern and northern China. By 1954 he was a member of the Politburo and number four in the party.

In 1967, during the Cultural Revolution, he was condemned for, among other infractions, being too pragmatic and insufficiently ideological: he used the slogan 'What matter black cat, white cat? So long as it catches mice it's a good cat' in relation to agricultural policy. He was banished to Jiangxi province where he did manual work. In 1973 he returned to Beijing to his earlier position as vice-premier. But in 1976 he was dismissed again, when Mao said that Deng 'knows nothing of Marxism–Leninism'. Finally in July 1977 he was reappointed and eventually took over Mao's reins.

Under Deng's leadership, economic reform proceeded in spurts and its pace varied from region to region. One reason for this was that differences of view existed between moderate and radical reformers. (In China those more in favour of reform are said to be on the right side of the political spectrum in contrast to ideological Marxists on the left; in the former Soviet Union these designations were reversed.) Another reason for the uneven pace of reform was that the economy experienced occasional bursts of inflation as central planning was relaxed.

Deng died in February 1997 and was succeeded by Jiang Zemin. Born in 1926, Jiang attended an American missionary school and likes to recite the beginning of Lincoln's Gettysburg Address. He joined the Communist Party as a student, spent a year in an automobile factory in Moscow and two years in Romania. He was mayor of Shanghai in the 1980s and after 1989 Deng selected him as general secretary of the Party. Following the Party Congress in September 1997, he made a successful visit to the United States. His selection of Zhu Rongji as prime minister in March 1998 testifies to his willingness to pursue economic reform.

Zhu was born into a poor family in 1928 in Mao's home town. He acquired a degree in engineering. Intellectully impressive from an early age, he was condemned as a rightist and purged in 1957 and again in 1965 during the Cultural Revolution. After Deng assumed power Zhu advanced rapidly. He too became mayor of Shanghai, in 1988, and encouraged foreign investors as one way of improving the economy of the city. Deng promoted him to deputy prime minister in 1991, stating that 'he understands economics'. As noted below, he took over the governorship of the central bank (the People's Bank of China) in 1993 in order to deal with inflation. In March 1998 he was elected premier, succeeding Li Peng, and became the third highest-ranking official in the country. He faced formidable problems: dealing with unprofitable state-owned enterprises and a banking system with a large volume of non-performing loans, while avoiding unemployment high enough to cause social unrest.

Zhu's efforts to reduce the size of government – reportedly cutting the number of civil servants in half – suggests a basic ideology in harmony with that of Tony Blair and Bill Clinton.

9.3   REFORM IN THE COUNTRYSIDE

The first spurt of reform under Deng focused on rural China. The communes were abolished and under the 'household responsibility system' farmers took over the management, though not the ownership, of land. Prices paid for agricultural products were raised and peasants were permitted to sell above-quota output at still higher prices and to retain the extra earnings. In 1985 the state's mandatory procurement quotas were replaced by a system of contracts with farm households for a limited number of products, giving even more freedom to farmers. Later, as output increased, the state introduced a system of support prices.

Under these improved incentives, agricultural productivity accelerated. Farm output, which had grown only 1.6 per cent per year in 1971–7, increased by 6.7 per cent per year in 1978–83.[7] This was, in Fairbank's words, 'a triumph for Deng's reforms'. But he goes on to write:

> Anyone who concludes that Chinese agriculture, having seen the light and wanting to be more like us, has gone 'capitalist' is making a grievous error. The contract system must be seen as the latest phase of statecraft in how to organize farmers in order to improve their welfare and also strengthen the state.[8]

Fairbank's observation is supported by the fact that local governments have often blockaded the grain market, prohibiting sales to traders, until the compulsory procurement quota is filled at the contract price, which is below the market price.

Rising income in the countryside created the savings that financed increased investment in the economy as a whole. The productivity increase also provided the basis, in terms of available labour, for towns and villages, and to a lesser extent private parties, to establish non-agricultural enterprises that operated outside the central plan, selling their products at market prices and reinvesting profits. Their output increased on average by 29 per cent per year in 1979–86. By 1994 TVEs numbered about 24 million, employing more than 150 million people and were responsible for about 40 per cent China's total output. The effect on living standards is striking. From the early 1980s to the early 1990s, average living space per person doubled in rural China and luxuries like refrigerators, washing machines and colour television sets became available. 'China has turned its back on Stalinist collectivism of agriculture, although it may be some time before it completely repudiates it.'[9]

Nevertheless one should not exaggerate the degree of prosperity in rural China. The benefits from the faster growth of productivity in agriculture are rather unequally distributed. In a number of provinces rural poverty is still acute. And peasants have demonstrated against higher taxes in some regions as they became aware that their incomes lag far behind those in urban areas. This led in June 1993 to cuts in a number of taxes and fees imposed on farmers.

The piecemeal raising of prices paid to farmers over the years was not passed on to consumers of rationed agricultural products such as grain and edible oils. As a result, subsidies grew large. In 1991 and 1992 the prices of these rationed products were raised sharply, contributing to the inflation that took hold, as discussed below.

In any event, the TVEs lost steam in the 1990s, as predicted by a number of authors. Given 'the tendency of these firms to bunch at the low end of the technology spectrum', it was argued that 'as underlying economic conditions change, rural industry will lose ground to large domestic firms, enterprise groups, and joint-venture companies during the course of the 1990s'.[10] By 1997, many TVEs suffered from 'crushing debt, narrow product lines, shallow management and, most troubling, questions about who owns them'. And many towns 'treat their enterprises as cash cows, skimming off money to finance municipal budgets instead of reinvesting in the company or reducing debt'.[11] In January 1997, a law went into effect providing that the 'property rights of township enterprises set up by groups of farmers or individual farmers are owned by the investors'.[12]

9.4   INDUSTRIAL REFORM

Reform came later and less comprehensively in industry (apart from TVEs). In 1978 state-owned enterprises accounted for more than 80 per cent of industrial output. As in other centrally-planned

economies, these enterprises were not subject to a hard budget constraint. Despite some reforms, a large proportion of them have operated at a loss and are kept going by subsidies and bank loans at low
interest rates.

Initially, after 1978, state-owned enterprises were permitted to
undertake some production outside the plan but state control
remained pervasive. One reason is the so-called 'iron rice bowl': the
enterprises provide housing, medical care and education to workers
and their families along with lifetime employment. Social peace
depends on the continuation of these arrangements.

Other reforms followed. In the mid-1980s the 'contract responsibility
system' – similar to the household system applied successfully in rural
areas – was introduced for state enterprises. It sought to separate management from ownership and appeared to shift authority from state
planners to plant managers. The latter were permitted to sell above-
plan output at negotiated, rather than at governmentally fixed, prices
and to reinvest the profits where they exist. And some prices were liberalised. Later, wholesale markets developed for the sale of output not
subject to the central plan and for the purchase of inputs. Nevertheless
the lack of incentives in centrally-planned systems that we have
observed in Eastern Europe and Russia is also evident in China's state-
owned enterprises. While the proportion of inputs and outputs of state
enterprises that is subject to central planning is shrinking, these enterprises are not the dynamic factor in China's economy. The share of
state enterprises in total output decreased from 76 per cent in 1980 to
41 per cent in 1996. The private sector share was 24 per cent.[13]

Deng Xiaoping gave a boost to the non-state sector in early 1992 by
visiting southern China, where such activity flourishes, and simply
saying 'Do it faster'. In March of that year references to a planned
economy were deleted from the country's constitution. And in
October 1992, the CCP 'formally embraced paramount leader Deng
Xiaoping's view that the market system was not incompatible with the
ideas of socialism and called for the establishment of a socialist
market economy'.[14] According to Sheryl Wudunn, after Deng's trip,
'the entire country seemed to change its personality. As if he had
flicked a switch, politics was out, business was in.'[15]

In the summer of 1993 the government 'announced plans to transform one-third of state-owned companies into limited-liability corporations responsible for their own profits and losses. That would mean
that if the companies suffered persistent losses, the Government
would not bail them out and they could go bankrupt.'[16]

In November 1993, the Party embraced the goal of establishing a 'socialist market economy' by the end of the century. At a Communist Party Congress in September 1997, there was agreement on selling shares of state-owned enterprises. The word 'privatisation' was not used; the euphemisms are 'public ownership' and 'corporatisation'.

In the mid-1980s concern over the fiscal deficit led to the decision to reduce state subsidies to state-owned enterprises and to replace them with loans from banks. As a result, by 1997 the enterprises were heavily indebted and the banks were loaded with a large volume of non-performing loans – estimated at $200 billion. This became an acute issue for the government and for Prime Minister Zhu in particular. In March 1998, the government announced its intention to issue bonds in the amount of Yuan 264 billion (equivalent to $32.5 billion) and to use the proceeds to recapitalise the four large state banks that handle 80 per cent of the country's banking.[17] That action was probably aimed at warding off a banking crisis and a 'run' on the banks based on withdrawals by depositors. Such a crisis was not at all unlikely before the announced bond issue.[18] In April 1998, the governor of the central bank announced that a decision had been taken to set up a deposit guarantee system. though he gave no details. It seems clear that the authorities are worried about the stability of the banking system.

While 'corporatisation' is planned, the problem is to restructure or close down loss-making firms without causing serious social unrest as the 'iron rice bowl' is diminished and unemployment increases. Zhu's intention is to replace the 'iron rice bowl' with social insurance and welfare programmes. Those reforms had started in a small way but they had not, as of 1997, affected most enterprises.[19]

In a speech in London in early April 1998, Zhu said that reform of state enterprises could not be a classic privatisation because of the problem of dealing with surplus workers. He invited the city of London to list Chinese enterprises on its stock exchanges. 'You're welcome to acquire state enterprises,' he said, 'but with one condition – that you don't lay off a single worker.'[20]

Thus China faces serious structural problems in the industrial sector. Related to the effort to deal with those problems was a decision in March 1998 to slim down the central government by reducing the number of ministries and cutting the number of civil servants by 50 per cent. One of the reasons given for that decision was that there was a 'lack of separation between government and enterprises'.[21]

Other sectors are also in trouble. In some cities, including Beijing and Shanghai, there has been overbuilding and many structures stand empty while banks hold non-performing loans based on them. There are even luxury villas that are unsold.

Shanghai, China's largest and most advanced city, has been building a financial and manufacturing centre – Pudong – in the 1990s. It is said to be creating more office space in one decade than Hong Kong built in four. Its mayor has boasted that one-fifth of the world's construction cranes were in his city. Unfortunately, 70 per cent of the office space was vacant in early 1998 and property values were falling as rents declined sharply. The completion of the world's tallest skyscraper (10 metres higher than the one in Kuala Lumpur – see Chapter 10) was delayed owing to the property glut.

9.5 MACROECONOMIC DEVELOPMENTS

Neither fiscal nor monetary policy has been especially effective in China, partly because the country is decentralised. The central government budget is burdened with subsidies to loss-making state enterprises, and revenues from profitable enterprises decreased after they were permitted to retain earnings. The People's Bank, which has been converted to a central bank and deprived of its commercial banking functions, appeared, until recent years, to have limited influence on the lending activities of the state-owned commercial banks. And the formulation of monetary policy was complicated by the fact that the agricultural sector was being monetised – that is, the farming community was increasingly using and holding cash and bank deposits.

In early July 1993 the governor of the People's Bank was forced to resign and was replaced temporarily by Vice Premier Zhu Rongji. One reason for concern at the highest level was the unrest – even violence – among peasants suffering from inflation and aware that they were not keeping up in terms of income with their urban countrymen. But the leadership appeared also to be concerned that too stringent a crackdown on credit in order to reduce inflation could lead to higher unemployment and social unrest. In 1998, a similar problem was being faced, involving not inflation but inefficient and loss-making state-owned enterprises.

Consumer prices rose 18 per cent in 1988–9, according to official statistics that are of questionable accuracy, and 24 per cent in 1994 but only 2.8 per cent in 1997. In 1998, consumer prices fell along with the costs of imports.

The official statistics apparently exaggerate China's growth rate. Angus Maddison has made a number of technical adjustments to the official data and finds that real GDP grew 7.5 per cent per year from 1978 to 1995 compared with the official data that show a growth rate of 10.5 per cent per year. Even if the data displayed in Figure 9.1 are reduced by 30 per cent, they represent an impressive performance – 3 times the growth of the United States, and $2\frac{1}{3}$ times that of China. It resulted from a high rate of gross investment – so high that capital productivity declined by 1.25 per cent per year from 1978 to 1995. But labour productivity rose at an average annual rate of 4.75 per cent. As a result, the increase in total factor productivity – at 2.23 per cent per year – was a large multiple of that in the United States and Japan. Much of the explanation lies in a massive shift out of agriculture to industry, where the level and growth rate of productivity was much higher. The share of industry in GDP rose from less than 12 per cent in 1952 to 47 per cent in 1995.[22]

9.6   INTERNATIONAL TRADE AND INVESTMENT

Since 1980 China's exports have grown about twice as fast as world trade. Shoppers in many countries are well aware of the great variety of Chinese goods available, particularly labour-intensive manufactured consumer goods. To a large extent, this increase in China's exports displaced exports of similar products from Hong Kong, South Korea and Taiwan.

The process started with the establishment of four 'special economic zones' (SEZs) in two coastal provinces in 1979–80. Firms in these zones, both state-owned and others, were permitted to operate outside the central plan and to attract foreign investment. In 1984 14 coastal cities were allowed to operate in a similar manner. Later, still other areas were declared to be 'open economic zones'.

Economic reform of the trade regime has made it possible for 'thousands of individual manufacturing firms and local foreign trade companies ... to conduct international trade transactions'.[23]

The striking export performance is related, in part, to foreign direct investment in China, which rose from less than $400 million in 1982 to $44 billion in 1997. At first much of this investment took the form of joint ventures. In 1997 the number of new wholly-owned

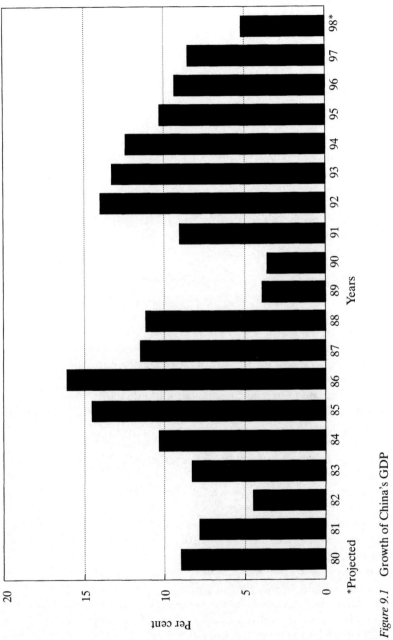

Figure 9.1 Growth of China's GDP

foreign enterprises was greater than the number of new joint ventures.[24] Much of this investment came from (or possibly through) Hong Kong as well as Taiwan and Macao and is located mainly in the coastal provinces. Hong Kong entrepreneurs began shifting manufacturing facilities to China in the mid-1980s, attracted by lower labour costs as wages rose rapidly at home. But some of the investment from Hong Kong has involved the purchase of state-owned firms. Taiwanese businesses followed suit more recently, especially in the case of labour-intensive products. It is likely that the figures on incoming direct investment are overstated since they reflect 'substantial amounts of domestic funds [that] are being recycled through Hong Kong in order to take advantage of the large tax concessions provided to foreign investors'.[25]

In general, China has become much more open to the world economy. From 1980 to 1997 both exports and imports more than tripled as a proportion of GDP.

9.7   POLITICAL AND SOCIAL CONDITIONS

China today is a far different country from what it was under the ideological zealotry of Mao Zedong.

It is true that Deng Xiaoping, while encouraging economic reform, attempted to maintain the Communist Party's political control. In 1979 he enunciated the 'Four Cardinal Principles' that China was expected to abide by: the socialist path, the dictatorship of the proletariat, the leadership of the Party and Marxism–Leninism–Mao Zedong thought.

Much has changed since then. Living standards have soared. Not only are Chinese citizens eating better, they are also enjoying modern conveniences. In 1981 there was one colour television for each 100 urban households; 10 years later there were 70. The number of washing machines per 100 urban households rose from six to 80 and the number of refrigerators from 0.2 to 50.2.[26] In its effort to cool the overheated economy in the early 1990s, the government banned the building of new golf courses!

It has to be stressed that this well-being is not equally distributed. It is most evident in the coastal provinces. In about one-third of the provinces, income per capita has been growing at about 3 per cent annually, compared with 6 per cent or more in Guangdong, Xingjiang, Yunnan and other coastal provinces.

Along with this economic improvement has come the spread of education and greater political freedom. The CCP is still firmly entrenched in power but it no longer attempts to control as much of the details of peoples' private lives as in the past. 'The world should be relieved that, for the Chinese, going into business has replaced joining the Communist Party as the way to success.'[27] The populace has become much more aware of ways of life outside China, thanks to television and a proliferation of satellite dishes. Here again we encounter the political and economic effects of the telecommunications revolution. The CCP no longer has a monopoly on news.

Short-wave radios, direct dial international telephones, fax machines and personal computers have also become available, facilitating international communication. It is questionable, given these facts and the reforms of the economy, whether the CCP can maintain its control. According to Nicolas Kristof, former *New York Times* bureau chief in Beijing:

> the Government sometimes resembles not so much a Communist monolith as a disorganized conglomerate. The Politburo, acting as a fractious board of directors, often ignores tacit disobedience.
>
> Even if the central Government ordered a major crackdown [on TV] it is unclear that it would be enforced outside the capital. Local governments, always lethargic about implementing edicts they dislike, are making money by running cable television systems that depend on satellite television.[28]

It should also be noted that greater economic freedom has brought back corruption, crime, and prostitution.

9.8 THE OUTLOOK

China's economic performance is likely to continue on an impressive scale for some time even if the growth rate slows somewhat. In 1998 the recession in China's Asian neighbours was slowing its exports and raising doubts about whether it could maintain its exchange rate. The state-enterprise sector of the economy will probably continue to shrink. While much economic reform has occurred, China has not become a full-fledged market economy.

Politically, China is nominally a Communist nation but as Kristof writes, 'No Communist country, at least, has ever so fully embraced stock markets, satellite television, private colleges, Avon ladies, music video and radio talk shows.'[29]

Questions remain. What model of politics will succeed communism which is disappearing as an economic ideology? Will new pro-democracy movements arise in a more educated society, as happened before the Tiananmen Square massacre of June 1989? And, given the communications revolution, which made the entire world aware of what happened at Tiananmen Square, would the Communist authorities dare to crack down again?

For the longer run we may hope that economist Lawrence Summers was correct when he wrote in 1992:

It may well be that when the history of the late 20th century is written, in a hundred years, the most significant event will be the revolutionary changes in China, which will soon be communist only in a theoretical sense. The rise of China may well be the transcendent event.[30]

10 Other Asia: Dragons, Tigers and an Elephant

The economic dynamism so evident in China was a feature of Hong Kong, South Korea, Singapore and Taiwan for many years. These four countries have been called 'the four little dragons' in Asia – China being the large dragon – and 'the four tigers' in the west. The dragon is a symbol of serene and prestigious power in Asia. The tiger, while also powerful, is regarded as less majestic and self-confident.

The four countries became industrialised and grew rapidly in the 1960s and 1970s as 'newly-industrialised countries' (NICs) and 'newly-industrialised economies' (NIEs). That process persisted in the 1980s and early 1990s as the composition of their output continued to shift away from labour-intensive products towards those embodying more capital and higher technology. Also in the 1980s Malaysia, Thailand and Indonesia emerged as fast-growing industrial powers. A distinguishing feature of most of these countries is that they combined rapid growth with increasing income equality. The entire area, including China and Japan, became more integrated economically as intra-regional trade and investment flows swelled. More recently India, symbolised by the large but slow-moving elephant, joined the parade by undertaking fundamental structural reforms and beginning to open its economy to the rest of the world.

In 1997 a financial and economic crisis broke out first in Thailand, and then in Malaysia, South Korea and Indonesia. The crisis revealed that serious structural weaknesses, both economic and financial, were present to varying degrees in the fast-growing tigers.

10.1 THE FOUR TIGERS

In the 1970s the economic performance of the four tigers was remarkable. Their growth rates ranged from 8 to 10 per cent per year. While they continued to prosper in the 1980s their manufacturers had to adapt to competition from both labour-intensive goods from lower-wage countries nearby and high-technology products from industrial countries.[1] This pattern of regional development, as comparative advantage shifts from the technological leaders to their neighbours, has often been likened to a formation of flying geese.

In the 1990s these countries were on the receiving end of a large volume of capital from abroad: direct investment, portfolio capital and bank loans. Malaysia and Indonesia were among the top 10 recipients of direct investment among all developing countries.

10.2   THE EAST ASIAN MIRACLE

A study published by the World Bank in 1993 – *The East Asian Miracle* – recounts and analyses the remarkable economic performance of the countries of East Asia. Among the characteristics of that performance are high growth rates based on heavy investment, rather low inflation, 'shared growth' in the sense that income is distributed relatively equally, rapid export expansion and industrialisation towards higher value-added and technologically more advanced products. What are the explanations for this record and what can other developing countries learn from it?

As the study and a number of commentaries on it pointed out,[2] the East Asian nations got the fundamentals right. Their fiscal and monetary policies were effective. Beyond that necessary condition, they invested in education. They orientated their economies towards exports, which promoted competitiveness and efficiency. In addition they were open to investment from abroad.

More controversial is the fact that in various degrees their governments intervened in the economies to promote industrialisation and exports. As the report states:

Policy interventions took many forms: targeting and subsidizing credit to selected industries, keeping deposit rates low and maintaining ceilings on borrowing rates to increase profits and retained earnings, protecting domestic import substitutes, subsidizing declining industries, establishing and financially supporting government banks, making public investments in applied research, establishing firm- and industry-specific export targets, developing export marketing institutions, and sharing information widely between public and private sectors. Some industries were promoted while others were not.[3]

In evaluating these policies and their relevance for other developing countries, the report concludes that promotion of specific industries did not work and therefore holds little promise for other developing economies. Directed credit has worked in certain situations but carries high risk [in a world of very mobile capital where firms not favoured by directed credit can borrow abroad]. The export-push strategy has been by far the most successful of the three sets of policy intervention and holds the most promise for other developing countries.[4]

As we shall see, directed credit and poorly regulated banking systems created serious problems in most of the east Asian countries in 1997–8.

10.3 KOREA

Korea is somewhat typical and it has had a greater demonstration effect on other developing countries than Taiwan or the city states, Hong Kong and Singapore. In the 1950s South Korea was a very poor country, much of its economy having been destroyed in the war with North Korea. In 1961 its exports were mainly raw materials and agricultural products and its annual per capita income was less than $1000. Land reform and government assistance led to rapid advances in agricultural productivity so that in the 1970s Korea had the highest rice yields per acre in the world.[5]

Industrialisation in the 1960s, encouraged by General Park with tax incentives and low-interest loans from the government, involved high rates of investment – 25 per cent of GDP in 1965–70. In the 1970s, emphasis shifted to heavy industry, including chemicals. By 1979 manufacturing in Korea accounted for about one-third of total output compared with 12 per cent in 1967. Concurrently its exports had increased by 28 per cent per year in real terms, more than four times as fast as world trade. Exports were encouraged in a variety of ways: duty-free imports of raw materials for export industries, cheap credit and tax preferences. Korean construction companies took advantage of the economic boom in Middle East oil-exporting countries after 1973; in 1980 more than 130 000 Korean construction workers were in the Middle East, contributing to Korea's earnings of foreign exchange.

The entrepreneurial system was organised and industrialisation was encouraged on the basis of groupings somewhat similar to the *zaibatsu* in Japan. Governmental incentives were provided to successful firms that were permitted to diversify to become holding companies or conglomerates, known in Korea as *chaebols*. The larger of these conglomerates have names that are now familiar worldwide as producers of automobiles, semiconductors and personal computers: Hyundai, Samsung, Daewoo and Lucky-Goldstar. But beginning in the 1980s, small and medium enterprises also grew rapidly, favoured by export financing and credit guarantees.[6]

The banks were used by the government to implement its industrialisation policy – encouraging heavy industry such as machinery, construction equipment and petrochemicals – by making 'policy loans' to favoured sectors at negative real interest rates and depriving other sectors of credit (a condition known as financial repression). According to Cho Soon, former governor of Korea's central bank:

> Bank managers were deprived of autonomy in decision making on bank operations as well as on determination of interest rates. From the bankers' point of view, there was little incentive to review the economic rationality of proposed investment projects or to provide advice and other assistance to loan recipients. Banks had only to follow government direction in making loans, and thus they initiated little project screening, resulting in the loss of a powerful bulwark against unworthy investment.[7]

This helps to explain Korea's vulnerability when the crisis struck in 1997, as is discussed below.

Korea's heavy investment in the 1970s was based in part on external borrowing. Its current-account deficit averaged $1.2 billion per year and then increased sharply with the second oil shock. But rapid export growth held down the relative burden of debt service payments. In 1982 the IMF listed Korea among the 20 most heavily-indebted countries but by 1985 it was not among the 15 debtor nations singled out for the Baker plan.

In the years from 1981 through 1996, GDP grew on average by 8.6 per cent per year, among the highest in the world. Annual inflation averaged 5.6 per cent from 1982 through 1996, whereas it had been well above 10 per cent in the previous two decades.

Structural reforms included a move away from the policy of import substitution, at least for non-agricultural goods. Import quotas were liberalised and tariffs were lowered. The freeing of imports still left a ban on a list of some 30 products from Japan – a result of Korea's 35 years as a Japanese colony and its desire to avoid undue reliance on Japan. A start was also made on removing government controls over the financial system, especially regulation of interest rates on bank loans. More generally, the government tried to shift away from picking 'winners and losers' in its industrial policy towards a more 'generic' approach. According to the World Bank, government intervention 'since 1979 has focused on the restructuring of distressed industries, support for the development of technology, and the promotion of competition'.[8]

Still, as became evident in 1997–8, industrial policy left something to be desired. Korea's economy remains subject to a considerable amount of government intervention. Its philosophy of the relationship of government to industry is more like that of Japan than in the Anglo-Saxon tradition. As Cho Soon wrote:

> What the Korean economy most badly needs is reassessment of government's role. The structure of the government today, formed during the early days of economic planning, was suitable for achieving selected targets ... These are all out of date.[9]

In 1987 Korea's first democratic election in many years put a former general in the presidency. In 1992 a civilian, Kim Young Sam, was elected president on a platform that promised gradual withdrawal of the government's controls over the economy as well as a drive against corruption. In 1998 Kim Dae-jung – who had been jailed, survived five attempts on his life, tortured and exiled by military governments for his advocacy of democracy – was elected president at the age of 74 in the midst of the crisis. He has been critical of 'Asian values', including 'crony capitalism'.

When Thailand devalued in July 1997, some of the *chaebols* were already in financial difficulty and a number of smaller enterprises were bankrupt. Part of the explanation was the collapse of the prices of semiconductors – by more than 80 per cent from January 1996 to June 1997. The Bank of Korea loaned some of its reserves to banks that had to repay foreign currency debts and that limited its ability to support the exchange rate, which depreciated steeply in late 1997 and early 1998. Interest rates soared and economic activity declined. Korea applied to the IMF for a support programme which was arranged in December 1997.

In August 1998, industrial production was almost 12 per cent below the level of a year earlier but interest rates had come down from their peaks and foreign exchange reserves were above pre-crisis levels.

10.4   MALAYSIA

Malaysia, with a population of about 18 million, is rich in natural resources, including tin, rubber and petroleum. In the 1970s it developed exports of light manufactured products – textiles, shoes, and apparel – in free-trade and export-processing zones on the basis of direct investment from abroad. The stock of direct investment in 1980 was six times as large as that in Korea.

Malaysia industrialised rapidly in the 1980s. Manufactured goods as a share of total exports increased from 18.8 per cent in 1980 to 70 per cent in the 1990s. Among its manufactures are semiconductors, disk drives, other electronic products and automobiles. A domestically-produced car – the Proton – supplied two-thirds of the home market and was exported to 17 countries in the early 1990s.[10]

The economy grew by 8.5 per cent per year in 1987–96 and the inflation rate, though it moved up in the booming economy, was 3.4 per cent on average. Malaysia's prosperity led its government to undertake the construction of what was then the world's tallest structure, an office building in the capital city, Kuala Lumpur.

In 1997 Malaysia was also in financial crisis. The exchange rate depreciated by more than 40 per cent and stock prices fell more than 50 per cent from mid-1997 to mid-1998. The prime minister, Mahathir Mohamad, was particularly vocal in blaming 'westerners' among others for what he termed speculation against the Malaysian currency.

As was true elsewhere in Asia, the financial system had its weaknesses. Banks' lending standards were lax, their capital was inadequate and their supervision was weak. As a result, the banks found themselves with a large volume of non-performing loans when the crisis broke out in 1997.

In early September 1998, Prime Minister Mahathir fired his deputy and imposed exchange and capital controls.

10.5   INDONESIA

Much larger in area and population than the other countries covered above, Indonesia consists of more than 10 000 islands, many of which are uninhabited, stretching over about 3000 miles. With about 210 million people, Indonesia is the fourth most populous country on the planet – after China, India and the United States. The densely populated island of Java accounts for two-thirds of Indonesia's industrial output. Although large in area and population, Indonesia has not been a weighty country in international trade. Its exports have been smaller those of most of its neighbours, including Malaysia, whose population is less than 10 per cent of Indonesia's.

President Suharto, a former general, was in his sixth five-year term until his resignation in May 1998. He ran a strong, if not authoritarian, central government. Its economic policy was earlier dominated by so-called 'technocrats' or the 'Berkeley mafia', many of whom earned economics degrees in the United States. They imposed budgetary discipline and monetary stability.

As an oil and gas producer (and a member of OPEC) Indonesia enjoyed windfalls in the two oil shocks. Its export earnings rose from about $1 billion in 1970 to more than $22 billion in 1981, when oil and gas accounted for four-fifths of exports. The increased foreign exchange earnings were used to improve health services, public infrastructure and especially education. Primary school education is nearly universal. But the government also invested in state-owned enterprises in heavy industry that required tariff protection.

In recent years, with oil revenues lower, Indonesia was the recipient of foreign direct investment which has financed the creation of labour-intensive industries producing shoes, apparel and electronics no longer made in Korea and other higher-wage countries in Asia.

From 1986 to 1997 annual economic growth was 6.8 per cent and consumer prices rose 8.2 per cent per year on average. The crisis that began in mid-1997 revealed some of the weaknesses in Indonesia's economic as well as social arrangements. The term 'crony capitalism', which has been applied generally in the region, was especially evident in Indonesia, where members of President Suharto's family were accorded special privileges in their business dealings. As prices rose steeply – more than in other Asian countries in crisis – with the large depreciation of the rupiah, Chinese storekeepers were brutally attacked.

The combination of a political and an economic crisis had a large impact on Indonesia. Its output in 1998 was falling by much more than in other Asian countries and its outlook was uncertain.

10.6 THAILAND

Thailand, with a population of 58 million, saw its economy grow at about the same rate as Malaysia's and its inflation was a little higher. It too experienced a shift in output and exports from rice and other commodities to manufactures. An explicit export promotion policy was adopted in 1981 and import barriers began to be lowered. In other respects the Thai government has intervened less actively in the economy than Malaysia and Korea. In the latter part of the 1980s incoming direct investment increased sharply, to more than $2 billion per year, much of it from Japan. By 1990 more than three-fifths of Thailand's exports were manufactured products compared with one-fourth in 1980. Although Thailand too was beginning to feel the competition of lower-wage firms in China and Vietnam, its export volume quadrupled from 1987 to 1995.

Despite this impressive performance, some serious policy mistakes were made. The Thai *baht* was pegged to a dollar-denominated basket of currencies but inflation caused the real exchange rate to appreciate by about 5 per cent per year. To maintain the exchange rate, the central bank kept interest rates high. That in turn led Thai enterprises and banks to borrow abroad at lower interest rates. The budget was in surplus until 1997 but gross investment exceeded one-third of GDP. As a result, Thailand had a current-account deficit equal to 8 per cent of GDP in 1996. The IMF urged Thai officials on numerous occasions, beginning in 1993, to adopt measures to deal with its problems but it was rebuffed.[11]

The proximate cause of the crisis in east Asia in 1997–8 may be found in the previous paragraph. Speculation against the Thai *baht* arose in 1997 and Thailand's foreign exchange reserves began to decline. In July, the exchange rate was unpegged and it floated down sharply.

10.7   THE EAST ASIAN CRISIS

The depreciation of the Thai *baht* led to contagion, as speculation against other currencies in the region was touched off, and to the resulting crisis, which was dubbed the 'Asian flu' in the press and 'bahtulism' by Paul Krugman. In addition to the competitive effects of the Thai devaluation and the depressive effects of Japan's recession, on neighbouring countries, there occurred what Morris Goldstein has dubbed a 'wake-up call'. International investors reassessed the creditworthiness of Asian borrowers and found, in a number of them, 'weak financial sectors, with poor prudential supervision, large external deficits, appreciating real exchange rates, declining quality of investment, export slowdowns (in 1996), and overexpansion in certain key industries'.[12]

As a result, exchange rates and stock prices fell sharply as it was revealed that banks in the east Asian countries had heavy foreign debts and that foreign exchange reserves were smaller than published figures indicated; in Thailand, the central bank had sold dollars against *baht* in the forward market; in Korea, half of the published reserves had been loaned to domestic banks. Moreover, banks in a number of the countries were saddled with non-performing loans as the result of an earlier property boom or of losses by borrowing enterprises. In Indonesia, as noted, another factor driving down the exchange rate and stock prices was the political crisis.

It is noteworthy that China and Hong Kong managed to keep their exchange rates from depreciating (at least through September 1998) even though their trade was bound to be affected by what was happening elsewhere in the region. Both have large foreign exchange reserves and both presumably wished to avoid exacerbating the crisis.

While the crisis that overtook the east Asian countries in 1997 was mainly financial in origin, it was aggravated by the structural weaknesses that resulted from the relations between governments and enterprises. What is not clear is whether Korea, Malaysia and Indonesia would have fallen into crisis if Thailand had not been forced by its economic circumstances to let its exchange rate depreciate. All of the countries had performed successfully for a number of years despite the structural weaknesses.

In any event, output fell in some and slowed in other East Asian countries into mid-1998. The IMF estimated that GDP in 1998 would decline by 7 per cent in Korea, 8 per cent in Thailand, 15 per cent in Indonesia, and 6.4 per cent in Malaysia. At the same time, these countries were moving into current account surplus as imports decreased with economic activity and their exchange rates depreciated.

Financial markets in many other countries – including Russia, as we observed in Chapter 8 – were affected. Beyond that, the decline in imports in east Asia was bound to have an impact on economic activity in many other countries. The IMF lowered its projection of world output in 1998 from 4.4 per cent in May 1997 to 2 per cent in October 1998.[13]

10.8 INDIA

From the time of its independence in 1947 India has been one of the most democratic countries in the third world. It has, however, been subject to social unrest based on religious friction between Hindus and Muslims. The economy was, until recently, highly regulated and its performance was disappointing. Poverty and illiteracy are still widespread.

Jawarharlal Nehru, prime minister from 1947 to 1964, was influenced by Fabian socialist thinking in Britain and impressed by the Soviet Union's economic performance under central planning. Moreover the colonial heritage created a fear of foreign domination and hence a desire for self-sufficiency. A planning commission, presaged by a planning committee under Nehru in the 1930s, was established after independence, chaired by the prime minister. It prepared a series of five-year plans, beginning in 1951, that set out production goals and investment guidelines. An overriding purpose was to reduce poverty. Among the other objectives were the prevention of monopoly power, protection of small producers and the maintenance of a balance in economic development among India's diverse regions. These objectives were implemented by a system of licences regulating the activity of firms including the types of products they turned out and their ability to expand or contract their scale of production. It has been reported that, before recent reforms, 'a single application to set up an industrial plant had to satisfy as many as eighty-six different enactments and control agencies before receiving approval'.[14] In addition, many industries were nationalised. Of the 25 largest businesses in terms of sales in 1992, fourteen were owned by the government.

Imports were limited by both quantitative controls and very high tariffs (averaging over 100 per cent). Imports increased only 1.2 per cent per year in 1965–80. Direct investment from abroad was discouraged. As former finance minister Manmohan Singh wryly observed, India's experience of having one foreign trading company arrive (the East India Company in 1609) and end up ruling the country until 1947 had an influence on India's attitude towards direct investment from abroad.[15]

India's system of controls over industry has been characterised as follows by Columbia University Professor Jagdish Bhagwati:

> The Indian planners and bureaucrats sought to regulate both domestic entry and import competition, to eliminate product diversification beyond what was licensed, to penalize unauthorized expansion of capacity, to allocate and prevent the reallocation of imported inputs, and indeed to define and delineate virtually all aspects of investment and production through a maze of Kafkaesque controls. This all-encompassing bureaucratic intrusive-

ness and omnipotence has no rationale in economic or social logic; it is therefore hard for anyone who is not a victim of it even to begin to understand what it means.[16]

This set of policies did not yield impressive results in terms of economic growth, successful industrialisation or the alleviation of poverty. From 1950 to 1980 real GDP increased by 3.7 per cent annually and per capita GDP went up by 1.7 per cent per year. Manufacturing output as a share of GDP was 19 per cent in 1995, having risen from 16 per cent in 1965. In comparison manufacturing comprised 32 per cent of GDP in east Asia in 1995. Yet investment in India was not low. In the 1960s it averaged 16.5 per cent of GDP and in 1995 25 per cent. The problem was that resources were not being used efficiently and productivity rose only slowly.

The most positive development was not in industry but in agriculture. In the mid-1960s higher-yielding types of wheat and rice along with fertiliser, pesticides and improved irrigation were introduced. The result – the 'green revolution' – was a significant increase in the output of grains and the elimination of famines and the need to import grains. Nevertheless farm output increased only 2.6 per cent per year from 1965 to 1995. Almost two-thirds of the Indian workforce is in agriculture, but this sector produced only 29 per cent of the nation's total output in 1995.

India's experience of sluggish growth appears to be similar to what was observed in the Soviet Union: although saving and investment increased as a percentage of GDP, productivity growth was very slow. In the case of India, Bhagwati placed the blame for this poor record on (1) extensive bureaucratic controls over production, investment, and trade; (2) inward-looking trade and foreign investment policies; (3) a substantial public sector, going well beyond the conventional confines of public utilities and infrastructure. He adds another factor: 'India's failure to spread primary education and to raise literacy to anywhere near the levels that other countries have managed.'[17] In 1995 35 per cent of adult men and 62 per cent of adult women were estimated to be illiterate.

One result of the policies outlined above was a shortage of electric power, rail transportation and communications facilities. Under Rajiv Gandhi, who succeeded his mother, Indira Gandhi, as prime minister after her assassination in October 1984, expenditures aimed at enlarging the capacity of and modernising such infrastructure were increased. Given the magnitude of the needs for investment, efforts were made to attract private capital into these areas of economic activity.

More important, Rajiv Gandhi began a process of structural economic reforms. Bhagwati suggests that Gandhi, a former pilot with Indian Airlines (the domestic carrier) and therefore the first prime minister who had worked outside politics, understood the disadvantages of the comprehensive system of controls on industry.[18] Gandhi proceeded to dismantle licensing in 25 industries. This included, for some industries, what in India is called 'broad-banding' – that is, permitting a variety of products in the general field in which the firm was licensed.

These and other reforms put through by the Gandhi government were, according to Bhagwati, 'a small step in the right direction; they generated enthusiasm simply because India seemed finally to be going down the right road'.[19] The reforms encouraged a speed-up of economic activity. Industrial production rose 125 per cent from 1985 to 1997 compared with 87 per cent in the previous twelve years.

Rajiv Gandhi had to leave office in 1989 in a corruption scandal and was assassinated during an election campaign in 1991. That brought P. V. Narasimha Rao to the prime minister's office and Manmohan Singh to the ministry of finance. Their first task was to deal with a macroeconomic crisis. The budget deficit had increased markedly in the 1980s and the inflation rate rose to almost 14 per cent in 1991. The current-account deficit and the foreign debt also increased. Foreign exchange reserves fell from $5.4 billion at the end of 1986 to $1.2 billion at the end of 1990 and even less during 1991. Questions were beginning to arise about India's ability to service its foreign debt.

The crisis forced the new government to act on these macroeconomic problems but also led it to reconsider the structural policies that had been pursued for many years. The successful performance of Korea and other East Asian countries probably had an influence in this respect.

An agreement with the IMF, under which India borrowed about $2.5 billion in 1991–2, involved policy conditions calling for reforms that a number of Indian economists had been advocating, especially after Rajiv Gandhi started the process. Thus in 1991 the question became not whether to reform but 'in what sequence, with what speed, with what chance of success?'[20] It began in July 1991.

Economic growth accelerated from less than one-half per cent in 1991 to $7\frac{1}{2}$ per cent in 1996 and then slowed to about 5.2 per cent in

1998. Thus the average growth of real GDP in the 1990s was not very different from what it had been in the 1980s.

Among the structural reforms, the extent of industrial licensing was severely curtailed: licensing, which had been in effect for decades, was abolished for all but 18 industries. But the 'no exit' policy remained in effect: firms with more than 100 employees were not permitted to discharge workers or to close down. Also eliminated were barriers to entry of new firms in areas previously reserved for public enterprises. At the same time an anti-trust system was set up.

While privatisation has not occurred, shares in profitable public enterprises have been sold – first to financial institutions and later to private individuals as well. But, as Jagdish Bhagwati and Yale Professor T. N. Srinivasan have observed, 'the programme offered only a marginal stake in public sector enterprises to the private sector without any efficiency implications'.[21] Another reform measure reduced the potential size of the public sector by lowering the number of industries reserved to it from eighteen to eight. But the state enterprises are still not fully exposed to market competition or to a hard budget constraint. Those making losses are subsidised through the budget.

With regard to foreign trade, export subsidies were abolished when the rupee was devalued and exporters were permitted to retain 30 per cent of their foreign exchange earnings. In March 1992 fairly complete convertibility on current account was introduced, though with a dual exchange rate – one of which was more favourable to essential imports. A year later the exchange-rate system was unified. Tariffs were lowered in both 1992 and 1993 but they still supplied a substantial portion of government revenue. In 1994 India accepted the IMF's Article VIII on current-account convertibility. Approval of foreign investment in India was made much more automatic in a wide range of industries. Such investment rose from less than $100 million in 1991 to an annual rate of $3.5 billion in January–September 1997 – still a small amount for a country of India's economic size. In the financial system a number of liberalising and deregulating measures were taken.

The Congress Party, which had been in power almost continuously since independence in 1947, was defeated in 1996. Following two years of political uncertainty, elections in March 1998 led to a coalition government in which the main party was the Hindu nationalist Bharatiya Janata Party (BJP) and the prime minister was its leader, Atal Bihari Vajpayee. A favourable omen was the appointment of

Yashwant Sinha as finance minister, known as a believer in market-orientated reforms.

Although less exposed than countries to its east, India was somewhat affected by the Asian crisis, but it is difficult to disentangle that effect from the prospective election in early 1998. The rupee depreciated in the second half of 1997 and early 1998 and stock prices fell as foreign capital moved out.

In the second week of May 1998, India conducted several nuclear bomb tests, which Pakistan soon emulated. Despite disapproval abroad, many Indians reacted with pride. The United States, but not other countries, imposed economic sanctions and cut off aid while the World Bank put loans to the two countries on hold. The immediate impact was a sharp depreciation of the rupee and a decline of stock prices. Whether there would be longer-term effects was not clear.

In general India has clearly started down the road to a significantly less state-controlled economy but much remains to be done. Many restrictions on economic activity still exist. Public enterprises, even when they are not loss-makers, are inefficient and a drain on the budget. A good case can be made for major privatisation, even of loss-making enterprises.[22] Foreign trade needs much more liberalisation especially in the case of consumer goods, which are subject to both quantitative restrictions and high tariffs. Finally, the financial system needs to be freed up so that it can perform its function of allocating credit where it does the most good in promoting efficiency and growth.

India managed, on the whole, to avoid contagion from the 'Asian flu' in 1997–8. It remains to be seen whether the elephant can be induced to move more rapidly.

11 Middle East and Africa: Oil, Wealth and Poverty

This chapter is concerned with a vast area running from the oil-rich Arabian peninsula with its sparse population through Egypt and its North African neighbours and on to the diverse but relatively under-developed countries of Sub-Saharan Africa. The term 'Middle East' does not denote a clearly defined geographical area. It sometimes refers to the entire region from Afghanistan to Mauritania, including Turkey. Other designations separate the so-called Maghreb countries: Algeria, Morocco, Tunisia and Libya; with Mauritania, they are also referred to as North Africa as distinct from the Middle East. Whatever the grouping, these countries are mostly Islamic and, except for Iran and Turkey, make up a large part of the Arab world.

A precise designation is not necessary for our purposes. As in the case of other parts of the globe, we shall examine a few countries in which significant transformation has occurred. First it is necessary to take account of the impact of OPEC.

11.1 THE RISE AND FALL OF OPEC

The Organisation of Petroleum Exporting Countries (OPEC) was founded in 1960 at a meeting in Baghdad among four Middle East oil-exporting countries – Iran, Iraq, Kuwait and Saudi Arabia – and Venezuela, the largest oil exporter in the Western Hemisphere. Although its membership grew to 13 nations – including, among larger ones, Algeria, Indonesia, Libya and Nigeria – OPEC attracted little attention until 1973 when it became a household word by inflicting the severest shock to the world economy since the Second World War. After a partial oil embargo was declared by its Arab members during the Arab–Israeli War in October 1973, OPEC announced two price increases. The oil price tripled from 1974 to 1975 (and crept up an additional 25 per cent by 1978). OPEC had become, at least for the time being, an effective cartel. Since in the short run the demand for oil is inelastic – that is, a change in price induces a relatively small change in the amount demanded – the cartel can increase its revenue by restricting the amount supplied as it raises the price. But, as became clear later, the OPEC members were not able to apply this simple principle. They could not agree on the division of the cartel's total output and it tended to exceed desired levels. Later, as the share of non-OPEC countries in world oil output increased, the cartel weakened further.

The sharply higher oil price in 1974–5, on top of already fast-rising commodity prices, aggravated inflation in oil-importing countries. The average price of all imports of industrial countries and non-oil developing countries rose about 75 per cent between 1972 and 1974. The oil-price increase also depressed the economies of the importing countries. As was noted in Chapter 2, the effect was similar to that of a large new sales tax.

The current-account surplus of the OPEC nations as a group rose spectacularly in one year, 1974, from $9 billion to $65 billion and, as noted in Chapter 2, they acquired large amounts of assets abroad. As a result of the newly-found power of the oil cartel, a number of fears arose among people in oil-importing countries: would OPEC raise the price again? Would it withhold oil, causing hardships of many kinds in importing countries? Would OPEC nations disrupt financial markets by withdrawing their substantial holdings of newly-acquired foreign assets or use them to buy up large parts of the economies of other countries? Given these worldwide concerns, journalists flocked to meetings of OPEC ministers. And they reported on every word and change in facial expression of Saudi Arabia's long-time oil minister, Sheik Ahmed Zaki Yamani.

As it happened, the oil-exporting countries quickly expanded their domestic spending and therefore their imports. By 1978 the OPEC current-account surplus had disappeared. Then the second oil shock occurred in 1979–80, as the result not of an OPEC decision but of the drop in Iran's oil output and a worldwide scramble to acquire oil in anticipation of still higher prices. The price advanced sharply once more, by about 160 per cent. Again the OPEC current-account surplus shot up, to reach $104 billion in 1980. As in 1975, the industrial world went into recession while inflation skyrocketed. The average import prices of industrial countries rose 46 per cent from 1978 to 1980. The non-oil developing countries were hit hard again by this combination of events.

The higher oil prices beginning in the early 1970s had predictable long-run effects on demand and supply. The price system worked, in the sense that new sources of supply of oil were developed in non-

OPEC countries and the demand for oil decreased in response to the higher prices. New oil supplies came from the United Kingdom, Norway, the North Slope of Alaska, Mexico and other developing countries. Consequently OPEC's share in world oil production fell from 54 per cent in 1973 to 39 per cent in 1996. At the same time energy consumption in general and oil use in particular were economised. Automobiles became smaller and more fuel efficient, especially in the United States. Supplies of other forms of energy increased. After rising rapidly for many years, oil consumption in the industrial countries fell by more than 18 per cent between 1979 and 1985; it rose only 1.6 per cent per year during the next 10 years.

The members of OPEC were unable to agree on a concerted reduction in the total amount they supplied. This led Saudi Arabia, which had been acting as the 'balance wheel' – cutting its exports almost 75 per cent from 1980 to 1985 – to increase its output and 'flood the market' in order to force the price down.[1] The average price of crude oil, which had decreased a little in 1981–3, dropped from $28.56 per barrel in 1984 to $14.72 per barrel in 1986. In this 'third oil shock', the effects in oil-importing countries were just the reverse of those when the price rose. And the current account of oil-exporting countries, which had already moved into deficit, registered a $28.6 billion deficit in 1986.

After a temporary rise during the Gulf War, the price of oil declined in 1991–4, rose in 1995–6 and fell off again in 1997 and 1998 to below $12 per barrel. In mid-1998 the real price of oil – the price adjusted for the rise in the average price of exports of oil-importing countries – was not far above where it had been before the first oil shock.

An agreement among oil producers, including several non-members of OPEC, in March 1998 to cut output by about 1.7 million barrels per day – about 2.7 per cent – led to only a temporary spurt in prices, partly because the agreed cuts were not fully met. In June 1998, OPEC members decided upon another reduction in output by about 1.4 million barrels. Apparently led by Saudi Arabia's oil minister, Ali Nuaimi, an effort was being made to get major producers, both OPEC and non-OPEC, to agree to adjust their output and sales flexibly in an effort to maintain a price satisfactory to them. Whether they would succeed remained to be seen.[2]

It is well known that new technologies and new discoveries – in non-OPEC nations as well as in OPEC members – mean that the potential supply of oil is above present output by a sizeable margin and is growing, while technology and conservation have dampened the advance in the demand for oil. World output of goods and services more than doubled from 1973 to 1997 but global oil production increased by less than 28 per cent.

11.2 TURKEY

A member not of OPEC but of the industrial countries' Organisation for Economic Cooperation and Development (OECD), Turkey is one of the larger nations in the Middle East in terms of both area and population (63.5 million). Mostly in Asia, partly in Europe, Turkey has been a crossroads for many centuries. On a visit to Antalya on the southern coast, I walked on the remains of a street on which Alexander the Great trod. Turkey has a common border with no less than seven countries: Syria, Iraq, Iran, Armenia, Georgia, Bulgaria and Greece.

In 1923 it became the first republic in the region. Mustapha Kemal Ataturk succeeded in converting his country into a modern, democratic, industrial, secular state, in which education and industrialisation were encouraged. In 1932, in advance of a number of European countries, he established women's suffrage. Turkey had the first woman prime minister among Muslim Middle Eastern countries and women account for two-fifths of the physicists and chemists and one-sixth of the lawyers and doctors.

In economic, but not in social, policy Turkey under Ataturk became a model for other Middle Eastern countries after the Second World War. In the 1930s Ataturk had nurtured Turkey's industrialisation and development with pervasive state intervention, including 'five-year plans' and import substitution. Many public enterprises were established, protected by high tariffs and import restrictions. Here as in Latin America (see Chapter 12) the doctrine of *dependencia* flourished.

Turkey since 1980

The interventionist policies introduced by Ataturk did not prevent the development of a private sector in the economy:

> The public sector, concentrated in capital-intensive industries with large economies of scale, was to provide the inputs necessary for

private industry and agriculture. Indeed, by 1980, the private sector, typically operating smaller plants producing consumer goods, accounted for about 70% of manufacturing value added.[3]

The economy had grown at respectable rates – about 6 per cent per year – in the post-war period up to the late 1970s. Then an economic crisis emerged. Unemployment was close to 10 per cent and concentrated in the cities. The state-owned enterprises required support from the budget – in amounts above 3 per cent of GDP – and inflation exceeded 10 per cent in 1980 while the current-account deficit soared. These were among the reasons, along with political unrest, for the military coup in that year. Trade unions were 'weakened or destroyed with the usual violence [of a military government]'.[4] That was the third military coup since 1960.

Somewhat as in Chile, as we shall see, the military government initiated a process of economic reform and macroeconomic stabilisation, relying on able technicians including Turgut Ozal, who continued to pursue these policies as prime minister after a return to civilian rule and elections in 1983. Export-led growth was adopted in place of import substitution. Over the years tariffs have been reduced and import controls have been eased. Many prices were raised in an effort to make state-owned enterprises profitable and reduce the budgetary support they were receiving. A process of privatisation was begun, partly motivated by the government's desire for increased revenue, which has been used to retire debt. The government has proceeded haltingly as the political balance has shifted one way or the other. From 1981 to 1990 Turkey's GDP growth averaged 5.4 per cent per year and the current-account deficit shrank to manageable size. In the 1990s, except for 1994, Turkey had one of the higher rates of growth, and the highest inflation rate, among OECD countries. The inflation is fuelled by a large budget deficit.

Turkey has a customs union with the European Union and is aiming to join it but was not included among the 10 countries selected as potential members in December 1997.

While reform has much further to go, Turkey is a less regulated, more outward-orientated country than it was in 1980. But it has not solved the problem of maintaining macroeconomic stability. And politically it faces several problems, including Kurdish separatism in the south-eastern part of the country, a dispute with Greece over Cyprus and the frequent clashes between the military and the Islamist political movement. As John Barham wrote in the *Financial Times*:

'Most Turks see the military as defenders of national unity and the secular republic, created by Kemal Ataturk in 1923 out of the wreckage of the Ottoman empire.'[5]

11.3 SAUDI ARABIA

The desert kingdom of Saudi Arabia is the largest oil producer in the area and will be the focus of our attention among countries in the Gulf region. Its population in 1973 was 6.8 million in a land area one-third the size of the United States. Even before the first large oil-price advance, Saudi Arabia had been developing. It has been called 'a unique model of nation building in which a country has been able to transform its polity from the conditions of the eighteenth century to those of the twentieth century within three decades'.[6] In 1973 its exports, consisting almost entirely of oil, exceeded its imports of goods and services and it was accumulating reserves. The dollar value of its exports more than quadrupled in 1974. Foreign exchange reserves reached a peak of $24 billion in 1981, but that was only a fraction of the government's foreign holdings. According to *The Economist*, government assets abroad in 1981 amounted to $110 billion and private Saudis had about $50 billion abroad.[7]

The enormous increase in export earnings, virtually all of which went to the government, provided the basis for a variety of infrastructure and other investment expenditures, including ports, airports, roads, schools, hospitals, housing, desalinisation plants, electric power facilities, new cities and heavy industries, especially petrochemicals and oil refineries. Even wheat is being grown, at a reported cost of $300 per ton[8] – considerably above the world price – supported by heavy subsidies and irrigated with water from underground aquifers that were discovered in the process of drilling for oil.

Substantial expenditures on a military build-up were also undertaken. Defence spending amounted to nearly one-fifth of GDP in the years 1973–85. In addition, many social services, including education, were enlarged and supplied free to the Saudi population, who pay no taxes. The labour force to carry out many of these activities was supplemented by a sizeable influx of foreign workers – not only from other Arab countries. According to official Saudi statistics – about which some doubts exist, given the difficulty of carrying out censuses – 43 per cent of all employees in 1979–80 were non-Saudis (and only 0.4 per cent were Saudi women).[9] Workers' remittances from Saudi Arabia reached a peak of $18.1 billion in 1994 and then decreased.

As a result of the step-up in economic activity, Saudi Arabia's real GDP tripled between 1970 and 1980, while its population increased by one-half. Inflation averaged nearly 16 per cent per year in 1973–9. The face and economic structure of the country changed enormously in the 1970s. And so did the lives of Saudi Arabians. The proportion of the population living in the desert declined from about 60 to 46 per cent and in small towns it fell from 20 to 12 per cent. By 1980 more than two-fifths lived in cities of 100 000 or more people.

In international relations the country plays a major role in OPEC. Its aim has been to keep the price from going too high in opposition to OPEC members with much smaller oil reserves – and therefore shorter time horizons – or with political motivations in relation to oil-importing countries. In the management of its foreign exchange reserves the finance ministry and the Saudi Arabian Monetary Authority were well aware that they had a stake in the stability of the western markets in which their assets were invested. Belying a number of predictions, they did not try to use the assets abroad as leverage to gain political or economic advantage. It was clear to them that a threat to pull their funds out of a market would lead to a sharp fall in prices in that market long before their assets had been fully withdrawn.

Developments since 1980

In 1980 manufacturing other than that based on oil accounted for less than 3 per cent of Saudi Arabia's GDP. The government was encouraging the development of diversified manufacturing firms including those involving joint ventures with investors abroad. Two new cities, Jubail and Yanbu, were constructed by the government, complete with all the infrastructure needed to support manufacturing activity. By 1992 (latest data available) 7 per cent of GDP came from manufacturing.

The oil boom faded in the early 1980s. The volume of Saudi Arabia's oil exports in 1985 was only 27 per cent of its level in 1980. The current account was in deficit from 1983 to 1995. With both the price and volume of oil exports down, the trade surplus declined from a peak of $82.5 billion in 1981 to a trough of $3.1 billion in 1986. In the 1990s, Saudi Arabia's trade surplus rose again but in 1997 was only 41 per cent of the 1981 level. Large payments abroad for services, workers' remittances and official transfers kept the current account in deficit. After rising sharply in connection with the Gulf War, the current-account deficit fell off and moved into a small surplus in 1996 and 1997, Saudi Arabia's foreign exchange reserves decreased from a peak of almost $28 billion at the end of 1981 to $6.4 billion in August 1998. But the banks had net assets abroad of about $27 billion.

Saudi Arabia's development programme in the 1970s and 1980s was undertaken largely by the government, whether directly or through the Saudi Basic Industries Corporation (SABIC). In the second half of the 1980s some privatisation was carried out and the development plan aimed at promoting the private sector. Part of the motivation was the declining income of the government as oil prices sagged. At the beginning of 1994 King Fahd announced that budgeted expenditures would be cut by 20 per cent, as revenues had fallen off with the decline in oil prices. Until this announcement, Saudi Arabia represented an exception to the general tendency we have observed towards less government involvement in the economy. The reasons were more pragmatic than ideological, given the enormous revenues accruing to the government during the oil boom.

Saudi Arabia's real GDP declined by one-sixth from 1981 to 1985 and then advanced, on average by 3.2 per cent annually through 1996. Population grew by 3.7 per cent per year in 1985–96 to reach more than 18 million. As a result, per capita real GDP decreased by about two-fifths from 1980 to 1996. That left it 21 per cent higher than in 1970 for an annual growth rate in per capita GDP of less than 1 per cent over the quarter century. While Saudi Arabia encouraged the immigration of foreign workers in the earlier years, more recently it has banned the hiring of non-Saudis in some industries.

Nevertheless the quality of life has improved. From 1980 to 1996 life expectancy increased from 61 to 70 years and adult literacy rose from 25 to 63 per cent. Between 1980 and 1995 the proportion of girls enrolled in primary school increased from 49 to 76 per cent, and their secondary school enrolment went up from 23 to 54 per cent.

Saudi Arabia continues as an absolute monarchy in which the large royal family functions in leadership roles throughout the economic and political systems. 'In Saudi Arabia, the state has in essence been privatised and control lies in the hands of the ruling elite.'[10]

11.4   EGYPT

Egypt came into the 1980s with a highly-regulated economy in which public enterprises were responsible for 27 per cent of GDP and 60 per cent of value added in manufacturing. These enterprises often required subsidies and were protected by high tariffs and import substitution policies. Like many Middle East countries, Egypt had been influenced by developments in Turkey under Ataturk. In the 1970s and early 1980s Egypt benefited, as an oil producer, from the high oil prices and also received remittances ($2.7 billion in 1980) from its migrant workers who were employed in Saudi Arabia and elsewhere. The end of the oil boom led the government to undertake sizeable public expenditures, which enlarged both the budget deficit and the current-account deficit and created a heavy foreign debt burden.

A reform programme – pursuit of *infitah* (economic opening or liberalisation), which started in the 1970s under Anwar Sadat – was revived in 1990. It involves improving the efficiency of loss-making public enterprises, some privatisation and some reduction of tariffs, as well as macroeconomic policies aimed at budget-deficit reduction and a lowering of inflation. The reform programme has been pursued cautiously, partly because President Mubarak is concerned that worsening unemployment will encourage the militant Islamic fundamentalist movement, which has made itself felt, among other acts, by attacking tourists (thereby harming an important source of foreign exchange) and attempting to assassinate officials.

Nevertheless under an IMF programme the budget deficit was brought down drastically and almost disappeared in 1996–7. Inflation dropped from near 20 per cent in the 1980s to about 3.6 per cent in the 12 months ending June 1998 while the economy grew by almost 6 per cent in 1997. Meanwhile unemployment remains high and Egypt faces the problem, both economic and political, of absorbing a half million or more new workers each year into employment as its population grows by $2\frac{1}{2}$ per cent annually.

The privatisation program was energised in 1996. Shares in 87 state-owned enterprises have been sold but, as of May 1998, only nine involved majority sales to so-called anchor investors. Meanwhile direct investment from abroad, which amounted to about $600 million in 1996, is being encouraged.[11]

Egypt's biggest challenge is to move much of its population out of poverty.

11.5   OTHER MIDDLE EASTERN COUNTRIES

The story varies from one country to another in the region. While some have benefited more than others from oil resources, they share the experience of coping with high unemployment despite overmanning in state-owned enterprises. In some nations, such as Algeria, high unemployment, especially among those more educated, nourishes Islamic fundamentalism. There has been movement away from the Ataturk model towards less state intervention in economies, encouragement of private activity and greater openness to the outside world. But it is far from complete. According to Said El-Naggar, former professor at Cairo University:

> It is difficult to justify that, in many Arab countries, the government continues to be involved in such activities as grocery and department stores, bakeries, flour mills, printing, bookshops, advertising, hotels, travel agencies, contracting, cattle and poultry farming, fisheries, and scores of other activities. These are normally the kinds of activities that are better and more effectively undertaken by the private sector.[12]

11.6   SUB-SAHARAN AFRICA

The economies in Sub-Saharan Africa have picked up steam since 1994. In the period from 1980 to 1983, Sub-Saharan Africa other than South Africa experienced declining income per capita, rapid population growth, the worst drought of this century in 1992, the spread of Aids, rising foreign debt (mainly to official lenders) and environmental degradation. In some countries civil strife, if not civil war, existed and governments barely functioned. Life expectancy at birth was 52 years in 1995 and more than 40 per cent of the population was illiterate. Daniel Cohen's explanation for 'the African tragedy' is low investment, mismanagement of the economies, and ethnic diversity.[13] No wonder that IMF Managing Director Michel Camdessus described it as 'the continent of woe'.

Part of the explanation for the economic woe was that most of these countries are highly dependent on basic commodities – including oil, copper, cocoa, coffee, cotton, tea and tobacco – for export earnings and the prices of these products tended to decline, especially during the recession of the early 1990s. Moreover, there was a loss of market share in some of these commodities to other developing countries.

More broadly, with a few exceptions the Sub-Saharan countries failed to diversify beyond the production of primary commodities. Domestic investment – especially private investment was relatively low, foreign investment went mainly to oil-exporting countries and foreign aid was insufficient even where it was used effectively.

There are some exceptions to this sad economic story. Botswana, with its diamonds, grew by more than 11 per cent per year in the 1980s. Burkina Faso, Burundi, Chad, Congo, and Mauritius had GDP growth rates above 5 per cent per year. They were joined since 1985 by Djibouti, Gambia and Mali. These nine countries accounted for less than 7 per cent of the population of Sub-Saharan Africa in 1995.

While not all of these features have changed, the 'economic performance and prospects in Sub-Saharan Africa have improved considerably. Growth of real GDP across the 49 countries averaged 4.3 per cent a year during 1995–97, compared with 1.6 per cent during 1990–94 and 2.6 per cent during 1980–89.' Excluding Nigeria and South Africa, the average growth rate during 1995–7 was 4.7 per cent per year and it was apparently rather widely shared among countries in the region. Apart from temporary factors such as favorable weather and higher commodity prices, the principal explanation seems to be improved and sustanied macroeconomic stability and policy reforms.[14]

As a result, per capita GDP turned up after falling for several years. At the same time the fertility rate for the entire region decreased from 6.7 to 5.6 between 1980 and 1996; in Botswana it fell from 6.7 to 4.3, in Zimbabwe from 6.8 to 3.9 and in Kenya from 7.8 to 4.6 but in Chad and Niger it remained almost unchanged at high levels.[15]

In these conditions, Sub-Saharan Africa as a region began to share in the flow of private capital to developing countries.[16] Net incoming foreign direct investment averaged $3.3 billion per year in 1994–7, of which South Africa accounted for only about 7 per cent.[17]

Although Nigeria, the most populous country in the area, has been mired in political turmoil, it too experienced a pickup in its growth rate in 1995–7, despite 'decades of mismanagement and corruption'. It is a major oil exporter but the country has been suffering from a scarcity of fuel since its four state-run oil refineries have 'ground to a halt'. That has led to cuts in electric power, which in turn is affecting economic activity.[18] A sharp slowdown in output growth apparently occurred in 1998.

Its military dictator, General Abacha, died in early June 1998, leaving the country's future uncertain.

Ethnic conflict has occurred elsewhere in Africa with dire economic effects. This is not the place for prescription. For that one may turn to the World Bank and the International Monetary Fund with their structural adjustment programmes, some of which have produced successful results. It is worth noting that even if Sub-Saharan Africa succeeds in growing at about 4 per cent per year in the next decade – twice the rate in 1987–96 – its per capita income would be no higher than it was in 1982, given the increase of its population by 3 per cent annually. Thus much remains to be accomplished.

11.7   SOUTH AFRICA

South Africa has experienced a remarkably peaceful, and historic, political transformation. The country has been described by Sir William Ryrie as 'a special case, where a First World economy is mixed with a Third World economy'.[19] The relationships between these two worlds appears to be evolving in a positive way, and that should have favourable economic consequences.

GDP growth accelerated in recent years – to 2.7 per cent per year in 1994–7 – after declining in 1990–2, but it slowed again in 1997–8. The volume of gold mined declined by almost two-fifths from 1970 to 1992 (latest data available).

Since the end of apartheid, South Africa's trade – especially its export trade – has increased with its continental neighbours. Negotiations are proceeding to form a 14-nation free trade area, the Southern African Development Community. But it is reported that South Africa has to tread carefully to avoid being regarded as a 'big brother'.[20]

12 Democratisation and Reform in Latin America

The 1980s became known as 'the lost decade' in Latin America. For the region as a whole, GDP grew little more than 1 per cent per year compared with 6 per cent in the previous decade. As a result, per capita GDP fell by more than 10 per cent in the 1980s. There were few exceptions – Chile and Colombia among them – to this declining trend in real income. The recession of 1981–2 in the industrial countries and the debt crisis that erupted in the summer of 1982 had much to do with the sharp turnaround in the economic well-being of Latin America in the 1980s. But the 1990s saw substantial improvement as economic reforms were adopted, some debt relief was obtained and capital inflows increased greatly. The Mexican crisis of 1994–5 had a 'tequila effect' on a number of countries in the hemisphere. In 1997 and 1998, some nations in Latin America felt the effects of the 'Asian flu' – the financial and economic crisis in the East Asian countries – as capital inflows slackened. They tightened their monetary policies, thereby slowing their economies somewhat. Nevertheless, 1997 and the first half of 1998 saw the most favourable combination of relatively high growth and low inflation in many years.

Meanwhile, and perhaps remarkably, Latin America moved towards more democratic political regimes despite the economic tribulations of the 1980s. In 1979 military dictatorships or juntas ruled in much of South and Central America. Elected presidents governed only in Colombia, Venezuela and Costa Rica. In 1998 every country in South America had a popularly-elected president.

This chapter first considers Latin America as a whole and then examines Mexico's reforms and subsequent crisis of 1994–5, followed by briefer observations on Argentina, Chile and Brazil.

12.1 BACKGROUND

Most nations of Latin America grew at a rapid pace in the 1960s and 1970s – an average of 5.7 per cent per year in the entire region. After 1973, a number of these countries became heavy borrowers from banks in the industrial world. As noted in Chapter 2, the banks were accumulating deposits on a massive scale from oil-exporting countries and were looking for profitable outlets for these funds. They used the technique of syndicated loans – shared by many banks – denominated mainly in dollars and bearing variable interest rates tied to the 6-month Eurodollar rate in London (London interbank offer rate, or Libor). The banks actively peddled these loans to South American borrowers, both governmental and private. The term 'loan pushing' came into use as the surpluses of OPEC nations were 'recycled' to promising-looking developing countries. The borrowers in turn welcomed the loans as a means of financing both the increased cost of imported oil and higher domestic investment.

During most of the 1970s the interest rates on these loans were very low when measured in real terms. It became conventional to judge real interest rates by comparing nominal rates with the annual increase in the export prices of the borrowers. For the heavy debtors, most of which were in South America, the average interest rate on loans from private creditors – mainly commercial banks – ranged from 7.5 to 9 per cent while export prices were rising on average by more than 14 per cent per year. To debtors it looked like a bargain. And the debt piled up. In Latin America as a whole, total long-term debt – that with a maturity of more than one year – increased from $27.6 billion in 1970 to $238.5 billion in 1982. The ratio of long-term debt to GNP rose from 18.3 to 33.5 per cent.[1]

How were these sizeable capital inflows used by the borrowing countries? They were able to finance enlarged current-account deficits. The deficit of the region rose from $7.6 billion in 1974 to $41.3 billion in 1982. While interest payments also increased, as noted, the debtors were in receipt of 'net transfers' – the excess of new borrowing over interest payments. That in turn financed higher domestic investment. In some countries it also financed capital flight, motivated by tax evasion or fear of political instability or expected inflation and currency depreciation.

Nevertheless, the process looked sustainable to many observers as the debtors appeared to thrive. Therefore the maturing loans were easily rolled over or refinanced with new loans. Among the more memorable statements of the period was that of Walter Wriston, Chairman of Citicorp in New York, to the effect that governments do not go bankrupt. It is only fair to report that I wrote in 1981: 'Given the high rate of investment, the strong rate of growth, and the availability of oil, it is hard to believe that Mexico will not continue to look like a good credit risk.' But I also noted that 'if real interest rates [in industrial countries] do not come down soon, the outlook for debt-financed economic development is bleak'.[2]

12.2 ONSET OF THE DEBT CRISIS

Whether or not the recycling could have continued smoothly under normal conditions is a moot question. The disruption of the process began with the Iranian revolution and the fall-off of Iran's oil exports, which had accounted for nearly 10 per cent of world oil output. The international price of oil rose in a series of jumps in 1979–80, cumulating to a price increase of almost 150 per cent.

As in 1973–4, inflation speeded up and economic activity slowed in many countries. To combat the inflation, central banks in industrial countries tightened monetary policy and interest rates rose steeply. Libor, which had averaged 9.2 per cent in 1978, was 16.7 per cent in 1981. That in turn caused the interest payments of the debtors to balloon. Latin American interest payments increased from 12.2 per cent of export earnings in 1978 to 30.3 per cent in 1982.

The combination of sharply higher interest rates, slackening exports to industrial countries in recession and higher costs of imported oil enlarged the balance-of-payments deficits of the debtor countries. Ironically the debt crisis started not in what looked like the most vulnerable country, Brazil, but in an oil-exporting nation, Mexico, that had appeared as highly creditworthy. In August 1982 Mexico temporarily suspended its debt service.[3]

When Mexico suspended, the banks quickly cut back their lending to all debtors and that threw all of them into crisis. In order to continue to meet the interest obligations on their debts to banks and other creditors abroad, the debtors had to conserve foreign exchange by reducing their imports. That required them to slash their domestic investment. In Latin America the volume of imports fell by 37.7 per cent in 1982–3 and investment as a proportion of GDP declined from 24.9 per cent to 17.5 per cent from 1980 to 1984. The result was a drastic slowdown in economic growth and in per capita output.

Why did the debtor governments not default – that is, stop paying interest so that they could use their scarce foreign exchange to buy imports? Various answers can be given. It has been said that the heads of state of the largest debtors did not want to disconnect their economies from the world financial system nor to risk a foreign policy rupture with the United States. More specifically, they depended on foreign commercial banks for short-term credit to finance their trade and did not want to see it withdrawn. And the debtor governments must have been motivated by the wish to maintain creditworthiness in the hope of future inflows of capital. Also, if they were to stop all debt service, capital flight probably would have intensified.[4]

12.3   DEALING WITH THE DEBT CRISIS

Initially the debt crisis had two aspects: the squeeze on debtor countries as noted above and the danger that many banks in industrial countries would be in serious trouble if the debtors defaulted. Motivated by these two concerns the IMF, then under the leadership of Managing Director Jacques de Larosière, induced the banks to undertake 'concerted lending' to many of the debtor countries as a condition for loans to the debtors by the IMF along with its 'seal of approval' on their policies. But such lending soon petered out. The banks were reluctant to put additional loans on their books when repayment was uncertain and the market prices for such loans – which were traded among banks and other investors – were at a fraction of their face value.

In the autumn of 1985 US Treasury Secretary James Baker announced a plan aimed at restoring growth in the debtor countries. He may have been motivated by a fear that Mexico would suspend its interest payments again in the face of the decline in oil prices.[5] The Baker plan called on the commercial banks in industrial countries and on the multilateral development banks (the World Bank and its regional counterparts in Latin America, Asia, and Africa) to increase their lending to the debtor countries by a total of $40 billion over three years. As William Cline has pointed out, new bank lending came close to the Baker goal, despite widespread views to the contrary.[6]

Then in March 1989 Baker's successor, Nicholas Brady, proposed a plan involving debt and debt service reduction as well as new lending by the commercial banks – all of which was to be assisted by new credits to the debtors from the IMF and World Bank. Debt reduction programmes were worked out for many countries.

Although the result was a relatively small decrease in the annual interest payments of the debtors, the Brady plan appears to have had a catalytic effect, especially in Mexico. In combination with Mexico's economic reforms, it led to a large inflow of private capital – both a return flow of Mexican capital that had fled the peso and foreign direct and portfolio investment. A similar inflow of funds occurred in other debtor countries.

Since 1989, when the Brady plan was announced, the debt burden has decreased significantly. For the 17 most heavily-indebted developing countries (most of which are in Latin America) the ratio of interest payments abroad to exports of goods and services fell from 24.1 per cent to 12.1 per cent between 1988 and 1997. In Mexico, that ratio declined from 37.8 per cent in 1982 to 10.2 per cent in 1996. In addition, substantial inflows of capital enabled the debtor countries once again to incur and finance current-account deficits. The aggregate current-account deficit of Latin American countries increased from $1.3 billion in 1990 to $64.4 billion in 1997. That in turn facilitated higher rates of domestic investment and a resumption of economic growth. In Latin America as a whole, GDP growth was 5.1 per cent in 1997 – more than twice the rate in the 1980–9 period.

What made all this possible was a return of confidence on the part of both foreign investors and domestic residents who had engaged in capital flight. The Latin American countries appeared more attractive to investors as the result of the economic reforms. That exerted a pull on funds from abroad. But there was also a push, as both short-term and long-term interest rates declined substantially in industrial countries.

Much of the inflow took the form of purchases of stock (some through the many emerging market mutual funds that have sprung up) and direct investment. Portfolio equity flows to Latin America and the Carribean were non-existent in 1980, $1.1 billion in 1990 and were estimated at $15.5 billion in 1997. Net foreign direct investment rose from $6.1 billion in 1980 to $42 billion in 1997.[7] About half of the capital inflow consisted of what the IMF calls 'non-debt-creating flows'. The inflows were so substantial that reserves in Latin America more than quintupled from 1989 to mid-1998, reaching $186 billion. While welcome, the large inflows created some problems for the monetary authorities. Prices of real estate and equities rose. In some countries the exchange rate appreciated, and restrictive monetary policy was undermined, leading central banks to seek ways to sterilize the inflows.

Chile led the way in this respect. It aimed at curbing short-term flows by imposing a non-interest bearing reserve requirement of 30 per cent for one year on banks and firms that borrow abroad. Incoming foreign direct and portfolio investment could not be repatriated during the first year. In June 1998, that deterrent to capital inflows was relaxed somewhat.

Meanwhile structural economic reforms of various types continued to be pursued in Latin America, including deregulation, privatisation, and the lowering of trade barriers. The latter includes Mercosur, a trade agreement among Argentina, Brazil, Paraguay and Uruguay.

Perhaps the most striking example of economic transformation in Latin America since 1980 is that of Mexico, which also suffered a severe crisis in 1994–5.

12.4 MEXICO

Mexico is the second most populous country in Latin America, and its history, both political and economic, has been very much influenced by its contiguity with the United States. 'Poor Mexico, so far from God and so near to the United States', said Porfirio Diaz, long-time dictatorial president in the late nineteenth and early twentieth centuries.

Much structural economic reform has occurred in Mexico since the early 1980s. Although reform started under the presidency of Miguel de la Madrid Hurtado (1982–8), it moved rapidly and comprehensively after Carlos Salinas de Gortari succeeded him in December 1988. The reforms, it has been written,

> are part of a fundamental shift in the government's development strategy, which aims at a substantial increase in the role of market forces and private incentives in the economy, while limiting that of the state to establishing the appropriate legislative and administrative framework for the private sector to create productive employment and wealth.[8]

The Mexican government appears to have discarded three elements that influenced its economic philosophy for many years: fear of domination by the United States, a large ownership and regulatory role for the public sector and import substitution rather than open trade. Salinas's enthusiastic embrace of NAFTA is evidence of these changes.

In other words, Mexico has abandoned dependency theory (*dependencia*), which earlier had widespread popularity in Latin America and elsewhere. According to that thesis, developing countries were dependent on industrial countries and were exploited by them. This was thought to hinder development in the Third World while industrial nations profited from their economic relationships with those developing countries.[9]

Mexico's economic reforms show up, according to former finance minister Aspe, in land tenure and use, deregulation of industry, privatisation of state-owned enterprises, import liberalisation, tariff reductions and promotion of direct investment from abroad, freeing of the financial system and an improved budget policy.[10] As it undertook these reforms, Mexico also succeeded in lowering its inflation rate to well under 10 per cent (until the crisis of 1994–5 – covered below) compared with an average of more than 90 per cent per year in 1983–8. It also achieved an apparent budget surplus, but that surplus included receipts from privatisation – a dubious revenue source little different from borrowing in its economic effects – and omitted loans by development banks from reported budget expenditures. In any event, Mexico attracted enormous amounts of both Mexican flight capital and foreign capital, as noted.

While economic reform proceeded in an impressive manner, Mexico's political system continued to be dominated by the Institutional Revolutionary Party (PRI) until July 1997, when it lost its majority in the lower house of the Congress. That led President Zedillo to state that 'for the first time in our history, we can achieve healthy, durable economic growth, along with a full, pluralistic and harmonious democracy – this is the opportunity of our generation'.[11]

Approach of Debt Crisis

Under the presidency of José Lopez Portillo (1976–82), large new oil discoveries were made, raising Mexico's proven reserves from 6 billion to more than 70 billion barrels between 1975 and 1982. Oil revenues increased from less than one-fifth to more than half of export proceeds. On the basis of this bonanza – at the higher oil price engineered by OPEC in 1973 – Lopez Portillo was able to 'administer the abundance' by undertaking massive public sector expenditures. The budget deficit rose from 4.7 per cent to 15.4 per cent of GDP in the Portillo years. Mexico's larger oil reserves also enhanced its creditworthiness in the eyes of bankers abroad. As a result, its long-term external debt increased from $6 billion in 1970 to $41 billion in 1980 and its interest payments abroad rose to more than one-fourth of its export revenues.

Although Mexico looked like a good credit risk, its prospects began to deteriorate in 1981. The price of oil, which had risen sharply again in the second oil shock, turned down. The United States, Mexico's chief trade partner, went into recession. As noted earlier, interest rates on dollar obligations rose steeply. When policymakers failed to react quickly to these unfavourable developments, private Mexican capital poured out of the country in anticipation of a depreciation of the peso. Capital flight is estimated to have exceeded $11 billion in 1981 – about 40 per cent of export earnings. In early 1982, with foreign exchange reserves dropping, the peso was devalued and a moderate budget-deficit reduction was announced.

In these conditions banks abroad cut back on their lending and Mexico's reserves ran low in 1982. The Federal Reserve propped them up for a while with overnight loans to the Bank of Mexico at the end of each month, thereby 'window dressing' the size of Mexico's published reserves.[12] The rationale was that Mexico needed to buy time until the new president – already known to be Miguel de la Madrid – took office and would agree to a stabilisation pact with the IMF.

But the banks had stopped lending and capital flight had increased as Mexico's inflation soared. Foreign exchange reserves were exhausted and in August the Mexican authorities declared a temporary standstill on debt service payments to creditor banks. The Mexican government, in Lopez Portillo's last months in office, imposed exchange controls in an effort to stem the flight of capital, devalued the peso again, and, as noted, nationalised the banks.

Many reasons can be cited for this débâcle in Mexico.[13] One faulty assumption, held by both the lending banks abroad and the Mexican authorities, was that the oil boom would go on indefinitely.

Coping with the Debt Crisis

De la Madrid's government, with Jesus Silva Herzog remaining as finance minister and Angel Gurria as chief debt negotiator, achieved greater consensus than that of his predecessor. It set about reducing the outsized fiscal deficit and devaluing the peso – a combination of policies aimed at improving the trade balance but which also worsened inflation. At the same time principal payments on the external debt were rescheduled and interest payments were resumed, helped by a credit agreement with the IMF. A medium-term goal of the government was to reduce inflation, which had risen from 17.5 per cent in

1978 to more than 100 per cent in 1983. One result was a sharp decline in real wages, by more than 30 per cent in 1983–5. Meanwhile net transfers, which had been a positive $6.4 billion in 1981, turned negative, amounting to $8.8 billion in 1984. Mexico's GDP declined by 3.5 per cent in 1983 and, partly for this reason, the target for the current account of the balance of payments was over-achieved: there was a surplus in 1983–5. Considering that net transfers were negative and foreign exchange reserves were low, Mexico did not have the means to finance a current-account deficit.

In 1985 a structural reform measure was adopted: trade liberalisation was begun. The proportion of imports not subject to licensing, which had been zero in December 1982, rose from 16.4 per cent in December 1984 to 64.1 per cent in July 1985.[14]

Mexico City suffered a severe earthquake in October 1985, which brought small amounts of financial relief from the IMF and World Bank. And then in 1986 the world price of oil fell. Mexico's export price dropped from over $25 to $12 per barrel. Although non-oil exports had been growing, oil still accounted for more than two-thirds of export proceeds in 1985. This loss of export earnings amounted to 6.7 per cent of GDP. As a result of this and the 1985 stabilisation programme, Mexico's GDP fell by 3.1 per cent in 1986 as domestic investment declined by more than one-fifth.

To deal with the loss of export earnings and continue to pay interest on its debt, the government had to devalue the peso again. This led to another acceleration of inflation as import prices shot up but the trade balance remained in surplus and foreign exchange reserves rose somewhat. This devaluation was successful in part because real wages were flexible downwards: nominal wages did not rise in line with prices. In this as well as other respects, Mexico differed from some other Latin American countries.

With the advent of the Baker plan, Mexico received in late 1986 $6 billion in new loans and much of its public and private debt was rescheduled with longer maturities and a seven-year grace period. The easing of Mexico's external financial position provided the basis for the government to initiate several reforms in 1987–8: an 'economic solidarity pact' aimed at lowering inflation by reduction in the budget deficit, moderate wage indexation, agreements with industry on inflation targets, additional trade liberalisation and privatisation of public enterprises.[15]

The pact brought the inflation rate down in 1988 but economic growth was only 1.3 per cent. That led the new government that took office in December 1988 under Carlos Salinas de Gortari to announce a 'pact for economic stability and growth'. It was aimed at holding inflation down and attracting capital inflow by Mexicans and foreign investors. Such an inflow of funds would reduce or reverse net outward transfers, which had averaged $7.2 billion per year in 1983–8 (not counting capital flight).

Then in March 1989 the Brady plan was proposed and Mexico became the second country to take advantage of it. Although the final agreement with the commercial banks was not signed until February 1990, it was retroactive to July 1989. The agreement provided debt relief in three forms: a reduction of principal by 35 per cent on a portion of the debt, a lower and fixed interest rate of 6.25 per cent on another portion, and new 15-year loans.[16] The banks were free to choose among these three options. The net result was a decrease in Mexico's annual interest payments by $1.4 billion and additional loans of about $670 per year for four years.

While the annual interest saving was not large, the agreement was greeted by the Mexican authorities with a degree of enthusiasm that was puzzling at the time. I later concluded that 'they accepted the best bargain they could get and, having done so, tried to strengthen the confidence of investors at home and abroad in the economic prospects of their economy'.[17] The agreement was followed, at least for a while, by a drop in domestic interest rates. It also provided the backdrop for a number of structural reforms. The tax system was reformed in 1987 and 1989 in order to encourage private investment. In May 1990 the Salinas government announced its intention to re-privatise the banks, which Lopez Portillo had nationalised in 1982. This announcement had a highly favourable effect on market sentiment and apparently induced a return of some flight capital. As a result, short-term interest rates fell from 46 per cent to 32 per cent in the second quarter of 1990 when inflation was running at an annual rate of about 20 per cent.

For many years government ownership of enterprises was widespread, in fields of economic activity that included oil production, sugar refining, automobile manufacturing and insurance. Privatisation of state enterprises began under de la Madrid: from 1982 to 1988 the number of state-owned firms was reduced from 1100 to 420 through mergers, liquidations and sales.[18] The process was accelerated after 1988 by the Salinas government. 'More than 80 per cent of the 1115 state-run companies that existed in 1982 were no longer in the hands of the government by the end of 1991.'[19] The largest privatisation was of Teléfonos de México, with a value of $1.8 billion.

As Aspe has observed, the private sector was privatised first, by removing subsidies on inputs and interest rates and by dismantling trade barriers so as to 'wean private industry away from an unhealthy dependence on the public sector'.[20]

Another basic reform under President Salinas was in rural Mexico, where the *ejidos* – akin to communes – can now be transformed into privately-owned farms. Mexican agriculture had been inefficient and output was stagnant.

Benedicte Larre has written that the reform of trade policy in Mexico since 1985

> is one of the most drastic breaks with the country's interventionist traditions; it is designed to expose the economy to international competition and to reverse the legacy of several decades of import substitution policy, which has led to a steady decline in the ratio of exports to GDP.[21]

Mexico joined the General Agreement on Tariffs and Trade (GATT) in 1986. Its trade liberalisation measures consisted of the elimination of import licences for many products, tariff reductions and the encouragement of direct investment from abroad. Import licences covered 83 per cent of imports in 1984 and 9 per cent in 1991. The average tariff dropped from 27 per cent in 1982 to 13 per cent in 1991. The flow of foreign direct investment to Mexico increased from less than $2 billion in 1985 to almost $11 billion in 1994.

The financial system was also reformed. Not only were the banks privatised but interest rates were deregulated and banks were given greater freedom of action to move in the direction of universal banks, as in Germany.

In the summer of 1990 President Salinas suggested talks with the United States on a free trade agreement, which led to the NAFTA proposal, later joined by Canada. This was the final step in Mexico's discarding of its fear of American dominance as well as the culmination of Mexico's actions to liberalise its trade. The major benefit to Mexico from NAFTA would come from an increased inflow of investment capital from the United States. In 1994 Mexico became a member of the Organisation for Economic Cooperation and Development (OECD) in Paris, which is generally regarded as an association of industrial countries.

The Crisis of 1994–5

In the midst of these favourable developments, domestic investment rose and saving diminished as consumer spending accelerated. The result was that Mexico's current-account deficit crept up year by year from $5.8 billion in 1989 to $29.7 billion in 1994. That amounted to 7 per cent of Mexico's GDP but it was financed – through 1993 – by even larger inflows of capital with the result that foreign exchange reserves increased. Meanwhile the exchange rate, which had crawled down relative to the dollar, was stabilized beginning in mid-1992. Given that the inflation rate was above that in the United States, the real exchange rate was appreciating.

1994 turned out to be a crucial year. A presidential election was scheduled for August and that was presumably one of several reasons why the exchange rate was kept stable and a tightening of fiscal and monetary policy was avoided. Other reasons might have been a concern that a devaluation would discourage foreign portfolio investors, would lead labour to demand larger wage increases, and would increase the peso burden of the banks' foreign liabilities.[22]

An uprising began in Chiapas, in southern Mexico, in January. A presidential candidate was assassinated in March, as was the secretary general of the major party – the PRI (Institutional Revolutionary Party) – in September. Meanwhile, American interest rates were rising as the Federal Reserve increased the Federal funds rate a number of times beginning in February.

The result was a falloff of capital inflow and, perhaps equally important, outflows of Mexican capital. In fact, it appears that Mexican residents began to shift funds out of peso securities into dollars before foreign investors.[23] As foreign exchange reserves declined, the Government issued peso securities whose principal and interest was linked to the dollar – *tesobonos*; by the end of 1994, about $30 billion were outstanding.

Shortly after the new president – Ernesto Zedillo – was installed on 1 December, the exchange rate of the peso was permitted to depreciate by about 13 per cent. But that action was not accompanied by a programme of macroeconomic policies designed to support the exchange rate or reduce the current-account deficit. That disappointed investors, who lost 'confidence in Mexico, its institutions and its leaders'[24] and they acted accordingly. Both reserves and the exchange rate dropped and on 22 December the rate was permitted to float. At the end of 1994, the peso was 42 per cent below its year-earlier level in terms of dollars. The new finance minister Jaime Serra resigned and was succeeded by Guillermo Ortiz.

The crisis in Mexico was felt in many other countries, where both exchange rates and stock prices declined as portfolio investors withdrew. This so-called 'tequila effect' was most severe in Argentina and Brazil but it was also evident in Asia.

Mexico received a large IMF loan along with credits from the United States and other industrial countries based on the adoption by the Mexican government of a more restrictive policy and limits on wage increases designed to prevent a wage–price spiral. The peso stabilised in the autumn of 1995, when real GDP was 15 per cent lower than in the fourth quarter of 1994. It then turned up and rose irregularly.

By the fourth quarter of 1996, real GDP was somewhat above the 1994 level. It rose 7 per cent in 1997. According to a *Financial Times* survey of 'Mexican Finance and Investment':

> The economic recovery from Mexico's deep recession in 1995 has been faster than foreseen by even the most optimistic forecasters. The economy is larger in real terms than before the crisis in 1994 and the 1m jobs destroyed in 1995 have been more than recouped.[25]

But real wages had not recovered. Norminal wages in May 1998 were twice their level of 1994 while consumer prices were $2\frac{1}{2}$ times higher.

Thus ended what has been called the first financial crisis of the twenty- first century.

The Mexican crisis led to the establishment of a supplemental reserve facility (SRF) in the IMF to deal with balance-of-payments problems resulting from sudden and disruptive losses of market confidence. The Fund also adopted a new procedure designed to see to it that debtor countries reveal fully information about their economies and financial systems – the Special Data Dissemination Standard, available on the Internet.

The crisis served to make it clear that a world of highly mobile capital entails dangers as well as benefits.

In general Mexico has undergone a striking economic transformation. Of course the country still has many serious economic problems. Inflation, though diminishing, was about 20 per cent in 1997. Income distribution is highly unequal. Poverty is widespread and it worsened during the period of declining per capita GDP in the 1980s and again in 1995–6. Environmental pollution is severe, especially in Mexico City.

12.5   ARGENTINA

In the first three decades of this century Argentina was by far the wealthiest 'developing' country. Anyone who visits Buenos Aires is reminded more of Paris and Rome than of the capitals of third world countries. In 1900 and 1929 Argentina's per capita GDP was about three times that of Brazil, almost twice that of Japan and roughly equal to GDP per person in Austria, Italy and Norway. That early prosperity was based on Argentina's agricultural land. The pampas have been called 'the most fertile tract of land in the world'[26] and they provided ample export revenues in the decades before 1930. By 1987 Argentina's per capita GDP was slightly lower than Brazil's and only a little more than one-third that of Italy.[27]

A military junta ruled Argentina from 1976 to 1982 when, after the Falklands/Malvinas fiasco, it resigned. In 1983 Raul Alfonsin was elected to the presidency. The country had been plagued by economic instability and triple-digit inflation from the mid-1970s. In Alfonsin's first year the budget deficit was more than 14 per cent of GDP and consumer prices rose 344 per cent. Inflation was almost twice that rate in 1984–5. Various attempts by the Alfonsin government to stabilise the economy – mainly the Austral Plan of 1985 and the Primavera Plan of 1988 – were undermined by continued fiscal deficits. Inflation fell to 90 per cent in 1986 but only temporarily. In 1989 it exceeded 3000 per cent or more than 2 per cent per day. It is not surprising that Argentinians moved their funds out of pesos into dollars in large amounts.

In those conditions, real GDP fell on average by 1 per cent annually during the 1980s.

Carlos Menem, a member of the Peronist party and governor of the state of La Rioja, was elected president in 1989. He did not give the impression of being an economic reformer who would tackle both the macroeconomic and structural problems of Argentina. In the first peaceful transfer of power since 1928, the economic crisis led Alfonsin to resign and cede the office to Menem five months early – in July 1989.

The chaos created by hyperinflation made for a public mood that welcomed economic reform. Menem immediately announced a series of measures that included a sharp cut in the budget deficit through both expenditure restraints and tax increases, a tight rein on monetary policy, a devaluation of the currency, liberalisation of imports and tariff reductions and a privatisation programme. 'Mr. Menem has adroitly used his Peronist credentials to reverse almost everything Gen. Peron did.'[28]

Hyperinflation continued in 1990 as consumer prices rose 2300 per cent. In March 1991, Argentina adopted a monetary arrangement akin to a currency board, under which the exchange rate was pegged to the US dollar and the central bank may normally add to the domestic money supply only in a one-to-one ratio to its foreign exchange reserves.[29] The arrangement is spoken of as 'convertibility' in Argentina. This was not the first time Argentina had recourse to a type of currency board. It did so in the years leading up to the First World War and in the 1920s.

The price advance slowed sharply in 1991. By mid-1993 annual inflation was about 10 per cent and in 1997 less than one per cent. The exchange rate was also stabilised.

The economy's growth rate picked up to 8.9 per cent per year in 1991–4. But the 'tequila effect' of the Mexican crisis led in 1995 to a drop in foreign exchange reserves and a banking panic in which the central bank could not act as a lender of last resort. Interest rates rose sharply and Argentina's GDP fell by more than $4\frac{1}{2}$ per cent. Output recovered in 1996 and expanded by more than 8.6 per cent in 1997.

Meanwhile a highly regulated economy was liberalised. By presidential decree numerous restrictions on economic activity were eliminated. Tariffs were also slashed, confronting Argentine businesses with more intense competition from abroad. Privatisation has proceeded at a rapid pace and employment by the state (including state-owned enterprises) declined substantially. Among the firms sold off are the national oil company YPF (*Yacimientos Petroliferos Fiscales*), the railways, and the telephone system and other utilities. Privatisation brought revenues to the treasury and has led to more efficient management but it has also elicited demands for regulation of the prices charged by the utilities.

Privatisation has also strengthened confidence in the reform intentions of the government, thereby encouraging a repatriation of flight capital. That plus inflows of foreign capital enabled Argentina's foreign exchange reserves to rise from $1.5 billion at the end of 1989 to more than $24 billion in August 1998 despite the existence of a current-account deficit. The return of capital was also based on the fixed exchange-rate policy. But that policy, important as it is in instilling confidence, created a problem for Argentine exports. The real exchange rate appreciated in 1991–4 as the peso remained pegged to the dollar while other currencies depreciated. Although it was a hurdle for exporters, the policy had the advantage of putting pressure on domestic firms to increase efficiency so as to be able to compete with imports. At some point, though, greater flexibility in the exchange rate and in monetary policy will no doubt have to be introduced. For the time being the pegged peso is a symbol of the economic stability that the Menem government has brought to 'the new Argentina'.

But all is not well. The Asian crisis had an impact on Brazil and in turn on Argentina, where short-term interest rates had to be raised sharply to defend the exchange rate. Unemployment and corruption are troubling issues. Privatisation and increased efficiency have brought a substantial rise in unemployment. It increased from less than 6 per cent in 1991 to more than 16 per cent in 1996 and then fell off to about 13 per cent in late 1997. Also, corruption is said to exist not only in government but in the corporate sector. These are among the reasons for the decline in President Menem's popularity and for the defeat of his party in congressional elections in October 1997.

12.6 CHILE

Chile is the paradoxical case of a country that, under a repressive political regime, was the first in Latin America to undertake structural economic reforms. In a violent coup in 1973 General Augusto Pinochet took over from the so-called Marxist government of Salvador Allende. During Pinochet's 17 brutal years as dictator, a 'dirty war' was waged against opponents of the regime and human rights were violated. But economic reform was also carried out. It included privatisation, deregulation, substitution of a flat 10 per cent tariff for most import restrictions, elimination of price – but not wage – controls and pursuit of effective fiscal and monetary policies. Also, the composition of tax revenues was altered by the adoption of a value-added tax and a reduction of income tax rates, while the taxes on wealth and capital gains were abolished. By 1977 the economy was growing rapidly and consumer prices were rising at double rather than triple digit rates. 'Almost all of the economic reforms recommended to highly indebted countries after the onset of the debt crisis in 1982 were implemented in Chile in the 1970s.'[30] As John Williamson has observed:

For a long time the adoption of those policies by the Chilean government threatened to give them the kiss of death, partly because of the political odium the Chilean regime had earned by its ruthless seizure of power and by the authoritarian way in which it subsequently governed.[31]

Chile was affected by the debt crisis and experienced a 14 per cent drop in output in 1982. But in contrast to most of its Latin American neighbours, it recovered quickly and its economy grew vigorously – an average of 6.3 per cent per year – in 1983–9.

The privatisation in 1986–8 of state-owned enterprises – various public utilities and the national airline – was of greater magnitude, relative to the size of the country, than the British privatisations of 1980–7. A number of criticisms have been levelled at the Chilean privatisations, including a charge of favouritism toward high-income groups, subsidies to foreign investors and lack of regulation of privatised natural monopolies.[32] And the copper mines, nationalised by Allende, remain state-owned enterprises.

In 1990, after a democratic election, Patricio Aylwin took over the presidency on a platform that endorsed the ongoing economic policy. Some changes were introduced, including a rise in the minimum wage. In 1997, under President Eduardo Frei, the Chilean economy grew by about 7 per cent and consumer prices rose about 6 per cent.

About one-third of Chile's exports went to Asia, including Japan, in recent years. And the price of copper, its main export, fell steeply in 1997–8. Chile's balance of payments and economic activity were therefore vulnerable to the Asian crisis.

Regarding Chile's economic performance in the 1990s, Andres Bianchi former governor of the Central Bank of Chile, had this to say:

Although this improved economic performance is encouraging, it is not the most important recent development in Chile's economy. That place is taken by a revolutionary ideological change. Whereas in the past several deep ideological rifts on matters of economic management divided the Chilean establishment and the Chilean people at large, a broad consensus has now emerged about the essential elements of policy needed to grow and modernize the economy. This has far-reaching implications not only for economic growth but also for the country's social and political development.[33]

12.7   BRAZIL

Brazil is the largest country in the region in terms of both area and population and a major industrial, as well as agricultural, producer. It is second only to Russia, among all the countries in the world, in terms of its forest area.

Structural reform and therefore transformation occurred in Brazil only in the 1990s. On the other hand, Brazil has had a relatively favourable growth record. In the 1970s its GDP increased on average by 8.9 per cent annually, while its population rose 2.4 per cent per year. In the 1980s, when many Latin American economies stagnated or declined, it grew, irregularly, at an average rate of 3.1 per cent per year.

But Brazil has not achieved its full potential. It has suffered from bouts of hyperinflation: in only one year of the 1980s did its consumer prices rise at less than a three-digit rate. In 1994, inflation was about 2100 per cent. As both cause and effect of inflation, wages and many other prices were indexed to the cost of living.

At the beginning of the 1980s, Brazil was a highly regulated economy in which 60 per cent of industry consisted of state-owned enterprises. Numerous imports were banned and others were subject to extremely high tariffs – the highest in Latin America. And Brazil had, and still has, a very unequal distribution of income. Any visitor to Rio is conscious of the shanty-filled *favelas* that ring the surrounding hillsides. In contrast to residents of American cities, it is the poor who have the better views.

A new civilian government under President José Sarney (1985–90) attempted to stabilise the economy with the Cruzado plan, involving a price freeze, de-indexation, and a new currency, the *cruzado*, in which three zeros were removed from prices. The Cruzado plan and its successors failed, owing in large part to lax fiscal and monetary policies. In 1987 Sarney announced that Brazil was suspending interest payments on its foreign debt, piling up arrears.

The government of Fernando Collor de Mello, beginning in March 1990, initiated more thorough economic reforms. Especially after Marcilio Marques Moreira assumed the post of minister of economy in May 1991, the government's credibility regarding macroeconomic policy and structural reform was strengthened both at home and abroad. The budget deficit was reduced somewhat and monetary policy was tightened. On the structural side, deregulation and privatisation were begun. Import barriers were lowered and restrictions on direct investment from abroad were relaxed.

But President Collor was forced out of office as the result of a corruption scandal and in October 1992 was succeeded by his less decisive vice-president Itamar Franco, who brought in a new economic team. In his first six months in office there were four different ministers of economy and inflation soared.

Fernando Henrique Cardoso assumed the presidency on 1 January 1995. As finance minister he had nurtured a new currency – the *real* – and launched the '*real* plan' which pegged the currency to the US dollar in a slow downward crawl. He also accelerated privatisation, deregulation, and import liberalisation, among other reforms. Inflation was brought down to 6.9 per cent in 1997 and to a 3 per cent year-over-year rate in mid-1998. As a result, real wages increased and the real income of the lower income groups rose substantially.[34]

The privatisation programme has been reinforced and has served several purposes. It provides revenue to the government and thereby permits the large budget deficit to be financed with a smaller increase in government debt; it brings in foreign direct investment, which helps to finance the sizeable current-account deficit; it is expected to stimulate domestic investment by both foreign and domestic purchasers of former state-owned enterprises. The budget deficit, it may be noted, reflects mainly interest payments on government debt. The primary budget deficit, which excludes interest payments, is less than 1 per cent of GDP.

The Asian crisis strongly affected financial markets in Brazil and the central bank raised interest rate from 20 to 40 per cent in October 1997 to protect the exchange value of the *real*. The rates were later lowered but had to be raised sharply again after Russia defaulted on its debt in the summer of 1998.

As viewed in 1998, Brazil is a much more open economy than it was in 1980, with a smaller public sector and a strikingly lower rate of inflation than at the beginning of the 1990s.

Although economic progress has been achieved, Brazil is still, according to Rudiger Dornbusch, 'a reluctant and tardy performer'.[35] The distribution of income is highly unequal, much poverty exists, and there is a serious crime rate.

It is appropriate to conclude with the familiar Brazilian quip that Brazil will always have a great future.

13 Problems and Promises of an Uncertain Future

To assert that the world looked very different in 1998 from what it was in 1980 is an understatement. Who would have predicted in 1980 that the Soviet Union would cease to exist, that Russia would be a democracy that has privatised many of its state-owned enterprises or that Eastern Europe would be liberated to pursue democracy and free markets? Or that regions of China would become thriving market economies growing at a breathtaking pace? Or that the two Germanies would be unified and the process would create serious economic problems for western Germany? Or that François Mitterrand, after winning the presidency on a socialist platform would later in the 1980s be presiding over an economy hardly more socialist than its neighbours and having a strong currency and at times a lower inflation rate than Germany? Or that Mexico would abandon its import substitution policies, open its economy to the rest of the world and have shares in some of its privatised companies traded on the New York Stock Exchange along with those of many other 'emerging markets'? Or that India would rid itself of many of its tight controls over its industries and, despite memories of the East India Company, open itself to foreign investors? Or that Korea, already a 'newly industrialised country' in 1980, would achieve such a high level of real wages that some of its firms would migrate to China and Vietnam, attracted by lower wages? Or that Saudi Arabia would have a large balance-of-payments deficit? Or that in a single year more than $250 billion of private capital in various forms would flow from industrial to developing countries, bringing benefits but also creating potential problems. Or that a depreciation of Thailand's currency could ignite a crisis in East Asia that would shake the world economy?

The world has changed drastically. Because dynamic societies are much more unpredictable than those that are static, this book must end with some notes of uncertainty. My crystal ball is as cloudy as that of most economists. Someone has said that while weather forecasters can at least tell if it is currently raining, all the best economists can do is to figure out if it rained in the past. In any event the state of the world today is such that prediction would be hazardous.

Much of the transformation reviewed in this book is the story of reduced involvement of governments in economies. The point has been made again and again that governments have not done well at operating industrial enterprises and that they have over-regulated economic processes, including international transactions. Much of the world is cutting back those functions of government. Yet there are important roles for governments in seeing to it that economies operate so as to maximise the well-being of citizens. This chapter turns to that topic first. Then it presents some of the problems, challenges and hopes for the future that are thrown up by the transformations that have occurred since 1980.

13.1   THE ROLE OF GOVERNMENTS IN ECONOMIES

Precisely because so much of what has been recounted in earlier pages stresses the benefits of getting governments 'off the backs' of the public, to revert to the Thatcher–Reagan rhetoric, I want to stress here how vital some governmental activities are to the proper functioning of economies and societies. The lessening of government involvement that has been applauded has to do either with functions that the private sector is better able to carry out – such as the production and distribution of goods and services – or with excessive regulation of such functions both domestically and across national borders. What needs to be emphasised now is that there are other roles that only governments can perform and they need not be minimal.

The most obvious and least controversial governmental activities are macroeconomic policies. Monetary policy is necessarily a state function. The fact that there is a widespread trend towards making central banks independent[1] does not contradict this point. Central banks that are not required to take instructions from finance ministries are still governmental institutions. In the early years of decolonisation after the Second World War, newly-independent states made an effort to establish their identity by setting up both central banks and national airlines. The former are intrinsically in the public sector; the latter need not be, and there has been a recent tendency to privatise them.

Fiscal policy is the other arm of macroeconomic policy that is essentially a government activity. Through their budgets governments spend and tax and borrow, thereby affecting the income and output of their economies. These functions can sometimes be fashioned so as to combat recession or inflation and to encourage economic growth and price stability. At the same time the tax receipts and spending of governments vary automatically with changes in aggregate demand and in total economic activity, thereby mitigating the severity of inflations and recessions without any overt policy decisions.

The next section returns to a discussion of the present-day constraints on the utilisation of fiscal policy in the industrial countries. Here, the point is simply that monetary and fiscal policy are legitimate, and necessary, functions of government.

Those legitimate functions go well beyond macroeconomic policies. They include the provision of so-called 'public goods', and of goods and services for which there are benefits to society over and above those to the individuals consuming them – in the language of economists, 'externalities'. Governments also provide a social safety net, including unemployment compensation and other welfare payments. Regulation of the private economy in a broad range of activities from anti-trust enforcement to environmental protection is another function that only governments can perform.

Public goods are goods and services that the private economy cannot be expected to produce and sell to individual households or businesses either because they are indivisible (like national defence) or because a price cannot be charged for them (again like national defence as well as lighthouses and sidewalks) or because those who do not pay cannot be excluded from using them (like flood control). Other examples of public goods are fire and police protection and crime prevention, roads and bridges (although tolls are possible in some cases), traffic lights in cities, many forms of welfare payment, and basic research and development outlays (because the results become public knowledge and therefore private R&D activity cannot yield full financial benefits to its originators).

In other cases the goods or services could be supplied by the private sector but they are natural monopolies such as railways, ports, and public utilities. The alternatives are to let such goods or services be provided by private business with governmental regulation of their prices and terms of service or to have the government supply them. In continental Europe postal, telephone and telegraph services (PTT) are usually provided by governments while in the United States most of them are supplied privately but are regulated by government agencies.

Another category of government functions could technically be (and some are) left to the private sector but it is regarded as socially undesirable to ration them by price. Primary and secondary schools are the outstanding example here. In principle, governments could stay out of education, leaving it completely to the private economy. The result would be that those with lower incomes would be excluded at some point in the education process. Public education assures a minimum level of learning for the entire population, which is of benefit to society as a whole – not only to those who would otherwise be excluded. In other words each member of society is better off if his or her fellow-countrymen are educated. That justifies government participation, either by supplying the service directly or subsidising private education.

Enough has been said to make the point. The transformations of the period since 1980 have reduced the functions of governments. In some countries – particularly in Britain under Margaret Thatcher and in the United States under Ronald Reagan – the process went too far. Thatcher privatised natural monopolies. In America under Reagan public infrastructure was neglected to the degree that many bridges became unsafe. What requires emphasis is that in all countries – whether they already have relatively free market economies, or are in transition from central planning or are developing countries that are moving away from tight government controls and a large public enterprise sector – a significant role for government remains.

13.2 UNEMPLOYMENT IN INDUSTRIAL COUNTRIES

While inflation, along with slowing economies, were major concerns in most of Western Europe, North America and Japan in 1980, in 1998 high unemployment was a serious preoccupation in much of continental Europe. In Ireland and the United Kingdom economic growth was more vigorous than on the continent and unemployment was much lower. The US unemployment rate was 4.6 per cent in September 1998 while inflation remained surprisingly low. Japan was suffering from its worst post-war recession and deflation. Its measured unemployment rate had crept up above 4 per cent – compared with an average of 2.7 per cent in the years since 1980.

Unemployment in the European Community (which became the European Union, EU, with the coming into force of the Maastricht

Treaty in late 1993) was causing grave concern and was having political effects. It helped to bring the Socialist Party back into a majority in France in 1997 and the Social Democratic Party to power in Germany in 1998. As happened under Mitterrand in 1981, the French Socialist Party under Lionel Jospin vowed during the election campaign of 1997 to reduce the work week to 35 hours.

The unemployment problem provides a sharp contrast between Europe and the United States. US unemployment was much lower in 1998 than in 1980. In the EU, on the other hand, unemployment rose from 6.3 per cent in 1980 to a peak of 11.5 per cent in 1994 and declined to about 10.3 per cent in 1998.

The US economy created many more jobs than did Europe, not only since 1980 but in the 1970s as well. By the same token productivity rose faster in Europe. From 1979 to 1997, output per employed person in the business sector rose by 1.2 per cent per year in the United States and 2.2 per cent in the EU. But, as noted in Chapter 4, American productivity growth picked up in 1996 and 1997. Whether that was just a normal cyclical recovery or something more lasting remains to be seen.

The unemployment problem in Europe was mainly structural – 84 per cent of total unemployment in Germany and 82 per cent in France in 1992. The obvious solution to the structural umemployment problem is to reduce the cost of hiring workers. That does not require cutting wages. It does mean reducing high taxes on labour and other labour costs. In 1996 the implicit average tax rate on workers aged 55 to 64 was 49 per cent in France, 32 per cent in Germany and 12 per cent in the United States.

13.3　BALANCE-OF-PAYMENTS DEFICITS

While unemployment became a matter of greater concern in some industrial countries, worry about balance-of-payments problems receded, at least until the outbreak of the Asian crisis in 1997. In 1980 most oil-importing countries were in current-account deficit, including all industrial countries except oil-producing Norway, United Kingdom and the United States. The EC as a group moved into surplus in the mid-1980s, as did Japan. The United States current account shifted into large deficit. That same pattern prevailed in 1998. These imbalances were easily financed by private capital flows with very little attention from the general public, the financial community or governments, given the heightened mobility of capital that has been a feature of our period.

That does *not* mean that persistent current-account deficits should not be a matter for concern. If they are not matched by increased domestic investment and therefore higher growth, they can be a burden on future generations.

Beyond that, the experiences of Mexico and Thailand in the 1990s demonstrated that current-account deficits can become large enough to appear unsustainable to investors, both domestic and foreign. When that happens, the result can be a financial crisis.

13.4 THE CHANGING STATUS OF DEVELOPING COUNTRIES

A striking difference appears between the performance of the world economy in the early 1980s and the 1990s. In 1982 growth of world output slowed to 0.5 per cent as the GDP of industrial countries fell slightly and developing countries in all areas of the world except Asia experienced slowdowns in their growth rates. As is discussed in Chapter 6, in the 1990s much of the developing world, far from being dependent on what happened to the economies of industrial countries, was acting as a locomotive for them. This reversal in dependency also appears in current-account positions. The combined current account of all advanced countries shifted from a deficit of $87 billion in 1990 to a surplus of $72 billion in 1997. Much of the counterpart of that shift shows up in the enlarged deficit of LDCs, which rose from $25 billion in 1990 to $66 billion in 1997. Unemployment in the industrial countries would have been higher without this increase in demand from the developing world.

Lawrence Summers, then Chief Economist at the World Bank, wrote in 1992 about the 'linkage between industrialized country economic performance and developing country economic performance', stating that 'it appears that each 1 percentage point of growth in the industrialized world translates into an additional 4 percentage point of growth in the developing world'.[2] From the experience of recent years, that link may now have been broken.

More broadly, the philosophy of *dependencia* has been shown to be irrelevant and that should encourage further reforms along the lines of what we have observed in Mexico, among others.

13.5   COPING WITH CAPITAL MOBILITY

We have seen that the increase in capital mobility has brought benefits, particularly to developing countries. But it has also created problems or exacerbated problems that have led to crises.

In particular, banking crises and balance-of-payments crises have become more prevalent. IMF Managing Director Michel Camdessus stated at the annual meeting of the IMF in 1996: 'In many countries, a banking crisis is an accident waiting to happen.' He called the fragility of national banking systems 'the Achilles' heel of the global economy today'.[3]

Banking crises have been especially prevalent in the developing world in part because liberalisation of financial systems has been carried out in the absence of adequate regulation and supervision. Another reason is that banks are dominant in the financial systems of many developing countries; the share of banks in total financial assets in 1994 was 91 per cent in Indonesia, 75 per cent in Thailand, and 87 per cent in Mexico but only 23 per cent in the United States.[4] In those conditions, a banking crisis can either cause or result from a balance-of-payments crisis. That was evident in Asia in 1997–8, where, in some cases, banks borrowed abroad without hedging their foreign exchange risk and where banks were directed by public officials to lend to specific industries regardless of their creditworthiness.

The Basle Committee on Banking Supervision had recommended a capital adequacy standard of 8 per cent for internationally-active banks. That accord was amended in 1996 to incorporate market risks.

A number of other reports and recommendations have been made by various international bodies including the Group of Seven Summit meetings in Halifax in 1995 and in Lyon in 1996, the Deputies of the Group of Ten, and the Institute of International Finance. In September 1997, the BIS published 25 'Core Principles for Effective Banking Supervision'. Finally, the IMF in January 1998 disseminated a paper entitled 'Toward a Framework for Financial Stability'. It is concerned with financial sector issues that could have major macro-economic implications. Incorporating the Basle Core Principles, it outlines how IMF surveillance of member countries will focus on banking institutions 'that have the potential to create systemic problems domestically or internationally'.[5]

The expression that came to be used was 'global financial architecture'. According to Prime Minister Tony Blair, the Group of Seven Summit meeting in Birmingham on 15 May 1998 agreed that there was an urgent need to strengthen that architecture so as to reduce the risk of crises, such as that in Asia, and 'to produce a system more resistant to shocks when crises do occur'.[6]

13.6   THE ROLE OF THE INTERNATIONAL MONETARY FUND

While the IMF has been an active participant in the international efforts to deal with the Mexican and Asian crises, it has come in for criticisms in some quarters, especially in the United States in connection with the proposed enlargement of its resources.

The most common criticism is that the availability of credits from the Fund creates moral hazard – that is, it induces both governments and investors to take risks in the knowledge that the Fund will 'bail them out'. These critics would leave it to free markets to deal with international financial crises.

The weakness in these arguments is that they fail to acknowledge that governments borrowing from the IMF have to meet stringent policy conditions that are often painful. 'In other words, the IMF is not just a lending institution. It is also a disciplinarian, representing the rest of the world in its dealings with countries in need of balance-of-payments financing and economic and financial reform'.[7] Furthermore, most investors are not 'bailed out'. Surely, many buyers of securities in Thailand, Korea and Indonesia suffered heavy losses in 1997–8.

In this world of highly mobile capital there is a definite need for an international lender. That is a function of the IMF – the closest thing we have to a world central bank. Its purpose is to deal with crises in individual countries so as to minimise harmful effects on other countries. The notion that market forces could substitute for this function seems far-fetched.

13.7   GLOBALISATION

Implicit in much of the transformation we are concerned with is the phenomenon of 'globalisation' – a term that came into common use during the period we have covered. Although the word appears on page 1 of both the earlier and the present edition of this book, the concept was not focused on.

What is globalisation? It is the increase in economic and financial linkages among the countries of the world – often referred to as growing interdependence.[8] Those linkages occur through international trade in goods and services, flows of capital, migration and international travel. The striking increase in the movement of private capital to developing countries is brought out in Chapter 6. More generally, cross-border transactions in bonds and stocks rose from 9 per cent to 152 per cent of GDP between 1980 and 1996 in the United States, from 7.7 to 83 per cent in Japan, and from 7.5 to 197 per cent in Germany. Foreign direct investment from advanced countries quintupled from 1980 to 1996.

The volume of trade in goods and services grew one-third faster than world output in the 1980s and more than twice as fast as world output in the 1990s. That acceleration from one decade to the other was accounted for mainly by the speedup in the growth of both exports and imports of developing countries; while the exports of advanced countries (industrial countries plus the four Asian tigers and Israel) grew about one-fourth faster in the 1990s, the export growth of developing countries more than quadrupled from 2.1 per cent per year in the 1980s to 8.9 per cent annually in the 1990s. International travel receipts for all countries of the world rose from $95 billion in 1980 to about $390 billion in 1996.[9]

Much of the explanation for the increased globalisation lies in computer technology and the so-called information revolution, as is discussed in Chapter 6. Also important has been the declining relative cost of transportation, along with reduced tariffs and other trade barriers. As Martin Wolf has pointed out, the unit cost of sea freight 'fell 70 per cent in real terms between the beginning of the 1980s and 1996'.[10]

While these facts may be impressive, it is important to keep them in historical perspective. In the late nineteenth and early twentieth centuries trade was a large fraction of output in the United Kingdom and other European countries.[11] And capital flows were also of substantial magnitude in those years.[12]

As Paul Krugman has written,

It is a late-twentieth century conceit that we invented the global economy just yesterday. In fact, world markets achieved an impressive degree of integration during the second half of the nineteenth century. Indeed, if one wants a specific date for the beginning of a truly global economy, one might well choose 1869, the year in which both the Suez Canal and the Union Pacific railroad were completed. By the eve of the First World War steamships and railroads had created markets for standardized commodities, like wheat and wool, that were fully global in their reach. Even the global flow of information was better than modern observers, focused on electronic technology, tend to realize: the first submarine telegraph cable was laid under the Atlantic in 1858, and by 1900 all the world's major economic regions could effectively communicate instantaneously.[13]

What has changed are the facts that (1) a larger number of countries are participating in globalisation, as developing countries also export manufactured goods and advanced countries import them; (2) much of the commerce involves intra-industry trade and what has come to be called outsourcing; (3) manufactured products are much more complex and differentiated today; and (4) a significant amount of trade is now shipped by air freight.

It is also noteworthy that despite the apparently large outflows of capital from industrial countries recently, there remains a distinct 'home bias'. Their portfolio investment in developing countries in 1994 – amounting to $250 billion – represented less than one-half of one per cent of total portfolio holdings in industrial countries.[14]

While this process of increased international integration and interdependence brings clear economic benefits, it has its critics. Dani Rodrik has spelled out the nature of the problems created by globalisation: workers with low skills can be harmed; conflict arises as the result of competition from countries with lower norms for social institutions such as minimum wages and child labour; and social safety nets may be weakened. He concludes not that globalisation should be reversed but that, to prevent a backlash against it, social cohesion should be strengthened via various forms of social insurance and tax preferences.[15]

13.8 THE NEED FOR POLICY COORDINATION

A result of globalisation is that countries' economies have a bigger impact on each other than in the past. A policy change in any one country has greater significance for its neighbours than before, even when those neighbours are separated by oceans.

The obvious implication of these facts is that policymakers should take account of these linkages among their economies when making their decisions. A process of policy coordination was implemented in the 1980s among nations of the Group of Seven. That process need not be continuous. Only from time to time is coordinated action needed or possible. The process has been compared with the function of firefighters sitting idly in the firestation apparently wasting taxpayers' funds. Only when a fire breaks out does their usefulness to society become evident. A case can be made for nurturing that coordination process and widening it beyond the Group of Seven.[16]

13.9   NATIONALISM AND FUNDAMENTALISM

The barbarism in what was Yugoslavia is a flagrant expression of revived nationalism. Nationalism or ethnic conflict has been in evidence elsewhere too: in some regions of Africa, in some of the states of the former Soviet Union, in Turkey and Iraq and in attitudes and actions towards immigrants or long-resident foreign nationals in some European countries. A similar concern is the rise of militant religious fundamentalism evident from Afghanistan westward through parts of the Middle East and North Africa. In some places the two tendencies are combined in religious nationalism. There is little I can say about these worrying tendencies except to record their existence here as problems for the future.

13.10   THE UNCERTAIN FUTURE

As one looks to the future of the world economy in the autumn of 1998, two principal uncertainties present themselves.

One is how seriously the world economy will be affected by the crisis that started in Asia in 1997. In October 1998, the IMF lowered its projection for the growth of world output to 2 per cent in 1998 and $2\frac{1}{2}$ per cent in 1999. Japan's economy was contracting by $2\frac{1}{2}$ per cent in 1998 and Korea by 7 per cent. While Russia's economic performance has a relatively small real external effect, its crisis was having psychological contagion impacts and its political future is clearly of major concern to the rest of the world.

The other uncertainty, which does not necessarily involve a crisis, pertains to how EMU will work. Will this historically unique development – a common currency and single monetary policy among independent sovereign countries – bring prosperity and stability to the member countries of EMU? And how will it affect the functioning of the world economy and its international monetary arrangements?

13.11   THE BASIS FOR FUTURE PROSPERITY

One of the fundamental truths of economic life – self-evident though it may be – is that rising living standards depend on advancing productivity. Growth in output per person employed and per unit of capital equipment has been the explanation for the enormous increase in economic well-being in the world since the industrial revolution began in England. Output per person of a country can also rise if a greater proportion of the population is working. But there are limits to the extent to which that ratio can be increased. Basically we come back to productivity.

There is everything to be said therefore in favour of policies that enhance competition. The significant improvement in the attractiveness of American automobiles to consumers and the productivity of their producers can be attributed to the competition from Japanese cars. The striking economic progress that we have observed in numerous developing countries is based in part on the productivity-enhancing effects of competition from imports.

While we face a future fraught with uncertainties, it is well to remember that the good society is one in which economic and political freedom are maximised. The economic transformations since 1980 have improved well-being in most countries where they have occurred. The lesson is that economic and political freedom enhance welfare but that governments still have important roles to play.

Notes

1. Introduction

1 T. Gylfason, T. T. Herbertsson and G. Zoega, 'Ownership and Growth', *Centre for Economic Policy Research Discussion Paper Series,* no. 1900 (June 1998).
2. S. V. Zhukov and A. Y. Vorobyov, 'Reforming the Soviet Union: Lessons from Structural Experience', in *Wider Working Papers* (Helsinki: World Institute for Development Economic Research of the United Nations University, November 1991) p. 3.
3. 'Chinese Feel the Strain of a New Society', *Washington Post* (17 June 1993) p. Al.
4. *New York Times* (1 April 1993) Sec. IV, p. 1.
5. I. Berlin, 'The Hedgehog and the Fox', *Russian Thinkers* (New York: Viking, 1978) pp. 22–81.
6. I. Berlin, *Personal Impressions* (New York: Viking, 1980) pp. 27–8.

3 Changing Philosophies of Economic Policy

1. N. Lawson, *The View from No. 11: Memoirs of a Tory Radical* (London: Bantam 1992) pp. 946–7.
2. J. Newhouse, 'The Gamefish', *The New Yorker* (10 February 1986).
3. A. Walters, *Britain's Economic Renaissance* (Oxford University Press, 1986) p. 4.
4. D. D'Souza, *Ronald Reagan* (New York: The Free Press, 1997) pp. 33–84.
5. D. T. Regan, *For the Record: From Wall Street to Washington* (New York: Harcourt Brace Jovanovich, 1988) pp. 142ff.
6. D. Stockman, *The Triumph of Politics: How the Reagan Revolution Failed* (New York: Harper & Row, 1986) p. 76.
7. G. Gilder, *Wealth and Poverty* (New York: Basic Books, 1981).
8. R. L. Bartley, *The Seven Fat Years* (New York: The Free Press, 1992).
9. P. C. Roberts, 'The Keynesian Attack on Mr Reagan', *Wall Street Journal* (19 March 1981).
10. P. C. Roberts, *The Supply-Side Revolution* (Cambridge, Mass.: Harvard University Press, 1984).
11. O. J. Blanchard, 'Reaganomics', *Economic Policy,* 2 (October 1987) pp. 17–48.
12. Remarks at the New York Financial Writers' Dinner, 14 April 1981, *Department of the Treasury News.*
13. Letter to *New York Times* (5 June 1991).
14. Bartley, *The Seven Fat Years*, p. 6.
15. B. Bosworth and G. Burtless, 'Effects of Tax Reform on Factor Supply, Investment, and Saving', *Journal of Economic Perspectives*, 6 (Winter

1992) pp. 3–25; M. A. Akhtar and E. S. Harris, 'The Supply-Side Consequences of U.S. Fiscal Policy in the 1980s', *Quarterly Review*, Federal Reserve Bank of New York, 17 (Spring 1992) pp. 1–20.

16. Statement of the Honorable Beryl W. Sprinkel, Under Secretary for Monetary Affairs, Before the Joint Economic Committee, 4 May 1981, *Department of the Treasury News*.

17. *Washington Post* (17 October 1992) p. A1.

18. P. Favier and M. Martin-Roland, *La Décennie Mitterrand* (Paris: Editions du Seuil, vol. 1, 1991) p. 41. I draw on this valuable work and on volume 2 (1991) for the story of developments in France.

19. K. Okamura, 'Background Paper: Japan's Medium- and Long-Term Fiscal Challenges,' in B. B. Aghevli, T. Bayoumi and G. Meredith (eds), *Structural Change in Japan* (Washington: International Monetary Fund, 1998) pp. 217–20.

20. M. Hellwig and M. Neumann, 'Germany under Kohl', *Economic Policy*, 5 (October 1987) pp. 113–14.

21. J. Williamson, *The Progress of Policy Reform in Latin America* (Washington: Institute for International Economics, January 1990) pp. 9–33.

4 America and Britain

1. P. Volcker and T. Gyohten, *Changing Fortunes* (New York: Times Books, 1992) ch. 6.

2. Bank for International Settlements, *55th Annual Report* (10 June 1985) p. 147.

3. M. N. Baily, G. Burtless and R. E. Litan, *Growth with Equity: Economic Policymaking for the Next Century* (Washington: The Brookings Institution, 1993) ch. 3.

4. *Washington Post* (28 June 1998) p. A24.

5. P. Kennedy, *The Rise and Fall of the Great Powers* (New York: Random House, 1987).

6. J. S. Nye, Jr., *Bound to Lead* (New York: Basic Books, 1990); H. R. Nau, *The Myth of America's Decline* (New York: Oxford University Press, 1990).

7. McKinsey Global Institute, *Capital Productivity* (Washington, June 1996).

8. N. Lawson, *The View From No. 11: Memoirs of a Tory Radical* (London: Bantam, 1992) pp. 64–5.

9. Ibid., p. 415.

10. Ibid., p. 70.

11. C. Johnson, *The Economy Under Mrs Thatcher, 1979–90* (London: Penguin, 1991) p. 41.

12. *Journal of Commerce* (24 March 1981) p. 4.

13. Lawson, *The View from No. 11*, pp. 88–9.

14. K. Matthews and P. Minford, 'Mrs. Thatcher's Economic Policies, 1979–1987', *Economic Policy*, 5 (October 1987) pp. 62–3.

15. A. Walters, *Britain's Economic Renaissance* (New York: Oxford University Press, 1986) pp. 140–1.
16. Lawson, *The View from No. 11*, p. 652.
17. M. Thatcher, *The Downing Street Years* (New York: HarperCollins, 1993) p. 701.
18. M. Wolf, 'From Delusion to Devaluation', *Financial Times*, 30 September 1992, p. 14.
19. Lawson, *The View from No. 11*, p. 835.
20. Thatcher, *Downing Street Years*, pp. 715–18.
21. Lawson, *The View from No. 11*, pp. 867–73. He put this proposal in a memorandum to the prime minister in November 1988.
22. *The Economist* (16 September 1989) pp. 15–16.
23. Ibid. (7 October 1989) pp. 13–14.
24. D. Healey, *The Time of My Life* (New York: W. W. Norton, 1989) p. 150.
25. *New York Times* (28 February 1993) p. 9.
26. *Financial Times* (2 April 1998) p. 10.

5 Adjusting to Shocks in France, Germany and Japan

1. D. Singer, *Is Socialism Doomed? The Meaning of Mitterrand* (New York: Oxford University Press, 1988) pp. 78–92.
2. P. Favier and M. Martin-Roland, *La Décennie Mitterrand* (Paris: Editions Du Seuil, 1991) vol. 2, p. 389.
3. E. Aeschimann and P. Riché, *La Guerre de Sept Ans* (Paris: Calmann-Lévy, 1996) p. 85.
4. C. Imbert, 'The End of French Exceptionalism', *Foreign Affairs*, 68 (Fall 1989) pp. 48–60.
5. *Washington Post* (2 June 1998) p. A7.
6. Ibid.
7. K. Biedenkopf, 'Germany in a New Europe', in A. B. Shingleton, M. J. Gibbon and K. S. Mack (eds), *Dimensions of German Unification* (Boulder, Co. Westview, 1995) p. 212.
8. Deutsche Bundesbank, *Monthly Report* (October 1997) p. 28.
9. Interview in The *New York Times* (29 December 1992) p. C11.
10. In a preface to A. Stead, *Great Japan: A Study in National Efficiency*, cited in C. Wood, *The Bubble Economy* (New York: Atlantic Monthly Press, 1992) pp. 14–15.
11. A detailed presentation of financial market liberalisation may be found in *OECD Economic Surveys: Japan 1990–1991* (Paris: Organization for Economic Cooperation and Development, 1991) pp. 137–47.
12. Wood, *The Bubble Economy*, p. 50.
13. Ibid., p. 60.
14. *Wall Street Journal* (1 June 1998) p. A1.
15. A. Posen, *Restoring Japan's Economic Growth* (Washington: Institute for International Economics, 1998) p. 53.
16 *The Economist* (21 February 1998) p. 74.
17. *New York Times* (9 November 1993) p. A7.

18. E. J. Lincoln and R. E. Litan, 'The "Big Bang"', *The Brookings Review* (Winter 1998) pp. 37–40.
19. *Financial Times* Survey (19 September 1997) p. iv.

6 Economic Interactions and Economic Integration

1. This point is made in the Background Paper by R. Solomon in *Partners in Prosperity*, The Report of the Twentieth Century Fund Task Force on the International Coordination of National Economic Policies (New York: Priority Press, 1991) pp. 60–1.
2. M. Feldstein and C. Horioka, 'Domestic Saving and International Capital Flows', *Economic Journal*, 90 (1980) pp. 314–29.
3. A. Dean, M. Durand, J. Fallon and P. Hoeller, 'Saving Trends and Behavior in OECD Countries', *OECD Economic Studies*, 14 (Spring 1990) pp. 8–58; L. L. Tesar, 'Savings, Investment and International Capital Flows', *Journal of International Economics*, 31 (August 1991) pp. 55–78; W. J. Jansen, 'The Feldstein–Horioka Test of International Capital Mobility: Is It Feasible?', *Working Paper of the International Monetary Fund*, 96/100 (Washington: International Monetary Fund, September 1996).
4. R. Solomon, 'The United States as a Debtor in the 19th Century', *Brookings Discussion Papers in International Economics*, 28 (May 1985) and in 'Endettement, Flexibilité et Régulation des Financiers', in *Economies et Sociétés*, Cahiers de l'Institut de Sciences Mathématiques et Économiques Appliquées, XIX (September 1985).
5. R. O'Brien, *Global Financial Integration: The End of Geography* (New York: Royal Institute of International Affairs, Council on Foreign Relations, 1992) p. 48.
6. N. Lawson, *The View From No. 11: Memoirs of a Tory Radical* (London: Bantam 1992) p. 538.
7. D. T. Regan, *For the Record* (New York: Harcourt Brace Jovanovich, 1988).
8. For this and a detailed inside story on exchange-rate negotiations see Y. Funabashi, *Managing the Dollar: From the Plaza to the Louvre* (Washington: Institute for International Economics, 1988).
9. P. Volcker and T. Gyohten, *Changing Fortunes* (New York: Times Books, 1992) p. 279.
10. Ibid., p. 268.
11. E. Hoffmeyer, *The International Monetary System: An Essay in Interpretation* (Amsterdam: North-Holland, 1992) p. 215.
12. S. Marris, *Deficits and the Dollar: The World Economy at Risk* (Washington: Institute for International Economics, 1985).
13. M. Dealtry and J. Van't dack, 'The US External Deficit and Associated Shifts in International Portfolios', *BIS Economic Papers*, 25 (September 1989).
14. For a thorough treatment of these developments see H. Ungerer, *A Concise History of European Monetary Integration* (Westport, Conn.: Quorum Books 1997).

15. Ibid., p. 179.
16. Ibid., p. 266.
17. Speech by the Rt Hon. Baroness Thatcher, OM, FRS to the CNN World Economic Development Congress on Saturday, 19 September 1992, Washington, DC.
18. P. Cecchini, *The European Challenge: 1992* (Aldershot: Gower, 1988).
19. R. Baldwin, 'On the Growth Effects of 1992', *National Bureau of Economic Research Working Paper Series*, Working Paper no. 3119 (September 1989).
20. A. Szasz, 'Towards a Single European Currency: Ecu, Franc-Fort, Question-Mark', in O. K. Fair and R. Raymand (eds), *The New Europe: Evolving Economic and Financial Systems in East and West* (Dordrecht: Kluwer Academic, 1993) p. 221.
21. See, for example, P. B. Kenen, *EMU After Maastricht* (Washington: Group of Thirty, 1992); C. R. Bean, 'Economic and Monetary Union in Europe', *Centre for Economic Policy Research Discussion Paper Series*, no. 722 (October 1992); and W. H. Buiter, G. Corsetti, and N. Roubini, '"Excessive Deficits": Sense and Nonsense in the Treaty of Maastricht', *Centre for Economic Policy Research Discussion Paper Series*, no. 750 (December 1992).
22. Group of Ten, *International Capital Movements and Foreign Exchange Markets*, A Report to the Ministers and Governors by the Group of Deputies (9 April 1993) p. 37.
23. P. B. Kenen, *Economic and Monetary Union in Europe* (Cambridge University Press, 1995) pp. 88–90.
24. On these questions, see P. R. Masson, T. H. Krueger, and B. G. Turtelboom (eds), *EMU and the International Monetary System* (Washington: International Monetary Fund, 1997).
25. Bean, 'Economic and Monetary Union in Europe', p. 35.
26. Ungerer, *A Concise History of European Monetary Integration*, p. 253.
27. G. Hufbauer and J. J. Schott, *NAFTA: An Assessment* (Washington: Institute for International Economics, February 1993) p. 1.

7 The Elements of Economic Reform: Eastern Europe

1. S. Fischer, 'Privatization in East European Transformation', in C. Clague and G. C. Rausser (eds), *The Emergence of Market Economies in Eastern Europe* (Cambridge, Mass. and Oxford: Blackwell, 1992) p. 230.
2. A. Maddison, *The World Economy in the Twentieth Century* (Paris: Development Centre of the Organisation for Economic Cooperation and Development, 1989) pp. 38, 126.
3. S. Fischer, *Russia and the Soviet Union: Then and Now*, National Bureau of Economic Research, Working Paper no. 4077 (May 1992) pp. 17–18.
4. D. Lipton and J. Sachs, 'Creating a Market Economy in Eastern Europe: The Case of Poland', *Brookings Papers on Economic Activity* (1:1990) p. 78.

5. Quoted in S. Fischer and A. Gelb, 'The Process of Socialist Economic Transformation', *Journal of Economic Perspectives*, 5 (February 1991) p. 91.
6. L. Balcerowicz, 'Common Fallacies in the Debate on the Economic Transition in Central and Eastern Europe', European Bank for Reconstruction and Development, *Working Papers,* no. 11 (October 1993) p. 3.
7. European Bank for Reconstruction and Development, *Transition report update* (April 1998) p. 7.
8. International Monetary Fund, *World Economic Outlook* (October 1992), pp. 45–6.
9. S. Thomas, 'The Politics and Economics of Privatization in Central and Eastern Europe', *The Columbia Journal of World Business*, XXVIII (Spring 1993) p. 169.
10. EBRD, *Transition report update 1998*, p. 12.
11. *Financial Times* (6 April 1993) p. 2.
12. A. Robinson, *Financial Times* (3 July 1992) Sec. III, p. I.
13. *The Economist* (11 October 1997) p. 61.
14. *Financial Times* (12 May 1998), p. 2.
15. A. Schwartz, 'Market Failure and Corruption in the Czech Republic', *Transition* (The World Bank) (December 1997) pp. 4–5.
16. *Financial Times* (20 April 1998) p. 2.
17. For a good general discussion of these points see J. Nellis and S. Kikeri, 'The Privatization of Public Enterprises', in S. El-Naggar, *Privatization and Structural Adjustment in the Arab Countries* (Washington: International Monetary Fund, 1989) pp. 50–80 and European Bank for Reconstruction and Development *Annual Economic Outlook* (September 1993).
18. EBRD, *Transition report update 1998*, p. 21.
19. EBRD, *Transition report 1997*, pp. 148–213.
20. *EBRD, Transition report update 1998*, pp. 12–13.
21. IMF, *World Economic Outlook* (October 1997) p. 17.

8   Chaos and Reform in the Soviet Union and Russia

1. E. A. Hewett, *Reforming the Soviet Economy: Equity versus Efficiency* (Washington: The Brookings Institution, 1988) pp. 37–8.
2. M. Gorbachev, *Perestroika: New Thinking for Our Country and the World* (New York: Harper & Row, 1987) pp. 18–19.
3. *A Study of the Soviet Economy* (International Monetary Fund, World Bank, Organisation for Economic Cooperation and Development, European Bank for Reconstruction and Development, February 1991) vol. 1, p. 12.
4. A. Maddison, *The World Economy in the 20th Century* (Paris: Development Centre of the Organisation for Economic Cooperation and Development, 1989) pp. 81, 91.
5. K. Tidmarsh, 'Russia's Work Ethic', *Foreign Affairs*, 72 (Spring 1993) pp. 67–77.

6   Hewett, *Reforming the Soviet Economy*, p. 81.
7.   D. C. Diller (ed.), *Russia and the Independent States* (Washington: *Congressional Quarterly*, 1993) p. 108.
8.   E. A. Hewett with C. A. Gaddy, *Open for Business: Russia's Return to the Global Economy* (Washington: The Brookings Institution, 1992) p. 96.
9.   Hewett, *Reforming the Soviet Economy*, pp. 390–1.
10. A. Åslund, *How Russia Became a Market Economy* (Washington: The Brookings Institution, 1995) p. 27.
11. *The Economist* (8 May 1993) p. 79.
12. D. Remnick, *Lenin's Tomb: The Last Days of the Soviet Empire* (New York: Random House, 1993) p. 477.
13. G. Arbatov, *The System* (New York: Times Books, 1992) pp. 345–6.
14. Remnick, *Lenin's Tomb*, p. 500.
15. R. G. Kaiser, *Why Gorbachev Happened* (New York: Touchstone, 1992) p. 437.
16. G. W. Breslauer, 'Evaluating Gorbachev as Leader', in E. A. Hewitt and V. H. Winston (eds), *Milestones in Glasnost and Perestroika*, vol. 2, *Politics and People* (Washington: The Brookings Institution, 1991) pp. 390–430.
17. Kaiser, *Why Gorbachev Happened*, p. 460
18. Diller, *Russia and the Independent States*, p. 306.
19. *Financial Times* (27 May 1993) 'Survey of Russia', p. I.
20. *New York Times* (21 January 1994) p. A1.
21. Åslund, *How Russia Became A Market Economy*, p. 205.
22. IMF, *World Economic Outlook* (May 1998) p. 100.
23. EBRD, *Transition Report Update 1998* p. 12.
24. EBRD, *Transition Report, 1997*, p. 14.
25. *OECD Economic Surveys, 1997–1998: Russian Federation* (Paris: OECD, 1997) pp. 139–42.
26. D. Remnick, *Resurrection: The Struggle for a New Russia* (New York: Random House, 1997) p. 177.
27. EBRD, *Transition Report, 1997*, p. 195.
28   C. G. Gaddy and B. W. Ickes, 'Russia: Virtual Economy' *Foreign Affairs*, September/October 1998.
29. A. Åslund, 'If the Ruble Goes Under, So Could the Region', *Washington Post* (12 July 1998) p. C2.

9   From Mao to Zhu: Economic Reform in China

1.   'A Survey of China', *The Economist* (28 November 1992) p. 6.
2.   *China 2020* (Washington: The World Bank, 1997) p. 97.
3.   J. K. Fairbank, *China: A New History* (Cambridge, Mass.: Harvard University Press, 1992) p. 385. I rely on this valuable work for descriptions of the Great Leap Forward and the Cultural Revolution.
4.   Ibid., pp. 402–3.
5.   Ibid., p. 410.
6.   H. Harding, *China's Second Revolution* (Washington: The Brookings Institution, 1987) p. 30. For the period up to 1987 I rely heavily on this valuable book.

7. A. Hussein and N. Stern, 'Effective Demand, Enterprise Reforms and Public Finance in China', *Economic Policy*, 12 (April 1991) p. 145.
8. Fairbank, *China*, p. 412.
9. *Financial Times*, Survey (16 June 1992) p. vi.
10. H. Cheng, 'Promoting Township and Village Enterprises as a Growth Strategy in China', in M. Guitian and R. Mundell (eds), *Inflation and Growth in China* (Washington: International Monetary Fund, 1996) p. 171.
11. C. C. Smith, 'Municipal-Run Firms Helped Build China; Now, They're Faltering', *Wall Street Journal* (8 October 1997) p. A1.
12. *China 2020*, p. 32.
13. World Bank, *Transition* (October 1997) p. 3.
14. M. W. Bell, H. E. Khor and K. Kochhar, *China at the Threshold of a Market Economy* (Washington: International Monetary Fund, Occasional Paper 107, September 1993) pp. 3–4.
15. S. Wudunn, 'The God of Wealth', in N. D. Kristof and S. Wudunn, *China Wakes* (New York: Times Books, 1994) p. 343
16. *New York Times* (15 August 1993) Sec. I, p. 7.
17. *Financial Times* (2 March 1998) p. 3.
18. N. Lardy, 'Banking as a Constraint to China's Growth', paper presented at Allied Social Science Associations Annual Convention, 5 January 1998.
19. *China 2020*, p. 29.
20. *Financial Times* (2 April 1998) p. 4.
21. *Financial Times* (7–8 March 1998) p. 3.
22. A. Maddison, *Chinese Economic Performance in the Long Run* (Paris: Development Centre of the OECD, 1988).
23. *Financial Times* (20 January 1994) p. 4.
24. C. C. Smith, 'Foreign Investors Break Loose From Chinese Partners', *Wall Street Journal* (11 June 1998) p. A17.
25. B. P. Bosworth and G. Ofer, *Reforming Planned Economies in an Integrating World Economy* (Washington: The Brookings Institution, 1995) pp. 59–60.
26. 'A Survey of China', *The Economist* (28 November 1992) p. 4.
27. *Wall Street Journal* (3 September 1993) p. A6
28. *New York Times* (11 April 1993) Sec.I, p. 1.
29. *New York Times* (6 September 1993) p. A1.
30. L. Summers, 'The Rise of China', *International Economic Insights*, 3 (May/June 1992) p. 17.

10 Other Asia: Dragons, Tigers and an Elephant

1. World Bank, *The East Asian Miracle* (New York: Oxford University Press, 1993) p. 133.
2. See, for example, *The Economist* (2 October 1993) pp. 18–20, 41–2; *Financial Times* (27 September 1993) pp. 3, 27; A. Fishlow, C. Gwin, A. Haggard, D. Rodrik, R. Wade, *Miracle or Design? Lessons From The East Asian Experience* (Washington: Overseas Development Council,

1994); J. E. Campos and H. L. Root, *The Key to the Asian Miracle: Making Shared Growth Credible* (Washington: The Brookings Institution, 1996).
3. World Bank, *The East Asian Miracle*, pp. 5–6.
4. Ibid., p. 354.
5. E. F. Vogel, *The Four Little Dragons: The Spread of Industrialization in East Asia* (Cambridge, Mass.: Harvard University Press, 1991) p. 50.
6. Campos and Root, *The Key to the Asian Miracle*, p. 65.
7. C. Soon, *The Dynamics of Korean Economic Development* (Washington: Institute for International Economics, 1994) p. 118.
8. World Bank, *The East Asian Miracle*, p. 130.
9. Soon, *The Dynamics of Korean Economic Development*, p. 192.
10. *Financial Times*, Survey (31 August 1992) p. III.
11. *Financial Times* (30 March 1998) p. 3.
12. M. Goldstein, *The Asian Financial Crisis: Causes, Cures, and Systemic Implications* (Washington: Institute for International Economics, June 1998) p. 18.
13. IMF, *World Economic Outlook* (May 1997) p. 131; (October 1998) Advance Copy, p. 34.
14. J. Eccheverri-Gent, 'Economic Reform in India: A Long and Winding Road', in *Economic Reform in Three Giants, U.S.–Third World Policies Perspectives*, no. 11, Overseas Development Council (New Brunswick, NJ: Transaction Books, 1990) p. 104.
15. *Washington Post* (19 September 1997) p. A16.
16. J. Bhagwati, *India in Transition: Freeing the Economy* (Oxford: Clarendon Press, 1993) pp. 49–50.
17. Ibid., pp. 46–7.
18. Ibid., p. 79.
19. Ibid., p. 80.
20. Ibid., p. 69.
21. J. Bhagwati and T. N. Srinivasan, *India's Economic Reforms* (New Delhi: Ministry of Finance, July 1993). A report prepared at the invitation of Finance Minister Manmohan Singh.
22. Ibid., pp. 48–52.

11 Middle East and Africa: Oil, Wealth and Poverty

1. E. R. Fried and P. H. Trezise, *Oil Security: Retrospect and Prospect* (Washington: The Brookings Institution, 1993) p. 10.
2. M. H. Hamilton, 'Oil Powers Consider Broader Group Than OPEC', *Washington Post* (30 June 1998) p. E3.
3. A. Richards and J. Waterbury, *A Political Economy of the Middle East* (Boulder, Colo.: Westview, 1990) p. 247.
4. Ibid., p. 248.
5. J. Barham, 'Turkish Ministers Bow to the Generals', *Financial Times* (8 July 1998) p. 3.
6. F. Al-Farsy, *Modernity and Tradition: The Saudi Equation* (London: Kegan Paul International, 1990) p. xxii.

7. *The Economist*, Survey (13 February 1982) p. 4.
8. *New York Times* (3 January 1994) p. A3.
9. *Financial Times*, Survey (5 May 1981) p. x. Data from World Bank, *World Development Report* (New York: Oxford University Press, various issues).
10. M. Huband, 'Control stays with the ruling families,' *Financial Times* (26 March 1998) Survey, p. III.
11. *Financial Times*, Survey (12 May 1998) p. XII.
12. S. El-Naggar, 'Investment Policies in the Arab Countries: The Basic Issues', in S. El-Naggar (ed.), *Investment Policies in the Arab Countries* (Washington: International Monetary Fund, 1990) p. 8.
13. D. Cohen, 'Growth and External Debt: A New Perspective on the African and Latin American Tragedies,' Centre for Economic Policy Research Discussion Paper no. 1753 (December 1997).
14. UN, *World Economic and Social Survey 1997*, pp. 29–30.
15. *World Development Indicators, 1998* (The World Bank, 1998, CD Rom).
16. See C. Madavo and J. Sarbib, 'Africa on the Move: Attracting Private Capital To A Changing Continent', *The Sais Review* (Summer-Fall 1997) pp. 111–126.
17. *Global Development Finance, 1998*, Country Tables (Washington, DC: The World Bank, 1998) pp. 38, 492.
18. *Wall Street Journal* (10 June 1998) p. A15.
19. W. Ryrie, *First World, Third World* (London: Macmillan, 1995) p. 214.
20. *Financial Times*, Survey (24 March 1998) p. IV.

12 Democratisation and Reform in Latin America

1. *World Debt Tables, 1989–90* (Washington, DC: The World Bank, 1989) p. 94.
2. R. Solomon, 'The Debt of Developing Countries: Another Look', *Brookings Papers on Economic Activity* 2 (1981) pp. 602, 605.
3. The details of the Mexican crisis and how it was handled are graphically set forth in J. Kraft, *The Mexican Rescue* (New York: Group of Thirty, 1984).
4. R. Solomon, 'An Overview of the International Debt Crisis', in H. Scholl (ed.), *International Finance and Financial Policy* (Westport, Conn.: Quorum Books, 1990) p. 136.
5. N. Lustig, *Mexico: The Remaking of an Economy* (Washington: The Brookings Institution, 1992) p. 46.
6. W. R. Cline, *International Debt Reexamined* (Washington: Institute for International Economics, February 1995) pp. 209–10.
7. *Global Development Finance, 1998* (Washington: World Bank, 1998) p. 26.
8. B. Larre, 'Mexico', *The OECD Observer*, 178 (November 1992) p. 40.
9. M. J. Francis, 'Dependency: Ideology, Fad, and Fact', in M. Novak and M. P. Jackson (eds), *Latin America: Dependency or Interdependence?* (Washington: American Enterprise Institute for Public Policy Research, 1985) pp. 88–105.

10.   P. Aspe, *Economic Transformation: The Mexican Way* (Cambridge: MIT Press, 1993) p. 224.
11.   *The Economist* (6 September 1997) p. 31.
12.   Volcker and Gyohten, *Changing Fortunes*, p. 199.
13.   See Lustig, *Mexico*, pp. 26–8.
14.   Ibid., p. 39.
15.   Aspe, *Economic Transformation*, pp. 22–4.
16.   The complex details of the arrangement may be found in *World Debt Tables 1990–91* (Washington, DC: World Bank, 1990) pp. 58–9.
17.   Solomon, 'An Overview of the International Debt Crisis', p. 154.
18.   C. Loser and E. Kalter (eds), *Mexico: The Strategy to Achieve Sustained Economic Growth*, Occasional Paper 99 (International Monetary Fund, September 1992) p. 7.
19.   Aspe, *Economic Transformation*, p. 31.
20.   P. Aspe, 'The Recent Experience of the Mexican Policymakers', in *Sea Changes in Latin America* (Washington: Group of Thirty, 1992) p. 5.
21.   Larre, 'Mexico', pp. 40–1.
22.   N. N. Auerbach, 'The Mexican Peso Crisis: Constituent Pressure and Exchange Rate Policy', *Claremont Policy Briefs* (Claremont, CA: Claremont Institute for Economic Policy Studies, December 1997) pp. 2, 3.
23.   J. A. Frankel and S. L. Schmukler, 'Country Fund Discounts and the Mexican Crisis of December 1994: Did Local Residents Turn Pessimistic Before International Investors?', *International Finance Discussion Papers, no. 563* (Washington: Board of Governors of the Federal Reserve System, September 1996) pp. 2–4.
24.   S. Edwards, 'The Mexican Peso Crisis: How Much Did We Know? When Did We Know It?', *National Bureau of Economic Research Working Paper Series*, Working Paper no. 6334 (December 1997) p. 25.
25.   *Financial Times*, Survey (16 December 1997) p. I
26.   *Financial Times*, Survey (14 May 1992) p. IV.
27.   A. Maddison, *The World Economy in the 20th Century* (Paris: OECD, 1989) p. 19.
28.   *Wall Street Journal* (29 June 1993) p. A 15.
29.   J. Williamson, *What Role for Currency Boards?* (Washington: Institute for International Economics, September 1995) pp. 9–10.
30.   P. Meller, 'Chile', in J. Williamson (ed.), *Latin American Adjustment: How Much Has Happened?* (Washington: Institute for International Economics, April 1990) p. 54.
31.   J. Williamson, *The Progress of Policy Reform in Latin America* (Washington: Institute for International Economics, January 1990) p. 37.
32.   Meller, 'Chile', pp. 80–4.
33   A. Bianchi, 'Chile: Economic Policies and Ideology during the Transition to Democracy', in *Sea Changes in Latin America* (Washington: Group of Thirty, 1992) p. 19.

34. For these and other aspects of developments in Brazil up to early 1997, see R. Dornbusch, 'Brazil's Incomplete Stabilization and Reform', *Brookings Papers on Economic Activity*, 1 (1997) pp. 367–401.
35. Ibid., p. 389.

13 Problems and Promises of an Uncertain Future

1. M. Deane and R. Pringle, *The Central Banks* (London: Hamish Hamilton, 1994).
2. L. Summers, 'Back to the Future', *The American Economy* (July/August 1992) p. 41.
3. IMF, *Summary Proceedings*, Annual Meeting 1996, p. 18.
4. M. Goldstein and P. Turner, 'Banking Crises in Emerging Economies: Origins and Policy Options', *BIS Economic Papers*, no. 46 (October 1996) p. 19.
5. Staff Team led by D. Folkerts-Landau and C. Lindgren, 'Toward a Framework for Financial Stability', IMF, *World Economic and Financial Surveys* (January 1998) p. 2.
6. *IMF Survey* (25 May 1998) p. 158.
7. R. Solomon, 'The IMF Can Stem the Crisis', *The World & I*, 20 (April 1998) pp. 68–70.
8. My Brookings colleague, Wolfgang Reinicke, has drawn a distinction between globalisation and interdependence but it is not necessary for our purposes. See W. Reinicke, *Global Public Policy* (Washington: The Brookings Institution, 1998).
9. UN, *World Economic and Social Survey 1997*, p. 184.
10. M. Wolf, 'The Heart of the New World Economy', *Financial Times* (1 October 1997) p. 12.
11. S. Kuznets, 'Quantitative Aspects of the Economic Growth of Nations', *Economic Development and Cultural Change* (15 January 1967) pp. 19–20.
12. A. I. Bloomfield, 'Patterns of Fluctuation in International Investment Before 1914', *Princeton Studies in International Finance*, no. 21 (December 1968) p. 13.
13. P. Krugman, 'Growing World Trade: Causes and Consequences', *Brookings Papers on Economic Activity*, 1:1995, p. 330.
14. E. M. Truman, 'The Mexican Peso Crisis: Implications for International Finance', *Federal Reserve Bulletin* (March 1996) pp. 202–3.
15. D. Rodrik, *Has Globalization Gone Too Far?* (Washington: Institute for International Economics, March 1997).
16. These propositions are spelled out in *Partners in Prosperity: The Report of the Twentieth Century Fund Task Force on the International Coordination of National Economic Policies* (New York: Priority Press, 1991).

Glossary

Current-account balance   Exports minus imports of goods, services, investment income and remittances

Gross domestic product (GDP)   The total value of the goods and services produced within the territory of the economy – that is, the economy's output. It is equal to expenditures by consumers, by businesses for investment goods and inventories, by governments and by foreigners for the country's exports minus expenditures for imports (which are included in the other spending categories). Real GDP values the output in the prices of a single year so as to measure physical output unaffected by price changes.

Gross national product (GNP)   The total value of the output of the nationals of the country – GDP plus their income from economic activity abroad minus income earned in the country by foreign nationals

Productivity   Output per hour of work (labour productivity) or output per unit of capital equipment (capital productivity) or output per unit of labour and capital (total factor productivity).

Real interest rates   Nominal interest rates minus the change in prices during the period in which the interest rates prevailed

Structural budget balance   The budget surplus or deficit adjusted for the effects of the business cycle on the budget – that is, the surplus or deficit that would prevail if the economy were at high employment and full capacity

Terms of trade   The ratio of a country's export prices to its import prices

Unit labour costs   Wage and salary costs per unit of output (equal to wage rate divided by labour productivity)

Value added   The value of output in a firm or sector or economy minus the value of materials bought from other firms, sectors or economies

Index